AYURVEDA AND THE BODY, MIND AND SOUL

AYURVEDA AND THE BODY, MIND AND SOUL

Roma Nanda

ABD PUBLISHERS
Jaipur ■ New Delhi

ABD PUBLISHERS

Regd. Off. "Bony Residency", Gate No. 2
Opp. Tilak Public School, Vishweswariya Nagar,
Gopalpura Road, Jaipur - 302018, India
Ph: 0141 - 2761280, Telefax: 2761381
Email: abdpublishersjpr@gmail.com

Delhi Office: 102, 1st Floor, Satyam House,
4327/3, Ansari Road, Darya Ganj,
New Delhi - 110002, India
Ph: 011-45652440

visit us: www.oxfordbookcompany.com

Distributed By
KEYA INTERNATIONAL PRESS LLP
E-mail: keyainternationalpressllp@gmail.com

Published in India, 2025

ISBN : 978-81-19343-70-6

Typeset by Shivangi Computer, Jaipur

Printed and bound in India by Thomson Press Ltd.,
New Delhi

Contents

	Preface	*vii*
1.	Ayurveda and the Body, Mind and Soul Connection	1
2.	Understanding the Body in Ayurveda	40
3.	Exploring the Mind in Ayurveda	89
4.	Nurturing the Soul in Ayurveda	143
5.	Ayurveda and Medicine	178
	Bibliography	213
	Index	215

Preface

Human beings face unprecedented challenges as we approach the next millennium. We are seeking new ways to meet the demands of modern life as its unrelenting flow of information demands our attention. Although in many ways, we have greater opportunities for a rich and fulfilling life than ever before, it is clear that we need to evolve new strategies if we are to survive and thrive as individuals and as a species. Ayurveda is the extraordinary mind-body medicine of India with its great yogic spiritual tradition, a tremendous resource for bringing wholeness to all levels of our existence. It is one of the world's oldest and most complete systems of natural healing, containing great wisdom for all humanity that all of us should know. The present volume examines the psychological aspect of Ayurveda, which is probably the most important part of the system and the least understood. This book goes into the Ayurvedic view of the mind and its relationship with both body and spirit, which is profound and intricate. It outlines a comprehensive Ayurvedic treatment for the mind, both for promoting health and for dealing with disease, using diverse methods from diet to meditation, These teachings derive from classical Ayurvedic texts, which commonly contain sections on the mind and its treatment. They also relate to yogic teachings, from which Ayurveda derives its view of consciousness and many of its modalities for treating the mind. However, I have not only examined the traditional psychological teachings of Ayurveda, I have also tried to make them relevant to the modern world. Ayurveda, as the science of life, is not a frozen science but one that grows with the movement of life itself, of which it partakes.

This book does not require that the reader possess prior knowledge of Ayurveda, though this is certainly helpful. It introduces the basic factors of Ayurveda, like the biologi-cal humors (doshas), particularly as related to psychology. On this foundation, however, the book does go deeply into its subject. It aims at providing the reader with sufficient knowledge to use the information and techniques of Ayurveda to improve his or her own life and consciousness on all levels. It is not simply introductory in nature and should be relevant to psychologists and therapists as well. I am not going to apologize for producing a more technical book on Ayurveda than the beginning reader might understand. There are already a number of introductory books on Ayurveda that can be examined for those who require this. Now there is a need for more advanced books to unfold this important subject further. Something of the depths of Ayurveda needs to be revealed to complement the general introductions now available. Unlike modern psychological science which has until very recently maintained the dichotomy of mind and body, Ayurvedic psychology clearly recognizes that the mind and the body are one. The mind is a field of ideas, the body is a field of molecules, but both are expressions of consciousness interacting with itself.

This book goes into the Ayurvedic view of the mind and its relationship with both body and spirit, which is profound and intricate. This book is a valuable resource to students of Ayurveda, Yoga, Tantra and psychology.

— ***Roma Nanda***

Chapter 1

Ayurveda and the Body, Mind and Soul Connection

Introduction

Ayurveda, the ancient Indian system of medicine, offers a holistic approach to health and well-being that encompasses the body, mind, and soul. Rooted in ancient texts such as the Charaka Samhita and Sushruta Samhita, Ayurveda views health as a state of balance between the body, mind, and spirit. It emphasizes the interconnectedness of all aspects of life and the importance of maintaining harmony within oneself and with the surrounding environment.

In Ayurveda, the body is seen as a microcosm of the universe, composed of five elements: earth, water, fire, air, and ether. These elements combine to form three fundamental energies or doshas known as Vata, Pitta, and Kapha. Each individual has a unique constitution or prakriti, determined by the predominance of these doshas at the time of conception. When the doshas are in balance, the body functions optimally, but imbalances can lead to disease and illness.

Understanding the body in Ayurveda goes beyond the physical anatomy to include subtle energies and life forces. Ayurvedic anatomy describes the body as a network of channels or nadis through which energy flows, and centers or chakras that regulate the flow of energy.

These concepts provide a holistic framework for understanding the body's structure and function and guiding health-promoting practices. In addition to the physical body, Ayurveda recognizes the importance of the mind in health and well-being. The mind-body connection is central to Ayurvedic philosophy, with mental and emotional factors playing a significant role in the development of disease. Ayurveda views the mind as a powerful force that can influence health through thoughts, emotions, and beliefs. Practices such as meditation, mindfulness, and yoga are recommended to cultivate mental clarity, emotional balance, and spiritual awareness.

Nurturing the soul is another key aspect of Ayurvedic healing. Ayurveda acknowledges the existence of a deeper dimension beyond the physical and mental realms, often referred to as the soul or spirit. This spiritual dimension is believed to be the source of consciousness and the seat of inner wisdom.

Ayurvedic teachings emphasize the importance of connecting with this inner essence through practices such as self-reflection, self-awareness, and self-realization. Integrating Ayurveda into daily life involves adopting lifestyle practices that support health and well-being on all levels. Ayurvedic dietary principles emphasize the importance of eating fresh, seasonal, and locally sourced foods that are compatible with one's dosha.

Daily routines or dinacharya, including practices such as oil pulling, tongue scraping, and self-massage, are recommended to promote detoxification, relaxation, and rejuvenation. Ayurvedic therapies such as Panchakarma, herbal medicine, and Ayurvedic massage are also utilized to address specific health concerns and restore balance.

Ayurveda offers a comprehensive approach to health and healing that addresses the body, mind, and soul. By recognizing the interconnectedness of these aspects of human existence and providing practical tools for promoting balance and harmony, Ayurveda offers timeless wisdom for modern living. Through understanding the body, nurturing the mind, and connecting with the soul, individuals can cultivate vibrant health and well-being in all aspects of life.

Ayurveda and Mind, Body Health: Exploring the Connection

Ayurveda, an ancient holistic healing system from India, emphasizes the balance between mind, body, and spirit for optimal health and well-being.

This system has been in practice for over 5,000 years and has been gaining popularity in the West due to its effectiveness in managing various health conditions. In this article, we will explore the connection between Ayurveda and mind-body health and how it can benefit individuals seeking holistic healing.

Understanding Ayurveda

Figure: *Ayurveda is a Sanskrit term that translates to "the science of life." It is a holistic approach to health that emphasizes the balance between mind, body, and spirit for optimal well-being. The principles of Ayurveda are based on the belief that each individual is unique and there is no one-size-fits-all approach to health and healing.*

Ayurveda is gaining popularity in the West due to its effectiveness in managing various health conditions, including chronic pain, digestive issues, and mental health problems such as anxiety and depression. In this article, we will explore the connection between Ayurveda and mind-body health and how it can benefit individuals seeking holistic healing.

Ayurveda

Ayurveda is an ancient holistic healing system from India that dates back over 5,000 years. It is based on the belief that health and well-being depend on the balance between mind, body, and spirit. Ayurveda uses a personalized approach to health and healing, focusing on the individual's unique constitution, or "dosha."

Ayurvedic Principles

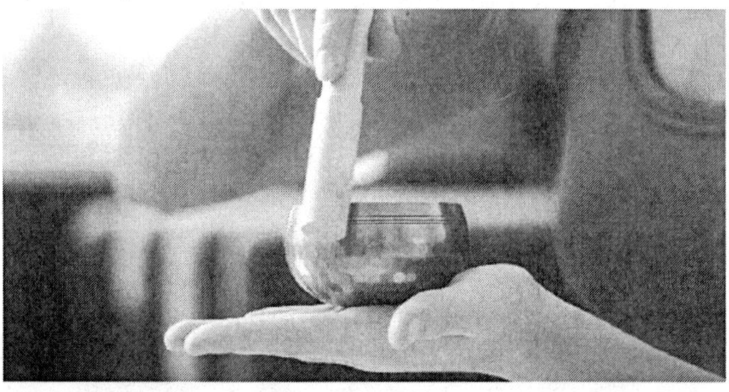

Five Elements and Three Doshas: Ayurveda is based on the principles of the five elements: ether, air, fire, water, and earth. These elements combine to form the three doshas: Vata (ether and air), Pitta (fire and water), and Kapha (water and earth). Each individual has a unique combination of doshas, which determines their physical and mental characteristics, such as body type, temperament, and preferences. Ayurvedic practitioners use this information to develop a personalized approach to health and healing.

Mind-Body Connection: Ayurveda recognizes the connection between the mind and body and the impact that mental health has on physical health. Negative emotions, stress, and anxiety can lead to physical health problems, while positive emotions and a calm mind can promote well-being. Ayurveda uses a holistic approach to mental health, focusing on lifestyle practices and treatments that promote balance and harmony between the mind and body.

Ayurvedic Lifestyle Practices for Mind-Body Health

Figure: *Ayurveda recommends various lifestyle practices for promoting mind-body health. These practices include:*

Proper Diet and Nutrition

Ayurveda recognizes the importance of proper nutrition for maintaining optimal health. Ayurvedic practitioners recommend a diet that is tailored to the individual's dosha and promotes balance and harmony between the mind and body.

The Ayurvedic diet is based on six tastes: sweet, sour, salty, bitter, pungent, and astringent. Each taste has a different effect on the body and mind, and the goal of the Ayurvedic diet is to balance the tastes based on the individual's dosha. For example, a person with a Vata dosha should eat warm, nourishing foods that are sweet, sour, and salty to balance their cold and dry qualities.

A person with a Pitta dosha should eat cooling, calming foods that are bitter, sweet, and astringent to balance their hot and sharp qualities.

A person with a Kapha dosha should eat light, spicy foods that are pungent, bitter, and astringent to balance their heavy and sluggish qualities.

Yoga and Meditation: Yoga and meditation are essential components of Ayurvedic practice for promoting mind-body health. It is a physical practice that involves various postures, or asanas, that promote flexibility, strength, and balance. Yoga also includes breathing techniques, or pranayama, that help calm the mind and reduce stress. Meditation is a mental practice that involves focusing the mind and achieving a state of calm awareness. Meditation can help reduce stress, anxiety, and depression and promote a sense of inner peace and well-being.

Aromatherapy: Aromatherapy is a form of holistic healing that uses essential oils to promote physical and emotional well-being. Ayurveda uses aromatherapy as a natural way to balance the doshas and promote mind-body health.

Massage Therapy: Ayurveda recognizes the healing power of touch and recommends various massage therapies for promoting relaxation and reducing stress. Abhyanga, a full-body oil massage, is a common Ayurvedic massage therapy that promotes mind-body health.

Ayurvedic Herbs and Supplements: Ayurveda uses a variety of herbs and supplements to promote mind-body health. These herbs and supplements are tailored to the individual's dosha and may include ginger, turmeric, ashwagandha, and Triphala.

A;c Treatments for Mind-Body Health

Ayurveda offers various treatments for promoting mind-body health. These treatments include:

Panchakarma

Panchakarma is a cleansing and detoxification process that removes toxins from the body and promotes mind-body health. This Ayurvedic treatment includes five procedures: Vamana (emesis), virechana (purgation), Basti (enema), Nasya (nasal medication), and rakta moksha (bloodletting).

Shirodhara: Shirodhara is an Ayurvedic treatment that involves pouring warm oil over the forehead in a continuous stream. This treatment promotes relaxation and reduces stress, anxiety, and insomnia.

Abhyanga: Abhyanga is a full-body oil massage that promotes relaxation and reduces stress. This Ayurvedic massage therapy also promotes lymphatic drainage and improves circulation.

Ayurvedic Approach to Mental Health

Figure: *Ayurveda takes a holistic approach to mental health, recognizing the connection between the mind and body. Ayurvedic treatments and lifestyle practices can help manage various mental health conditions, including:*

Anxiety and Depression: Ayurveda recommends various lifestyle practices, such as yoga, meditation, and aromatherapy, for managing anxiety and depression. Ayurvedic herbs and supplements, such as ashwagandha and Brahmi, can also help reduce anxiety and depression symptoms.

Stress Management: Ayurveda offers various lifestyle practices and treatments, such as massage therapy and Panchakarma, for managing stress. These practices promote relaxation and reduce the negative effects of stress on the mind and body.

Insomnia: Ayurveda recognizes the importance of proper sleep for maintaining optimal health. Ayurvedic treatments, such as Shirodhara, and lifestyle practices, such as yoga and meditation, can help promote relaxation and improve sleep quality.

The Benefits of a Balanced Mind-Body Connection:

- When the mind and body are in balance, we experience a wide range of benefits, including improved physical health, mental clarity, emotional stability, and spiritual growth.
- By promoting a balanced mind-body connection through Ayurvedic practices and lifestyle factors, we can experience greater vitality, happiness, and fulfillment in our lives.
- Ayurveda recognizes that each person is unique and offers personalized treatment plans to support individual health and well-being.

The Great Three Classics of Ayurveda

The Charaka Samhita is believed to have arisen around 400-200 BCE. It is felt to be one of the oldest and the most important ancient authoritative writings on Ayurveda. It is not known who this person was or, if indeed, this represents the work of a "school of thought." It could have been from a group of scholars or followers of a man known as Charaka or an original composition from a single person named Charaka.

This work is sometimes considered a redaction of an older and more voluminous work, Agnivesha Samhita (46,000 verses), which is no longer extant. Dridhabala, living about 400 AD, is believed to have filled in many verses of missing text (perhaps up to 20%) in the Chikitsasthana and elsewhere, which disappeared over time.

The language of Charaka is Sanskrit and its style is poetry, with meter and melody. Poetry was known to serve as a memory aid. Charaka contains over 8,400 metrical verses.It presents most of the theoretical edifice of Ayurveda and concentrates on the branch of Ayurveda called kayachikitsa (internal medicine). This is largely the theory of the internal fire-of digestion-or internal medicine, in modern terms. Charaka never discusses the sub-types of pitta and kapha, but does list and describe the 5 sub-types of vata.

Seen from a greater perspective, this work seems to represent a certain value of consciousness that is different from other works. It gives more discussion about the notion that life is fundamentally a field of intelligence and pure knowledge. This field is self-aware; it is the Knower as well as the object of perception, and for Charaka this is part of what is to be treated by the physician.

The P.V. Sharma translation comes in four volumes, two of original text and two of commentary about the original work. Sharma's English version is said to be a scholarly and relatively faithful work. It has numerous appendices and an extensive index. The B. Dash / R.K. Sharma version lacks these features but does have extensive commentary incorporated in with the original text. All three translators have excellent academic or/and clinical credentials supporting their works.

Sushruta Samhita

The Sushruta Samhita presents the field of Ayurvedic surgery (shalya). This branch of medicine arose in part from the exigencies of dealing with the effects of war. This work also is said to be a redaction of oral material passed down verbally from generation to generation. It is thought to have arisen about the same time period as the Charaka Samhita, slightly after or before it according to different authorities. Its style is both prose and poetry with poetry being the greater portion.

The Sushruta Samhita, while dealing with the practice and theory of surgery, is an important source of Ayurvedic aphorisms. the most comprehensive and frequently quoted definition of health is from Sushruta.

This work is unique in that it discusses blood in terms of the fourth doshic principle. This work is the first to enumerate and discuss the pitta sub-doshas and the marmas. With its emphasis on pitta, surgery, and blood, this work best represents the transformational value of life.

This work, also originally written in Sanskrit, is now available in English with Devanagari. Bhishagratna's translation is English and Sanskrit. P.V. Sharma has recently written a translation with both the Sanskrit/Devanagari and English that includes Dallana's commentary. Dallana has been regarded as the most influential commentator on Sushruta's work.

Ashtanga Hridayam and Ashtanga Sangraha

Ashtanga Sangraha and Ashtanga Hridayam are the work of a person named Vagbhata. There are two works by a person or persons with this name. The Ashtanga Sangraha is nearly 40% greater in size (by verse count) and is primarily poetry with prose. The Hridayam (about 7800 verses) is written in prose and seems to have a slightly different organization of material than the former. Both works have been dated about the same time and are thought to date after the Charaka and Sushruta Samhitas (400 CE).

The exposition is relatively straightforward and also deals primarily with kayachikitsa. In this work, we see the kapha sub-doshas are listed and described for the first time, completing our modern edifice of vata, pitta, and kapha with their five sub-types. Its emphasis on treating the physiology of the body and suggestions for therapeutic use of metals and minerals means the perspective of the treatise represents the gross, material value of life more than its counterparts Charaka and Sushruta. Srikantha Murthy's translation includes the Sanskrit/Devanagari for those who want to delve into the original text. S. Murthy has translated many of the ancient Ayurvedic writings into English, for which we are indebted. He has weighty credentials and brings them to bear in this work.

The Lesser Three Classics of Ayurveda

The Sharngadhara Samhita is a concise exposition of Ayurvedic principles. Its author, Sharngadhara, has offered his work as a digested version of Ayurvedic knowledge, deliberately omitting much detail because the works of The Great Three were already widely known. This treatise is thought to have originated in the 15th century AD.

The Sharngadhara Samhita is prized for its enumeration and description of numerous pharmacological formulations used in panchakarma and contains the first textual elaboration of diagnosis by means of the pulse.Its subject matter is again the field of kayachikitsa. This work is available in Sanskrit/Devanagari and English translation by Srikantha Murthy.

Bhava Prakasha: Bhava Prakasha is just now available in English translation. It is the most recent of the classical texts, written in the 16th century. It is a well-organized and compact re-presentation of the earlier classics. There are about 10,268 verses of varying meters. It deals with kayachikitsa generally and has a large section entitled Nighantu, which gives the characteristics of many foods, plants, and minerals. Many of it sutras are direct quotes from earlier writers. Sri Kantha Murthy again does this Sanskrit/Devanagari and English translation.

Madhava Nidanam: Madhava Nidanam, available here in Sanskrit/Devanagari and English translation by Srikantha Murthy, deals with the classification of diseases in Ayurveda. Its taxonomy is slightly different at times from those given by Charaka, Sushruta, and Vagbhata, while for the greater part its verses are seemingly direct quotes from them. This work is dated around 700 AD and is prized for covering a wide range of diseases in the fields of bala (children and women's disorders), shalya, damstra (toxicology), shalakya (ear, nose and throat), and kayachikitsa. While this treatise gives detailed description of disease etiology (disease doctrines), prodroma and cardinal signs and symptoms, it does not give explanation or suggestions for chikitsa (treatment).

Detoxification with Ayurveda Internal Cleaning

While the Western world has often taken a cynical view towards detoxification as a method of healing the body, an ancient medicinal art from India called Ayurveda has been prescribing detoxification and internal cleansing for thousands of years. They especially recommend it during the spring time, so body can take part in the rebirth of nature.Ayurveda believes in maintaining balance within the body. To achieve balance, one should not create a new imbalance in order to fix it.

Therefore, internal cleansing should be quick so that impurities embedded in the tissues can be released without compromising or disturbing the quality and the functions of other organs and tissues in other parts of the body. Internal cleansing can be achieved alone or with a supervisor to guide as go through the fast. Performing a self-detox is not highly recommended, because the nature of the toxins in body may be harder to release than imagine. Once the toxins manifest themselves in the form of fevers and body pain,need additional support to get through the cleansing process.

Ayurveda believes in three kinds of toxins that the act the body's defence systems. The first is the toxin of incomplete indigestion. This is usually caused by eating foods that are not in sync with body type, or by eating too little or too much, or by going to sleep with a full stomach. Incomplete indigestion also results from eating processed foods, fermented dishes, or leftover meals from the day before. They believe that the root cause is a weak or irregular digestive fire. If this toxin is allowed to continually build up, it will disrupt the flow of nutrients to the body, as well as impede the natural bowel movements. However, the digestive system can burn off this toxin with the aid of herbal supplements and by drinking a lot of water.

The second kind of toxin is a more reactive form of indigestion that is more dangerous and needs to be dealt with differently than the first toxin. This is the toxin they ascribe as the source of artherosclerosis and strokes. The last type of toxin is the kind that comes from the environment, such as heavy metals, pollution, synthetics and preservatives. They ascribe this as the root cause of painful diseases such as multiple sclerosis and fibromyalgia.

The aim of Ayurvedic medicine is to correct the imbalance in the body. It uses the body's own natural systems (liver, kidneys, sweat glands, lungs, etc.) to flesh out these toxins. Their methods are never forceful or painful, but are simply supportive of our own organs.

The danger in focusing on only one organ for cleansing such as the colon is the imbalance it brings to the rest of the organs. Some of the treatments recommended for detox are drinking herbal teas made of fennel and coriander seed. These herbs lubricate and flushes out the toxins found in the bowels and urinary system. They are even more powerful when supported by a prescribed Ayurvedic diet rich in vegetables and organic foods. The process follows three distinct stages: the preparation of the body, at the actual cleansing and the follow-up therapies after the detox. And because the Ayurvedic approach is holistic, Ayurvedic detoxification continues to work even after the detox is done.

Mind, Body and Behaviour

People function on three different levels-physical, behavioural, and cognitive. So far, each system has been dealt with separately, for the sake of clarity. But, in reality, they do not operate in isolation. People interact with the world constantly on all levels; and consequently, if a problem arises in one area, it can quickly effect functioning in the other two, and in one's relationship with the outside world.

Theoretical questions concerning these interactions and, specifically, as to the primary of thought, action, or affect, have become a source of major controversy in recent years; the debate continues. What we know is that, on a day-to-day basis, these three systems are not perfectly correlated; they do not work in complete harmony. For example, a person can be very "wound up" on a physical level and feel extremely tense and anxious while behaving efficiently and thinking quite clearly. Furthermore, although everyone experiences and responds to the world in these three ways, there are large individual differences in modes of response.

Some people, when stressed, consistently have difficulty in getting their thoughts together, or can feel like running-but do not experience any uncomfortable physical symptoms, for example. Another person might feel physically like a time bomb, but, at the same time, be able to think clearly and get on with their work. In other words, people have characteristic ways of responding to stress. Some people are more physical, whereas others are more cognitive or behavioural.

Such habitual styles of response have nothing to do with intelligence or background; nor do they result from conscious deliberations or choices. People do not, for example, decide early on in life to have panic attacks, rather than muzzy thoughts, when upsetting things occur. Response patterns develop over time and reflect the individual's personal vulnerabilities and unique learning experiences. These individual differences are extremely important in understanding both one's own patterns of stress response and those of the people around one. It can be difficult, for example, for the type of person who responds to stress by feeling ill or shaky, to understand another person who complains of not being able to concentrate, think straight, or get any work done; or yet another who rushes around doing even more than usual while claiming to be so pressurized that he or she cannot cope.

There are also large individual differences in people's areas of vulnerability. Some people develop fears and phobias, others get depressed, and yet others turn to food or alcohol. These differences are related to the nature of the stressor, but even more so to the individual's unique genetic makeup, learning history, and experiences. What generally happens, as already explained, is that existing tendencies to wind up or down-physically, behaviourally, or cognitively-come to the fore when under stress. A person who tends to overindulge will be particularly likely to eat or drink to excess after a shock, a disagreement, or when dissatisfied with a work situation, for example.

Someone who normally likes to keep her surroundings neat and tidy, might find herself being excessively fussy at times when a relationship is not going well or when worried about financial or marital prospects. A person who normally has a tendency to err on the side of pessimism, might, under pressure, react to bills, a slight weight increase, or an interpersonal letdown as if it were the end of the world.

A person with a sensitive stomach might find that, coming up to exams or deadlines, they cannot eat or keep food down at all. One such client said that he felt as if his stomach had been invaded by an army of butterflies. Everyone has such weak spots, which can give rise to problems, as well as greatly adding to the situation when pressure is coming from other areas. Unfortunately, one of the most insidious aspects of stress is its self-escalating nature.

What starts off as a problem in one area can quickly get lost in a web of confusion. Imagine, for example, that Barry is preoccupied about his job. As a result, he is not great company, and even puts people off by being uncharacteristically irritable or unduly reserved. Little support is offered from a spouse who has been embarrassed by a public outburst or retreat, which also caused upset for others.

Marital and sexual relations then suffer. Preoccupation over this renders Barry even less efficient at work, which leads to financial losses and threats from a boss or partner. Because things at home are becoming more frosty, a habit of staying late at the office or going for a few beers sets in. This results in a neglect of eating and, subsequently, weight loss. He then feels even more tired, listless, and unhappy, as well as more vulnerable to illnesses, both major and minor. Tension headaches and stomach upsets perpetuate an increasingly stressful existence. Sensing that things are unravelling adds to the pressure and panic. Not feeling in control colours his perception and interpretation of situations, making him increasingly dogmatic and unreasonable, and so on.

Whether the initial stressor is an external event, ill health, or faulty behaviour or thinking, and whether the initial problem response is physical, behavioural, or cognitive, it is in this way that problems gradually accumulate. They slowly grow and feed into one another in complex and subtle ways. The fact that people are such bad observers of themselves facilitates the process. Problems build up without their awareness. The time when they most need to take stock is when it is hardest to do so, because they are just too caught up in themselves.

When things finally do reach a level where a person can no longer cast a blind eye and is forced-by a boss, a massive panic attack, a significant weight change, or an exam failure, for example-to acknowledge that there is a problem and to take a look at things, it can be at a disaster area. Health, social relationships, and finances can all have taken a bruising. At this point, professional assistance, such as that of a clinical psychologist, is usually sought. The first step in helping any client to cope is to get them to simply stop and think. The next is to define exactly what is wrong, and to identify the problem or problems, and the sources of stress. The necessary changes then have to be carefully planned. This takes time and perseverance, but the skills acquired along the way serve for life.

Anxiety, Fears, and Phobias

An event is said to be stressful if it poses "a real or perceived threat to a person,"-that is, when they feel unable to cope or that they are not in control. Stress is, and always has been, an integral part of living, one of the basic ingredients of life. For this reason, as already explained, man has developed an adaptive coping mechanism-the "fight or flight response"-to deal with these inevitable pressures and problems. Up to a certain point, stress adds a dash of spice to life. It keeps us on our toes. It makes people perform even more efficiently on all levels-physically, behaviourally, and cognitively.

What happens beyond this point, however, is not so desirable. Most people have experienced the discomfort-maybe even embarrassment-of a dry mouth, shaky voice, pounding heart, sweaty hands, or wobbly legs, at some time or another. Everyone knows what it is to be frightened or worried about something; the "something" can be concrete, like a bill or illness, or less tangible, like the anticipation of a future unpleasantness-an exam, interview, or work deadline, for example. People can even get worked up at the prospect of something pleasant, such as a wedding, party, or date. Likewise, everyone has spent the occasional night lying awake, thinking over and over something that happened during the day or that might happen in the future. Most people occasionally avoid things, places, or people that make them feel uncomfortable or nervous.

For many people, however, fear and anxiety are a major problem. A large number of research studies (of psychiatric populations, general medical practices, and community surveys) suggest that about one third of the adult population suffers constantly from nervous complaints, especially anxiety, and that about 5%, or 1 in 20, have a constitutional predisposition to anxiety. Fortunately, in most cases, nervous reactions and anxiety related difficulties can be attributed to things other than constitutional factors, such as an inability to cope with an unconducive or threatening environment, an unhealthy lifestyle, bad habits, faulty learning, or distorted thinking. Generally speaking, anxiety is most common among women, the poor, and the aged, but the reasons for these trends are complex.

Anxiety is present in the mildest to the most severe emotional disturbances, from transient distress to mental illness. Consequently, fear and anxiety are present in all the major problems of living-fears and phobias, depression, obsessionality, interpersonal difficulties, marital and sexual problems, and problems of overindulgence. Five basic kinds of fear have been identified: fear of things and places, fear of internal fears (i.e., fear of bodily sensations of anxiety), fear of one's own thoughts, interpersonal and social fears, and derivative fears (i.e., fears and anxieties that arise as a result of other problems). This focuses on the first two of these-fear of things and places (phobias) and fear of internal fears (agoraphobia). The remaining fears are dealt with in the following, in the context of the other major problems of living.

Fears and Phobias

When a person is fearful of something to an extent that would be generally regarded as out of proportion to the stimulus, they are said to be phobic. For example, one young man I treated was so afraid of dogs that it totally curtailed his social life and, eventually, his professional life. His fear was irrational.

The most common phobias and fears are of animals, heights, spiders, thunder, fire, darkness and night, noise, storms, and lightning. A fear of flying is also quite prevalent and can occur in experienced passengers and even crew members. People can also develop phobias about illness, disease, and death, and other bodily things, such as swallowing, blood, or medical procedures in general. I could also list snakes, enclosed spaces, water, dirt, cancer, fire, birds; suffice it to say that people can become phobic of almost anything, from flies to tomatoes. Basically, it is a fear of the potential of the object to harm one. The number of people who suffer from phobias to the extent that it interferes with their getting on with life is relatively few (about 8% of the population). However, there are many people who, although not clinically "phobic", fear certain ordinary things in their environment much more than they realistically should. The Fear Survey Schedule was developed to measure responses to such commonly occurring fears.

Causes, Signs, and Symptoms

Seligman, an American psychologist, is of the opinion that humans have an in-built fear of certain things, for example, snakes; and that people are much more likely to develop phobias of these things. Be that as it may, the main way in which fears and phobias develop is through traumatic or faulty learning. We learn in three ways-by association, by consequence, and by observation. Fear can often be triggered by a single traumatic event or experience, such as being bitten by a dog or sexually assaulted.

The anxiety so generated can then lead to avoidance of the same or similar objects, persons, or situations thereafter. Anxieties can also arise as a consequence of vicarious conditioning. In other words, people can become fearful of things through observation, without even being directly involved. Sometimes, because certain phobias run in families, it can look as if they are genetically transmitted-for example, if all the children in a family are afraid of birds. The more reasonable explanation is that children learn to be fearful of the same things as their parents are, by a process of association, reinforcement, and observation. The physical symptoms of anxiety are dealt with in more detail in the following section on agoraphobia.

The basic phobic response includes all the autonomic concomitants of anxiety, heart palpitations, muscular tension, shaking, blushing, trembling, perspiration, nausea, numbness, tingling in the hands and feet, a desire to urinate, and stomach upsets.

These symptoms can occur not only in the presence of the feared object but also at the mere thought or anticipation of it. When people are in a constant or prolonged state of anxiety, sleep, appetite, and general health can suffer.

The most immediate behavioural reaction is that of "flight," which, in time, can develop into an avoidance response. Avoidance is self defeating, because it feeds the anxiety; the temporary relief that is experienced makes it more likely for the same and similar situations to be avoided again.

People can get to a point where their whole life is tailored by their avoidance of an increasingly large number of everyday situations, objects, and events. Their social, emotional, and professional lives take the toll.

Below are 51 different stimuli which can cause fear in people. Please rate how much fear you feel using the following rating scale and record your answer in the space provided:

Table Key:

1 = None

5 = Much fear

2 = Very little fear

6 = Very much fear

3 = A little fear

7 = Terror

4 = Some fear

There is a large cognitive component in phobic reactions because, objectively speaking, the stimulus or object of the fear is, to most other people, innocuous. It is what the source of the fear means to the person-their perception of the object or situation, and what they are saying to themselves about it-that keeps the anxiety alive: "It will bite me." "We are going to crash, I know we are." Unfortunately, such preoccupation makes it even more difficult for the individual to think straight, to concentrate, and to be objective.

Likewise, many phobics experience vivid visual images of themselves in their feared situations-being savaged by a dog, surrounded by screaming people in a plummeting airplane, or going totally blank at an exam or interview. Such images can be even more disturbing and less easily dismissed than anxiety-provoking self-talk.

Treatment

The recognized treatment of choice for phobias is called systematic desensitization. It is one of a family of flexible exposure techniques for overcoming fears. As with all the interventions described, the therapist starts off with a thorough evaluation interview or behavioural assessment. When a clear picture of the problem has been formed-and this may take a couple of consultations-an assessment of the client's motivation to change is carried out, after which the change plan is set up.

The client's ongoing diary-keeping then provides detailed information about the situations in which the problem occurs and the degree of anxiety generated. It also gives the therapist a feel for the client's "life space". This information facilitates the construction of a realistic and personalized hierarchy of increasingly more anxiety-provoking situations. The person is then trained in deep muscular relaxation and, over a number of therapy sessions, is systematically exposed to each item until the pinnacle of the hierarchy is reached.

Systematic desensitization can be carried out in imagination but, more often, real-life, or in vivo, exposure is preferred. If, as with many phobias, part of the client's fear stems from ignorance (lack of information), he or she is supplied with reading material on the subject. For example, a thanatophobic-somebody who is phobic of thunder-might be supplied with easy-to-read literature about thunder and how harmless it really is. Children's books can be ideal in delivering simple facts in an unthreatening way.

As important as the behavioural part of the intervention is the cognitive part. From their diary-keeping, clients are taught to identify and then to dispute the validity of maladaptive, anxiety-provoking self-statements, which occur during, as well as before and after, exposure to their feared objects or situations: "I know it's going to bite me," "I escaped this time-next time I won't be so lucky." They gradually learn to replace their negative self-talk with a new, more objective internal dialogue, which they can then utilize in the feared situations. This effectively breaks the fear spiral by replacing negative thoughts with incompatible, realistic, and reassuring appraisals. Sometimes, underlying beliefs, such as, "Because I am afraid of dogs, I am inferior," also have to be uncovered and explored. Finally, if the client's fear is generated and maintained by anticipatory visual images, strategies for dismissing and distracting have to be acquired, as well as guidelines supplied on how to utilize their imaginable capacity as a general coping tool.

How Mind Loses Its Body and World

We exercise our mental abilities all the time. Exercising mind, however, is different from thinking about mind; we use mind to think about a lot of things besides mind. Everyone exercises mind, but not everyone reflects on or thinks about the nature and characteristics of mind. Such reflections are mostly for scientists and philosophers. They are also the purpose of this book, which tries to frame some concepts and theoretical models to describe and explain mental phenomena as they occur in everyday life and in scientific laboratories.

The closed mind is so counterintuitive one wonders how it comes to dominate theoretical models. These models vary on a Cartesian theme in which an inner mental realm is closed off from the outer physical realm. They share some important concepts, the meanings of which have become muddled by overuse. Therefore I start by clarifying concepts and tracing their roots.

"Cartesian" is not a good word today. Descartes bashers are legion, but many are also avid vendors of Cartesian concepts dressed in high-tech jargon. The superficial bashing presents a frivolous or dogmatic Cartesian-ism, but this is unfair. The Cartesian theme is an earnest effort to find a theoretical representation for a complex phenomenon, providing simplifications to make the problem tractable. I reject it because I think its simplifications are on the wrong track, not because it addresses the wrong problem. Descartes identified important questions about mind that face us today. To see them more clearly, let us get a historical perspective.

Ancient Conceptions of Mind

We are naturally mindful and automatically wield mental abilities. Anthropological research has found no culture that is purely behaviourist in its conception; mental notions such as belief and false belief are universal. With subtle variations in meaning, psychological terms such as thinking, feeling, acting, perceiving, speaking, understanding, caring, craving, remembering, anticipating, willing, and dreaming are used in the daily conversations of people everywhere on Earth, from antiquity to now. They are phenomena to be observed and explained by sciences of mind. Nevertheless, they are practical and not theoretical. Although people understand and deal with each other by these concepts, they are hard put if asked to elaborate.

Theoretical concepts of mind, by which we do not merely use everyday mental notions but treat them and mental capacities themselves as objects of discourse or investigation, are less widespread and evolved haltingly. Some cultures do not have a concept analogous to our "mind," others have concepts that differ widely from those of modern Europeans and Americans.

For instance, Illongots of the Philippines hold a concept of mind that fuses what we now know as mentality and vitality (Lillard 1997). This cross-cultural variation is not surprising when we realize that the theoretical concept of mind familiar in the Western world is itself a late introduction. Aristotle, for example, would be more in tune with Illongots than with modern Greeks.

Homer did not have a unitary notion of mind or soul. Psyche, the word for soul in later Greek that is the stem for psychology, is in Homer the breath of life that leaves the mouth or escapes from wounds when a person dies. Nous, the word for mind or intellect in later Greek, is in Homer the capacity to realize and understand a situation, to imagine and plan, to penetrate appearances for deeper insight, as to recognize Aphrodite in the guise of an old woman. These are all practical intelligence, and realization and recognition dawn as immediately as vision. Noein, to know or to think, never means discursive reasoning in Homer.

Homer did not describe the functions of psyche in life. By the sixth century B.C.E., psyche became the body's vital principle present in all living organisms, holding together, controlling, and strengthening individuals. Besides thinking in humans and locomotion and perception in higher animals, activities of the soul also included digestion, growth, and reproduction, which we now classify not as psychological but as physiological.

Mind for the ancients always intimately tied to the world. Pre-Socratic philosophers, materialists one and all, regarded the soul as some stuff such as air that suffused the body and its surrounding, thus making the organism a part of the cosmic whole. They explained thoughts in terms of some peculiar mixtures of bodily constituents. Parmenides, for example, held that mind is inseparable from being. The pre-Socratics contrasted nous with aisthesis, sense perception. Sense perception has access only to the changing and partial surfaces of things that form the basis of beliefs in most people. Mind can penetrate into the constant real world as a whole that is the basis of truth. By making explicit the possibility of mind to be deceived and to err, these philosophers brought out the role of logical reasoning and discursive argument in attaining truth. Logos, which for Heraclitus was mainly the noun for "to say," became increasingly central to reason (Fritz 1974; Wright 1990).

Aristotle clarified the thoughts of his predecessors. Furthermore, he put the notion of the soul as the principle of living organisms with mind as its intellectual component into his own theoretical framework of form and matter, actuality and potentiality. As the form of organisms as wholes, the soul is the actuality for the potentiality of organic bodies. It is natural, because form and matter are both present in all things. Aristotle analyzed the soul in terms of its various functions: practical intelligence, technical know-how, reason, and theoretical knowledge. His definition of nous was rather narrow, confined to reason, the base for knowledge and belief. He sharply distinguished reason from perception and intelligence, denying the former but not the latter to animals. Like Aristotle, Thomas Aquinas did not include in mind passive sensory images, which we follow the British empiricists in regarding as quintessentially mental.

Continuing the Aristotelian practice of locating the study of soul within biological investigation, the Stoics and Epicureans took advantage of scientific and medical advancements in the Hellenic age and developed even a stronger materialist view of mind. Thus from the pre-Socratics onward, Western thinking has had a strong tradition for the monistic and naturalistic conceptions of mind. In this tradition mind is a part of the natural order and susceptible to study by natural science. Detailed formulations of it change as our scientific knowledge changes (Annas 1992).

Whereas the monistic conception has its roots reaching back to pre-Socratic thinkers, the dualistic conception also has a long root that traces back to Plato. Plato believed that the relationship between soul and body was deeply problematic and defied our understanding. In several of his dialogues, especially Phaedo, the soul appears as a substance separate from but on a par with body, it is immortal and, for it, the body with its desires and pleasures is a nuisance.

This dualist view was revived by Neoplaton-ists in the third century. Plotinus proposed a clear distinction between body and soul and used it as an approach to the Platonic distinction between the physical world and the immaterial world of forms. As something incorporeal and noncomposite, the soul is not subject to destruction. The idea of the immortal soul was seized enthusiastically by Christians, among whom was Augustine of Hippo, an avid reader of Plotinus. Augustine's writings were very much a part of the intellectual milieu of educated Christians in the seventeenth century, when mind-body dualism received its definitive formulation from René Descartes (Robinson 1970; O'meara 1993).

The Control Power of Mind Designers

The Trojans play God, controlling the fate of Greeks inside the original Cartesian Trojan horse. Mind designers in modern variants are godlike, possessing abilities that are categorically different from the closed mind and mysterious to it. However, their specific abilities vary. Some, such as the programmers in computationalism or the scientists stimulating the brain in a vat, claim access to both inside and outside of the veil of perception or formality. Others do not care about what goes on inside. They are like Trojans who seal the trap door in the horse and let the Greeks perish inside. Despite the difference, the two classes are equally domineering. This section concentrates on various forms of behaviourism that are mostly concerned with predicting and conditioning behaviours.

Theospectivism

Most mind designers retain remnants of divinity. When the human mind is identified with brain or computation and closed off from the world, those that assign meanings to mental representations must have capacities that transcend the human mind. They must be able to access the world without experience or thinking, otherwise they would be trapped like the ordinary human mind. Consequently the world accessed by mind designers is naked reality, whose furniture is given and totally uncontaminated by any conception. Knowing naked reality, mind designers are in possession of absolute truth. Extending these ideas, we arrive at the philosophical position whose "favourite point of view is God's Eye point of view," as Putnam put it. This view is not contaminated by ordinary mental process, so the world it accesses is absolute naked reality. Thus, Putnam (1981:49) wrote: "On this perspective, the world consists of some fixed totality of mind-independent objects. There is exactly one true and complete description of 'the way the world is.' Truth involves some sort of correspondence relation between words or thought-signs and external things and sets of things." He called this position, which he criticized, "metaphysical realism," others call it "objectivism." I prefer to call it theospectivism for clarity.

Some people think that science can be theoretical only if it attains God's-eye point of view that is free from all human perspectives; it can be objective only if it attains "the view from nowhere," in Thomas Nagel's (1986) words. They mistake objectivism for objectivity and theospectivism for the theoretical attitude, as if science can be objective and theoretical only if scientists become God. Science and theory have nothing to do with theospectivism. Theory derives from theoría, the Greek word for viewing and contemplation. Theospectivism issues from the perspective of theós, God. The two are distinct.

The aspiration of theospectivism is illusory. Those who claim that they have achieved divine neutrality devoid of all human perspectives are merely blind to their own inherent biases. They are more deeply prejudiced than those who lay on the table their own peculiar perspectives and try to compensate for them somehow. Scientists are not gods but human beings who have learned to view and contemplate critically and systematically.

Theoretical reason is basically common sense. It is not created but developed, refined, and applied in larger scales in scientific research. Science is never omniscient. No matter how much it develops, it remains a human endeavor and shares the finitude of the human mind. To explain how we humans can view and contemplate without pretending to be God is a major task for the science of mind. It is also an analysis and critique of the foundations of science, including the science of mind itself. One of its tasks is to discredit the Cartesian Trojan horse, which leads to theospectivism.

Interactive Behaviourism

It appears that one way to escape the Cartesian Trojan horse is to deny that anything is inside and consider only an entity's external behaviours and interactions. This is the approach of behaviourism, which generally regards mental entities as black boxes that behave in complicated ways and interact adeptly with their environment. All one needs to have mind, be-haviorists maintain, is to behave and interact appropriately, to respond to stimuli and be susceptible to behavioural conditioning. Therefore they prohibit scientists to use mental and psychological concepts in describing people.

Behaviourism dominated the study of mind in the first half of the twentieth century, but became the target of attack in the cognitive revolution of the 1950s. Although explicit behaviourist doctrines are discredited in cognitive science, behaviourist ideas survive quietly in various guises. For instance, critics of computationalism often complain that it is a form of behaviourism, as it leaves out experience and understanding and is concerned only with behavioural intelligence, which is essentially behavioural efficiency. The behavioural tendency becomes more pronounced with the recent rise of dynamicalism in AI, which builds robots.

Unlike good old-fashioned behaviourism, which concentrates on a system in isolation, recent models emphasize systems that interact with the environment. Variously called the ecological approach and situated cognition in AI, they are united by their rejection of the mental entity's first-person view. Consequently they have little if any use of psychological concepts. Presently, these models apply best to insects and insect-like robots, the meanings of whose interactive behaviours are assigned by ecologists, AI engineers, or other mind designers. They belong to a variant of behaviourism, interactive behaviourism.

All entities, animate or not, have behaviours and interactions. Why are some mindful and others not? Can criteria of mindfulness be articulated without referring to processes internal to the system or using mental and psychological concepts, as behaviourism claims? What is the status of behaviourists who are capable of prediction, a mental ability behaviourism denies to ordinary people?

Ecological Approach

James Gibson's (1979) ecological approach deprives perception of mental processes and holds that it can be explained by appropriate responses to what ecologists call environmental "information." The theory, based on Gibson's lifelong research on vision, is a big improvement over old-fashioned behaviourism. It makes at least three innovations. First, it replaces fixed-eye vision by mobile-eye vision. Electrodes on the brain in a vat may simulate sense stimuli, but they cannot simulate the brain's motion. Animals are mobile, and their motion contributes essentially to their perception of their surroundings. Second, it brings out the rich complexity of environment factors. The motion of the perceiver greatly enhances the complexity of the optical patterns that strikes the perceiver's retina, the analysis of which is Gibson's greatest contribution to vision research. Third, it replaces responses to arbitrary retinal features by responses only to some invariant features that can be correlated with specific properties in the environment. Thus perceivers attune to environmental properties directly without mediation of sense impressions or other mental representations.

When an animal moves, the optical stimulus on its retina is no longer fixed even if the environment is constant. It is an ever-changing optic array, an optic flow, as Gibson called it. Gibson emphasized the brimming richness of the flow's structural complexity and maintained that it contains all necessary information about the environment and distal objects. The chief information he called affordance, which depends on the features of both the environment and the animal, so that the animal directly resonates with specific environmental features and responds accordingly. Examples of affordances for the frog are small moving shapes and large looming shapes; the frog responds to the perception of the former by lashing out its tongue, to the latter by leaping away. No one doubts the complexity of optic flow. However, many dispute Gibson's assertion that structures of optic flow are already in the form of information that can be "picked up" by the perceiver with minimal process on its part (Fodor and Pylyshyn 1981).

Gibson rejected all mental processes and all conceptual involvements in perception. Memory, too, he deemed superfluous. In his ecological approach, an animal picks up and responds to certain features in the complex optic flow. Its motion contributes to the subsequent optic flow, establishing an automatic feedback between optics and responses. Thus a string of immediate responses constitute intelligent behaviours with little mental contribution. As the animal adapts to the environment, feedback becomes more fluent and resonates more to affordance. Thus perception involves no mental structure and is mostly unconscious. A heat-seeking missile is a good ecological perceiver; heat is the affordance it perceives, or the information it picks up, and its motion resonates with the heat source.

This approach regards an ecological perceiver as a part of the environment reacting appropriately to certain specific features in the optic flow that ecologists recognize as information on distal objects. It allows minimal structures for the mental subject, puts all complexity in the environment, and places so much emphasis on the interface between the subject and its environment that the two become fused together. Gibson insisted that affordance, what the perceiver perceives, is "both" and "neither" subjective and objective. That is because ecological perception has no means to distinguish subjectivity and objectivity. Perceivers are moving-sensing systems tied into their environment. No surprise, a persisting criticism is that the ecological approach leaves out the mental subject.

Many features of ecological perceivers described by Gibson have been proved by subsequent research on insects. Vision plays crucial roles in insect behaviours and is closely coordinated with self-motion. The compound eyes of insects have high temporal resolution, which makes them most sensitive to the flow of optical stimuli and adapt to detecting motion. The fly's deft flight, evasive maneuver, and precision landing make robot designers green with envy. To find out how the fly achieves these feats, scientists insert microelectrodes in the fly's brain, monitor the excitations of individual neurons, and correlate them with the optical input to the fly's eyes and its motor output in flying performance. They find specialized neurons that are finely tuned to the optic flow resulting from a specific type of flying motion, say, pitching or rolling, thus establishing a direct causal link between vision and motion. Thus the fly's complex abilities are managed by relatively simple nervous systems that coordinate visual and motor systems with minimal intermediate steps. This closed sensor-motor control loop serves the survival of insects admirably (Krapp and Hengstenberg 1996; Giurfa and Menzel 1997).

It is unclear how the ecological approach distinguishes insect perception from human perception. Humans do have perceptual experiences that fall within the ecological model; for instance, subjects stumble when optical flows on their retina generate the illusion that they are walking in a "moving room." However, we can do much more. We can recognize objects in perception, as things separate from us, as different kinds of things. Recognition seems to have no place in the ecological approach to perception.

Human Body : From the Viewpoint of Ayurveda

We have introduced ourselves to the human body by viewing it under various modern equipments, analysing and examining various elements of it through different chemicals and examining the entire system, and its parts. A question naturally arises as to why the same human body is to be considered through the ayurvedic perspective. Because even if the body is viewed from the angle of ayurveda, the nature of the body or its functioning does not change. It is not possible that the structure and the function of the body are different in ayurveda and modern sciences. But the method of study of the organs of the body is different though their structure and functions remain the same.

Though we have resorted to the modern science to study the structure and the functions of the human body, yet for a comprehensive study of the reasons and the results of the never ending complicated and numerous processes of the internal organs of the body, one must resort to the ayurveda which thinks about the power which is behind these processes. The yoga sadhakas assume inseparable relation of the body and the mind and try to go beyond it; it is useful for them to understand the view.

Hence, a student of yoga, should resort to modern sciences wherever necessary, and yet study the body from the ayurvedic point of view. Ayurveda has evolved the origin of the body by following "Je Pindi te Brahmandi" (principle found in a jiva is the same as that found in the universe) and "Je Brahmandi te Pindi " (principle found in the universe is the same as that found in a jiva), the two dictums as the basis. Since the nature is based on panchmahabhootas, the body should also be based on them. It is said that Prithvi (Earth), Aap (Water), Tej (Fire), Vayu (Air) and Aakash (Space) the panchmahabhootas and the soul together form the body. It is stated as " Shatdhatvatmaka Purushaha" while clarifying this Charaka has defined the body as under:

Tatra shariram naam chetanadhishtanabhutam |

Panchmahabhootvikar samudayatmakam samyogavahi | | C S 6.

Chaitanya (Consciousness) and the elements arising out of panchmahabhootas (Five basic principles earth, fire, water, air, space or ether) form the body.

As the body is formed out of panchmahabhootas (Five basic principles earth, fire, water, air, space or ether), the five sense organs in the body possess the virtues of these panchmahabhootas (Five basic principles earth, fire, water, air, space or ether). The characteristics of akasha (space or ether), that is shabda (sound) is received by the ears. The characteristics of vayu (air), that is sparsha (touch) is perceived through the skin. Characteristics of teja (Fire), that is roopa (view) is seen through the eyes. Characteristics of aapa (water), that is rasa (taste) is perceived through the tongue. The characteristics of the prithvi (earth), that is gandha (smell) is perceived through nose. That means the body formed out of panchamahabhootas (Five basic principles earth, fire, water, air, space or ether) through its five sensory organs perceives the characteristics of those panchamahbhootas. The nature of the panchamahabhootas in the other organs of the body is as under:

Parthiv Bhav (Earthly nature): Nails, bones, teeth, flesh, skin, excretion, beard, body hair, hair etc.

Jaliya Bhav (Nature of water): Fluids, kapha, pitta, urine, perspiration, and saliva.

Aagneya Bhav (Nature of fire): Pitta, heat, the glow of the body, view, eyesight etc.

Vayviya bhav (Nature of air): Breathing, blinking and opening of the eyelids, speed, inspiration, dharana etc.

Aakashiya bhav (Nature of space): All holes, hollow places, small and big strota, vocal system and ear system.

Thus, the body formed out of panchamahabhootas, while working gets burned down or degenerated. "Shiryate tat shariram", that which degenerates is known as body. The body elements degenerate and get lost again in panchmahabhootas. The same are again formed anew. The body actually demands for their new formation from the surrounding panchamahabhoutik nature. The elements in the surrounding panchmahabhoutic nature are picked up willingly by the body and assimilated. The symptoms such as desire, hunger, and thirst are commonly felt. Also, hatred towards the element, which has been created in excess is also born. In any natural process, these three things are included.

Visargadanvikshepe somsuryanila yatha |

Dharyanti jagddeham kaphapitta nilastatatha | | Sushrut | |

Visarg (giving strength), Aadan (taking away of strength), Vikshepa (movement), behind these three things, there are three strengths in the nature, Chandra, Surya and Vayu (moon, sun and wind). While thinking about the body, this work is done by kapha, pitta and vat. This is stated in Ayurveda.

These three principles (doshas -kapha, vat and pitta) do the disintegration and integration of the components in the body. The medium of these three doshas is responsible for these disintegration and integration actions. As these three doshas are endowed with their characteristics, they are termed as dravya (liquid).

The ayurvedic doctors too have different opinions about these tridoshas. There was a conference on tridosha in 1935 at Hindu Vishwavidyalaya at Kashi. There was discussion amongst renowned pandits and the following conclusions were drawn regarding tridoshas. The strengths cannot stay independently, and need support of liquids, hence vat, kapha and pitta are not strengths but liquids. But according to their locations, they are gross at some places and subtle at others (cannot be seen). They are exhibited through actions at such places.

Kapha is a white coloured substance, which is cold, heavy, slow, sticky and glossy type. Even if it is subtle or gross, it has these qualities. As per ayurveda, kapha amounts to six palm full. That means it can be in liquid form too. Even if the oily part of the kapha is demonstrated through the organs, its other characteristics are according to its functions. Pitta is hot, sharp, a little bit of expansive property, with particular smell or strong smell. Even if these are demonstrated through organs, other characteristics are as per functions. Pitta is five palmfuls. This also is a liquid substance.

Vat is dry, less cold as compared with kapha, tiny and movable. This substance is of moving nature and not related to body organs. This is at some places gross and at most of the places subtle. It is called as Avyaktovyaktakarma " that is even if it is not expressed on its own, it is expressed through actions.

The health or ill health of the body depends on these three substances. Also, most of the movements in the body are also dependent on this. Even if all the substances in the nature and in this body are panchmahabhoutik, the main functional ones are only three i e aap, tej and vayu. For carrying out their functions, these three substances have to seek help from the earth and the sky. Hence, the doshas are also three. There is another stream of thought that the life of the body and the most supportive element i e the blood is also the fourth dosha. But it is more proper to recognise blood as dhatu instead of dosha.

If these three doshas are equal in proportion in the body (individual), then the body functions all right. But when this equality is disturbed, ill health sets in. To reduce the substance, which has become excessive or to increase one, which is reduced, one has to plan proper medicine or other process. The nature has a number of substances surrounding the body. The substance, which is absorbed in the body affects it and causes certain symptoms. At times, the equality in the three doshas is damaged and ailments start. There are different characteristics of the elements of the body, they are of twenty types.

Heavyness, slowness, coldness, oilyness, smoothness, thickness, softness, firmness, minuteness, and the opposites of this that is lightweight, swift, warm, dry, rough, thin, hard, moving, gross, sticky etc. Out of these twenty characteristics, oily, cold, heavy, slow, soft, sticky and solid are reflected through the prithvi and aap elements out of the panchmahabhootas.

If these substances are absorbed more into the body than needed, and are demonstrated by the body through lithargy, heaviness, softness etc, then one can say kapha dosha is on the increase. Because these characteristics are of kapha dosha. Also, oily, sharp, small, hot etc characteristics are reflected in tej-based elements. If these substances are absorbed more into the body, and are demonstrated by symptoms such as thirst, burning, fever etc, then one can say pitta dosha is on the increase. Also, sensations such as dryness, smallness, coldness, roughness, minuteness and movement etc are reflected through the vayu and aakash or logical elements. If they are absorbed more into the body and are demonstrated through symptoms such as sleeplessness, dryness, lightweight etc then one can say vatdosha is on the increase.

If the three ḍoshas i e vat, pitta and kapha are equalised, then their functions support each other and the body remains healthy. The proportion of each dosha to the desired extent is known as doshasamya. If it increases or decreases it is known as doshavaishamya. So while studying the body the health or ill health, first one must consider the three doshas. After the three doshas, one has to consider dhatu and mal. Because it is stated that " Doshadhatumalamulam hi shariram | " Vakbhata has the following reference:

Vayuh pittam kaphascheti trayo doshah samasatah | V S 1.6

Vikruta vikruta deham ghananti the vardhayanticha | V S 1.7

The body contains three doshas kapha, pitta, vayu. When they go astray, they destroy the life. When they are equalised, they govern the life. Ras, Rakta, Mans, Med, Asthi, Majja and Shukra are seven dhatus. These are also called substances. Urine, stool and sweat are known as mal. They are also substances, both of these can be affected by the doshas.

Ras (Fluids) - This is a flowing dhatu. When one consumes food that is a square meal, based on panchmahabhootas, including six rasas, twenty characteristics and all types of viryas and when the food is digested properly after being processed by the fire in the stomach, the substance generated which is minute essence is known as rasa.

Its place is the heart and that is circulated through all the vessels due to the vyanvayu all over the body. It also supplies dhatus necessary for the growth of the children, dhatus which are weakened in the old people, and continues to maintain the stability in the middle aged persons. It stays alive in the body. Other dhatus are then made up of rasa.

Rakta (Blood) - When the rasa containing more water reaches the liver and the spleen, it becomes red in colour due to the ranjak pitta. Then it is known as blood. The characteristics of prithvi, aap, tej, vayu and aakash in that order i e peculiar smell, liquidity, red colour, speed and ? are exhibited in blood. Hence blood is known as panchamahabhoutic. When the blood is washed away from a cloth and does not leave any stain on the cloth, it is termed as healthy blood (defectless). That is the main function of this dhatu.

Mansa (Muscular Tissue or flesh) - On the supporting blood, the fire in the muscular tissue operates in the mansvah strotra and this dhatu is produced. The warmth or heat of the vayu and tej is mixed up in the blood and it becomes thick. It gets ripened due to the fire of the mansa and takes the form of mansa.

The cells and the muscles in the body are also forms of flesh... The cells do the act of covering and hence the organs are protected. The muscles bear the weight of the body. The joints move. All these movements are due to vyanvayu.

Med (Adipose Tissue)- On the supporting mansa (flesh), the fire in the med operates in medovah strota and the dhatu med is created. It strengthens the body.

Asthi (Bones) - On the panchmahabhootas in the supporting elements, the fire in the asthidhatu operates and creates roughness. This creates bones. Due to vayu, they can be porous. This function is carried on in asthivah strota. Due to this...

Majja (Bone Marrow) - Asthidhatu supporting majja gets operated upon by the fire in majja in majjavah strota. and majja dhatu is created. The.. in the holes in the bones is known as majja. The nature of it is different from the med...

Shukra (Generative Tissue) - Shukra dhatu is produced from majja due to uniting with fire. The origin of shukra dhatu is in shukradhar kala in shukravah strota all over the body. Though the testicles and the eggs are the main origins for this, actually shukra dhatu is produced all over the body in a miniscule form. It drizzles in the testicles and comes out through medhra. In a young age, it exists in invisible form and when the child comes of age, it becomes visible.

Female Shukr The shukra dhatu originating in the female body is termed as Aartava.

There are two types of this:

- o The monthly aartava which is produced in the uterus each month, this is known as bahihpushpa. This is not useful for conceiving, but this is necessary to purify the uterus.
- o The other aartava originates in a tiny form It takes part in the unity by absorbing the shukra, it is termed as Antarpushpa.
- o The brightness or the excellent glow in the shukra dhatu, of all seven dhatus, is termed as oj. The main place of oj is the heart, but it occupies the entire body. It is the main basis of living and the state of the body depends on it. Pranas reside in it. It is actually representative of the characteristics of all seven dhatus and as such need not be considered as the eighth dhatu.

There are upadhatus for all sapta dhatus.

They are as under:

Rasa: Stanya and Raj

Rakta: Kadara and Shira

Mansa: Vasaa and Twacha

Med: Snayu, Sandhibandha, Shira

Mal: These are of three types:

Purish: After the food has been fully digested, at the time of division of sarkitta, purish is produced by purishdharakarla in purishvah strota. According to the Charaka, the measure of it is 7 handfuls. Due to this, there is dharana of vayu and agni.

Mutra Urine): According to Charaka, the measure is 4 handfuls.

Sweda (Perspiration): This is mal of med. Due to this, the skin and hair become little moist.

Now, when the basic concept of tridosh, saptadhatu and their impurities is clear, we will consider the physical body. Ayurveda has clarified as under:

When friction is caused between the organs of the male and female body at the time of coitus, the vayu provocates the teja in the body. Due to the unity of teja and vayu, the shukra starts flowing, gets dislocated from its place and through the penis enters the vagina; there it gets united with aartava. Raj in the form of fire and shukra in the form of soma get united and the fetus is formed which moves to the uterus and stays there till the arrival of time to come out. Vaayu separates from this fetus, which is in the form of chaitanya, doshas, dhatus, mala and other organs. Teja does the work of digestion. Aap gives it moistness. Earth gives the form. When the grown fetus assumes hands, legs, tongue, ears, nose etc and other organs, then it gets the term body.

Ayurveda has considered the human body in four stages. First the shape of the body that is structural consideration of the body. In this, dhatus such as asthi and muscles (mansa) are considered. Then the prakriti of the body that means the internal processes of the body are thought of. Here, the processes of rasa, rakta, med, majja and shukra are considered. Then the vikruti, that means the disturbed rapport in the internal processes of the body. Here, all the diseases have been considered. Then nishkruti that means the process of examining the body with respect to the vikrutis. We will consider only the first two stages in this chapter (because it is outside the purview of this book, to consider the later two stages of vikruti and nishkruti)

The main basis of the human body is the skeleton of the bones. All the parts of the body function due to the support of the Asthi (bones) belong to the prithvi principle and are the most hard and most durable part in the body. Even when the body is burnt on the pyre, all the bones do not get burnt away. Bones stay for a very long time, hence skeletons from thousands of years ago are still available.

While thinking in detail about the bones in a full-grown body, it should be done considering the six aspects of the body. Sushrut, who is the pioneer of the traditional anatomy, has stated these six aspects as under - Main part of the body i e the torso and head. Two hands, two legs are the four branches. The hands and the legs are considered as if the main part has branched out. Even when the branches are cut, the main tree remains alive, thus even if the hands and legs are cut, the body stays alive. This proves the appropriateness of the terms used in Ayurveda.

The upper and lower part of the body each have 30 bones, thus there are 120 bones. While considering the middle part of the body, first the spinal cord should be considered. It is made up of 33 vertebrae. They are joined to each other. The 7 vertebrae in the upper portion are considered of neck and then 12 of the chest. From the first vertebra of the chest (i e the eighth vertebra), the ribs start. They are termed as Parshuka or vakri.

The cord is like a bamboo, thick at the base and goes on narrowing upwards. Like a bamboo, it is made up hollow. As the bamboo is hollow, the spine is also hollow and the cord passes through it. In the head, there is a cavity made up of eight flat bones, in which the brain is placed. Due to this cave, the brain is protected securely. The bones below the bones on both the sides are known as Shankasthi. They are very thin and from behind them a big blood vessel, which supplies blood to the brain, passes. Hence, a blow on this part can damage the brain severely and there are chances that person may die. In front of this cave, there are 14 bones of the face. The cavity of the ear also has a chain of small bones and the perception of the sound waves is carried through this chain to the nervous fibres.

Thus, the full-grown body has in all 206 bones, according to Sushrut 300 and according to Charaka 360 bones.

The bones are divided into six types:

Nalikasthi: These are long like tubes and hollow from within. They are stuffed with majja. Till the age of 20 years, the colour of this is red, then it turns yellow. These types of bones are in the hands and legs.

Kapalasthi: These are flat in nature. The above and below layer is separated and hollowed parts are made. Red majja is filled in it.

Valayasthi: These are round in shape. The ribs of the chest are of this type.

Tarunashthi: These are soft in nature. They are mainly in between joint of vertebrae, two vertebrae there is a circle of tarunasthi. Hence, any jolt to the body, till it reaches the brain becomes mild.

Ruchakasthi: The teeth which are different from all the other bones in the body are covered under this. They are 28 or 32 in all.

Aanvashti: The bones which are smaller and irregular in size and which do not fit under any of the above category fall in this. These bones have fat with blood.

The entire bone system is divided into two main parts, nails and teeth is whitish part. Since they do not have a layer of the skin, it is termed as bahyakankal. These bones can be used for detecting disease. All other bones are covered with skin, they are covered in antahkankal.

All the bones in the body are joined with each other. These joints are termed as sandhi. Sandhi are of two types. Sthir or achal. The sandhis of the skull fall under this type. The bones in the jaw and the teeth have sthir sandhi(fixed joints). They cannot move relative to each other. All other joints are chal or cheshthavant. They can be moved in a limited manner with respect to each other.

Generally all the bones coming under chal joints are covered with tarunashti. They are elastic in nature and can withstand the pushes. Above these tarunashti, there is another layer, which covers the joints like a bag, which is termed as sandhikosh. In this sandhikosh, above tarunashti, there is a double thin layer like a bag. Substances such as shleshak, shleshma exist in it. When the joints are moved, these are used as grease. When this substance reduces, then the joints start creaking while moving and there is pain.

In Ayurveda, there are eight types of sandhis:

Kor: Joints in Finger, wrist, ankle, elbow.

Ulukhal: The joint of the thigh, joint at he roots of teeth.

Samugad: Joints near the shoulder, anus, reproductive organs, hips etc.

Pratar: Joints like neck, vertebrae of the back etc.

Tunnasevani: Joints of the kapalashthi at face, waist etc.

Vaayastund: Joints near the chin on both the sides.

Mandal: Round - joints at heart, eyes etc.

Sankhavarta: Having circles - Joints at ears, shankha (inner ear.) etc.

If the number of joints are considered, each branch has 17, that all branches have 68, and at other places 83, i e in all 210 joints described in Ayurveda.

Muscles join all the bones with each other and the movement is made with expansion and contraction of the muscles.

The muscles are of four types:

Pratanvarti Muscles: Four branches and in all joints

Vruta: Kandara - All round muscles

Sushira: Contracting muscles in big intestine

Pruthul: Flat muscles - muscles at side, chest, back, head etc

If the number of muscles is seen, then in four branches (600), 150 in each branch, ? 70, at other places 230, thus in all there are 900 muscles in the body.

Simple Definition

Ayurveda is a wholistic system of medicine from India that uses a constitutional model. Its aim is to provide guidance regarding food and lifestyle so that healthy people can stay healthy and folks with health challenges can improve their health.

There are several aspects to Ayurveda that are quite unique:

1. Its recommendations will often be different for each person regarding which foods and which lifestyle they should follow in order to be completely healthy. This is due to it's use of a constitutional model.
2. Everything in Ayurveda is validated by observation, inquiry, direct examination and knowledge derived from the ancient texts.
3. It understands that there are energetic forces that influence nature and human beings. These forces are called the Tridoshas.
4. Because Ayurveda sees a strong connection between the mind and the body, a huge amount of information is available regarding this relationship.

Origin

Ayurveda is an intricate system of healing that originated in India thousands of years ago. We can find historical evidence of Ayurveda in the ancient books of wisdom known as the Vedas. In the Rig Veda, over 60 preparatison were mentioned that could be used to assist an individual in overcoming various ailments. The Rig Veda was written over 6,000 years ago, but really Ayurveda has been around even longer than that. What we see is that A yurveda is more than just a medical system. It is a Science of Life. We are all part and parcel of nature. Just as the animals and plants live in harmony with nature and utilize the Laws of Nature to create health and balance within their beings, we, too, adhere to these very same principles. Therefore, it is fair to say that Ayurveda is a system that helps maintain health in a person by using the inherent principles of nature to bring the individual back i nto equilibrium with their true self. In essence Ayurveda has been in existence since the beginning of time because we have always been governed by nature's laws.

Meaning

Ayurveda is made up of two Sanskrit words: Ayu which means life and Veda which means the knowledge of. To know about life is Ayurveda. However, to fully comprehend the vast s cope of Ayurveda let us first define "Ayu" or life. According to the ancient Ayurvedic scholar Charaka, "ayu" is comprised of four essential parts. The combination of mind, body, senses and the soul.

Mind, Body, and Sences

We tend to identify most with our physical bodies; yet, in actuality, there is more to us then what meets the eye. We can see that underlying our physical structure is the mind, which not only controls our thought processes but helps assist us in carrying out day-to-day activities such as respiration, circulation, digestion and elimination. The mind and the body work in conjunction with one another to regulate our physiology.

In order for the mind to act appropriately to assist the physical body, we must use our senses as information gatherers. We can think of the mind as a computer and the senses as the data which gets entered into the computer. Smell and taste are two important senses th at aid in the digestive process.

When the mind registers that a particular food is entering the gastrointestinal tract, it directs the body to act accordingly by releasing various digestive enzymes. However, if we overindulge the taste buds with too much of a certain taste, such as sweet, we may find that the ability of the mind to perceive the sweet taste is impaired; and thereby the body becomes challenged in its ability to process sweet foods. Maintaining the clarity of our senses is an essential part in allowing the mind and body to integrate their functions and help in keeping us healthy and happy individuals.

Soul

Ayurveda also sees that before we exist in physical form with the help of the mind and senses that we exist in a more subtle form known as the soul. The ancient seers of India believed tha t we were comprised of a certain energetic essence that precluded the inhabitance of our physical entity. In fact, they hypothesized that we may indeed occupy many physical bodies throughout the course of time but that our underlying self or soul remains unchanged. What we see to help illustrate this concept is what transpires at the time of death. When the individual nears the time to leave the physical body, many of his/her desires will cease to be present. As the soul no longer identifies with the bod y, the desire to eat food or indulge in a particular activity that used to be a great source of satisfaction for that person drops by the wayside. In fact, many individuals have been documented to experience the sensation of being "out of their bodies." These are just a few examples of how we are made up of these four components that we call life.

Principles

Now that we have a better understanding of what comprises life, let's look at some of the principles of Ayurveda and how they might affect us. In Ayurveda we view a person as a unique individual made up of five primary elements. The elements are ether (space), air, fire, water, and earth. Just as in nature, we too have these five elements in us. When any of these elements are present in the environment, they will in turn have an influence on us.

The foods we eat and the weather are just two examples of the presence of these elements. While we are a composite of these five primar y elements, certain elements are seen to have an ability to combine to create various physiological functions. Ether and air combine to form what is known in Ayurveda as the Vata dosha. Vata governs the principle of movement and therefore can be seen as the force which directs nerve impulses, circulation, respiration, and elimination. Fire and water are the elements that combine to form the Pitta dosha. The Pitta dosha is the process of transf ormation or metabolism. The transformation of foods into nutrients that our bodies can assimilate is an example of a pitta function. Pitta is also responsible for metabolism in the organ and tissue systems as well as cellular metabolism. Finally, it is pr edominantly the water and earth elements which combine to form the Kapha dosha. Kapha is what is responsible for growth, adding structure unit by unit. Another function of the Kapha dosha is to offer protection. Cerebral-sp inal fluid protects the brain and spinal column and is a type of Kapha found in the body. Also, the mucousal lining of the stomach is another example of the Kapha dosha protecting the tissues. We are all made up of unique proportions of Vata, Pitta and Ka pha. These ratios of the doshas vary in each individual; and because of this, Ayurveda sees each person as a special mixture that accounts for our diversity.

Ayurveda gives us a model to look at each individual as a unique makeup of the three doshas and to thereby design treatment protocols that specifically address a persons health challenges. When any of the doshas (Vata, Pitta or Kapha) become accumulated, Ayurveda will suggest specific lifestyle and nutritional guidelines to assist the individual in reducing the dosha that has become excessive. We may also suggest certain herbal supplemen ts to hasten the healing process. If toxins in the body are abundant, then a cleansing process known as Pancha Karma is recommended to eliminate these unwanted toxins.

Mind-Body-Soul Balance Through Ayurveda

Figure: *According To Ayurveda, A Person Is Made Up Of 3 Components-The Body (Physical- Sthula Sharir), The Mind (Psychological- Sukshma Sharir), And The Soul (Spiritual- Karana Sharir). It Is Essential To Maintain A Mind-Body-Soul Balance For One's Well Being. Hence, Ayurveda Suggests Following The Below Practices For Harmony Between The Body, Mind, And Soul.*

One Must Consume A Wide Range Of Foods That Inculcates All The 6 Tastes Of The Human Tongue, I.E., Sweet, Salty, Bitter, Sour, Spicy, And Astringent. By Doing This You Make Sure That The Food You Consume Has All The Essential Nutrients For The Body's Functioning And Health, Thus Harmonizing The Connection Between The Mind-Body-Soul Of An Individual.

Dincharya

Dincharya Is A Daily Regime, Prescribed By Ayurveda, That Is Synchronized With The Cycle Of The Sun During The Day. Waking Up Before Sunrise, Scraping Your Tongue, Washing Your Face, And Sipping Warm Water Daily Is A Part Of The Daily Routine. Following This Routine Helps To Cleanse Us From Within, Relaxes Our Minds, And Sharpens Our Cognitive Abilities, Thus Creating A Balance Between The Body, Soul, And Mind.

Yoga & Pranayama

Pranayam Is A Few Breathing Exercises That Help To Cleanse The Respiratory And Lymphatic Systems In The Body. It Maintains The Life Force Or Prana And Clears The Channels Of Energy Or Nadis In The Body By Employing Controlled Breathing Techniques. You Can Also Add Yoga To Your Schedule Which Helps In Increased Flexibility And Strength To The Body.

Meditation

Meditation Focuses On Building One's Spiritual Well Being. It Creates Awareness Of Your Intangible Being Living Within You And Makes You Experience Divine Bliss Or Ananda. It Helps To Improve Your Memory And Concentration Skills As Well.

Switch To A Natural Lifestyle

Instead Of Spending Time Indoors, Try And Spend Time With Nature. Be Amongst The Elements Of Nature Like The Sky, Earth, Fire, Air, And Water. You Can Spend Time Observing Them Gain Harmony And Holistic Well Being.

Chapter 2

Understanding the Body in Ayurveda

Introduction

In Ayurveda, the understanding of the body extends beyond its physical form to encompass subtle energies and life forces. According to Ayurvedic philosophy, the body is a microcosm of the universe, composed of five elements: earth, water, fire, air, and ether. These elements combine to form three fundamental energies or doshas known as Vata, Pitta, and Kapha. Each individual has a unique constitution or prakriti, determined by the predominance of these doshas at the time of conception.

Ayurvedic anatomy describes the body as a network of channels or nadis through which energy flows. These nadis correspond to the circulatory, nervous, and endocrine systems in modern anatomy. The flow of energy through the nadis is essential for maintaining health and vitality, and blockages or imbalances in the nadis can lead to disease and illness.

In addition to the nadis, Ayurveda recognizes the presence of centers or chakras in the body. Chakras are subtle energy centers that regulate the flow of energy throughout the body. There are seven main chakras aligned along the spinal column, each associated with specific physical, emotional, and spiritual qualities. Balancing the chakras is believed to promote health and well-being on all levels. Ayurvedic anatomy also includes the concept of dhatus, or tissues, which are the building blocks of the body. There are seven dhatus in total, including plasma, blood, muscle, fat, bone, bone marrow, and reproductive tissue. These dhatus are nourished by the digestive system and play essential roles in maintaining the structure and function of the body.

In Ayurveda, the understanding of the body is closely intertwined with the concept of doshas, which govern physiological processes and determine individual constitution. Vata dosha is associated with the elements of air and ether and governs movement and communication in the body. Pitta dosha is associated with the elements of fire and water and governs digestion, metabolism, and transformation. Kapha dosha is associated with the elements of earth and water and governs structure, stability, and lubrication.

Understanding the doshas and their influence on the body is key to maintaining health and well-being in Ayurveda. By recognizing one's unique constitution and balancing the doshas through diet, lifestyle, and herbal remedies, individuals can promote harmony and vitality in all aspects of life.

In this day and age when the world has become a global village, people from one socio-demographic location can be found across the world, with a lot of cross mingling of relationships that stretch the barriers of place and time. In this scenario, the need of the hour is to develop a theory of personality that transcends this problem of cultural and racial bias to propound one that is valid across the world. For this, the basic requirement is that it should be universally acceptable, be of an elemental nature, and be valid to people across all genres.

To understand this, the first source of knowledge that comes to mind to tackle the problem at hand is that of the Indian philosophical systems that have withstood the test of time to be applicable across millennia without losing their relevance and applicability to people from ages to the present day. The first discipline that comes to mind which is capable of identifying people is that of Ayurveda with its exact science of medicine and which is capable of giving answers to questions that are posed at a biological and physical level as to the constituents of man and the reasons for his biological behaviour.

"With the increasing realization that many of the western psychological concepts and methods lack relevance to different cultural systems, the need for developing indigenous psychologies was recognized all over the world (Kim and Berry, 1973)..."

Objectives

The main objectives of this paper are to consolidate a personality theory taking support of Ayurvedic literature from the psychological perspective and to make a case that personality testing taking Tridosha and Triguna could be a comprehensive perspective.

Ayurveda, with its defined constructs which are elemental and form the cornerstone of physiology as well as psychological delineations, their assessment, categorization and treatment options, is indispensable for developing a theory and methodology for assessment of Prakriti-more specifically, the psychological manifestation of the Tridoshas and the Trigunas combined-for a scientific, elemental and globally valid testing procedure and its obvious categorization. This would lead to globalizing the understanding of human behaviour irrespective of caste, creed and religion, leading to a universal typology of people, helping in the ultimate need for psychology, that of understanding and predicting of human behaviour and emotions. This has large implications in areas ranging from harnessing of human resources to early identification of diseases and their better management.

The Manifestation of the Five Proto-elements in Man

One of the basic tenets of Ayurveda is that man is a microcosm of the very world that he inhabits. This implies explicitly that whatever man is made up of, the world too is made up of those same things or elements, but of different combinations and degrees. Here, by elements is meant the five Mahabhutas-that is, Akasa, Vayu, Tejas, Ap and Prithvi. The earth and man are made up of these five elements. In fact, Ayurveda postulates that all living beings on the earth, including the non-living too, are made up of these same five elements in varying degrees, specific to each form, matter and species, and according to a predetermined ratio that cannot be changed. These five elements combine with each other to form the three humors of Vata, Pitta and Kapha (also called as the Tridoshas in unison) which is the cornerstone of Ayurvedic philosophy.

If changes do occur, then this leads to an imbalance in the organism, or a modified version of the organism is formed, the survival of which will depend upon its ability to adapt to its environment. Ayurvedic principles are drawn heavily from Samkhyan Philosophy.

"In Ayurveda, the three Doshas are considered to be universal principles that function in all aspects of material creation, including the mineral, plant, and animal kingdoms, the time of day, the seasons of the year, even the planets and galaxies. In this way, the human physiology is inexorably connected to the whole of existence. The Doshas have been correlated with systems theory in the field of physics, providing a sound theoretical basis for this Ayurvedic concept, and research utilizing a bio-statistical approach to quantify the Doshas reveals a sound empirical basis as well. A pilot study revealed the possibility of utilizing Prakriti to correlate phenotypes with genotypes in the human population, which could have wide-ranging implications for health care".

The five elements combine to form the Tridoshas in biodiversity

"According to Ayurveda, the universe evolved out of the 'un-manifested' (Avyakta), which implies Prakriti (primordial matter) and Purusa (primordial consciousness). Mahan (intellect) then evolves from Avyakta, and Ahamkara (ego) follows. Ego has three different qualities (Gunas): Sattva (the pure), Rajas (the dynamic), and Tamas (the inert). Sattva and Rajas together then produce eleven Indriyas (sense and motor organs known as Jnanendriyas and Karmendriyas) and Manas. The Gunas, Tamas and Rajas combine to produce five Tanmatras (energy quanta), which in their turn produce the five Mahabhutas (elements in the ancient sense, sometimes also called proto-elements). From these Mahabhutas the entire material world is made up... Living beings consist of the Mahabhutas as well as the Indriyas".

Dash, in his book Fundamentals of Ayurvedic Medicine (pg. 16, 17), has explained the inter-relatedness of man with the environment and how the Pancha Mahabhutas have evolved in man to form the different body organs and organ systems. He says, "...man has five senses and through these senses he perceives the external world in five different ways. The sense organs are the ears, the skin, the eyes, the tongue and the nose. Through these sense organs, the external object is not only perceived, but also absorbed into the human body in the form of energy. These five types of senses are the basis on which the entire universe is divided, grouped or classified in five different ways, and they are known as five Mahabhutas.... According to Ayurveda, the body of the individual is composed of five Mahabhutas. Similarly, other things of the world are also composed of five Mahabhutas. In the human body these five Mahabhutas are explained in terms of Doshas, Dhatus and Malas..."

The play of the five proto-elements or the Pancha Mahabhutas is not restricted to the physical body only. It finds expression in the mind too, which also is purported to be made up of the five elements. Frawley in his book Ayurveda and the Mind is of the opinion that the mind transcends all the five gross elements because through the mind we can perceive all the elements and their inter-relationships. He further says that all the forms of earth, water, fire, air and ether can be observed, imagined and contemplated on. "Yet the elements do provide a key to how the mind works. Though the elements in the mind are more subtle than those in the body, they retain the same basic attributes and actions. We can understand the mental elements through the analogy of the physical".

Charaka Samhita expresses this idea in verses 46-47 (as stated in Mental Health in Ayurveda) as follows: "Mind, Soul and the Body-these three constitute a tripod, upon the meaningful combination of which the world is sustained. They constitute the substratum for everything, which is endowed with life. This (combination of the above three) is Purusha who is sentient and who is the subject matter for this science. It is for this that Ayurveda has been brought to light". Verse 1-55 also states: "The body and the mind are the abodes of diseases as well as health. Proper body-mind interaction is the cause for happiness".

Review of Literature

"The concept of Tridosha, the Ayurvedic theory of physiologic regulation involving the integrated function of the three Doshas-Vata, Pitta, and Kapha-is a cornerstone of Ayurveda, named in the first chapter of the earliest text, Charaka Samhita (Angot, 1993; Sharma, 1981-1986). Its connection to modern science, showing that the Doshas constitute systems of regulatory function, each with a particular area of responsibility (Hankey, 2001) and its present preliminary validation, are first steps to bringing the discipline wider acceptance within modern medicine".

From the Ayurvedic source, what has already been studied and internalized in psychology is the concept of "Triguna". "The theoretical expositions on Triguna and their manifestations in human nature have attracted the attention of Indian psychologists. The concept has been examined theoretically (Bose, 1966; Misra et al., 2000; Parameshwaran, 1969; Rao, 1971) and empirically (Das, 1987, 1991; Kapur et al., 1997; Marutham, Balodhi and Misra, 1998; Mathew, 1995; Mohan and Sandhu, 1986, 1988; Pathak, Bhatt and Sharma, 1992; Rao and Harigopal, 1979; Sebastian and Mathew, 2002; Sharma, 1999; Singh, 1972; Sitamma, Sridevi and P.V.K. Rao, 1995; Uma, Lakshmi and Parameshwaran, 1971; Wolf, 1998)". So far, what has not been explored is the study of "Tridoshas", empirically from the domain of psychology.

"The ancient texts name many other properties of the Doshas. For example, all human beings can be classified according to the dominance of one or more Doshas in their physiology, their Prakriti (literally 'nature'). The classification gives a good indication of physiologic strengths and weaknesses, mental tendencies, and susceptibility to illnesses of different kinds. According to Ayurveda, the Prakriti, including its distortion by life history, is of fundamental importance in maintaining health: It provides a guide to lifestyle and ways of healthy living appropriately individualized for each person. Early, pre-pathologic stages of the development of illness depend on the pressure on the functioning of the Doshas. Do they have the ability to cope with challenges presented? Simple knowledge of how they function, and what their state is at any time, can prevent disease, and help restore health more quickly".

Hankey (Establishing the scientific validity of Tridosha) is also of the opinion, "the functions of Vata, Pitta and Kapha are fundamental is confirmed by the fact that each represents an independent definition of 'life' used in modern biology". He reinstates this statement by delineating the functions of the Tridoshas with the knowledge obtained by modern science, and more specifically, the area of biological, cellular, chemical sciences as we know them today. He is of the opinion, "...These three (homeostasis, the ongoing production of 'negative entropy', and inheritable structure)" (he is talking about the modern biological equivalents of Vata, Pitta and Kapha) "have all been used as definitions of life. Comprising all three makes Tridosha the most powerful definition of life ever formulated!"

"Being based on systems theory Tridosha would apply to living organisms other than those found on earth. ... The possibilities for speculation are endless. But whatever the chemical basis for its reproducing forms, each organism in such a system of life would necessarily have to possess the systems functions named, and their regulation could justifiably be identified as 'Vata, Pitta and Kapha'". Hankey said, "The analysis of Dosha function presented here confirms the experience of every practicing Vaidya: Tridosha is a simple and profound way to understand human physiological function, giving an accurate explanation of physiological function, including the means of regulation of all the major organ subsystems - and their principal organs. One of the most powerful aspects of Tridosha is that it presents physiological function from a holistic perspective.... In not losing sight of the whole when dealing with each component part, Tridosha reveals its sophistication as a description of physiological function from the perspective of the organism itself, 'the organism as a whole' is the primary concept, and the functioning of its parts is secondary. Wholeness of organism functioning can only be maintained by coordinated regulation of functioning of each successive level of parts. In Tridosha, Ayurveda gets it right, setting the scene for descriptions of how to maintain wholeness of organism functioning, and when compromised how to restore it. In other words, it lays the ground for programs of both prevention and cure of ill health". (Hankey, Establishing the scientific validity of Tridosha)

"Every individual is different. What determines the 'individuality' of a person? How do we identify genotypes associated with phenotypes and classify the human population? Systematic surveys of genetic variation form the basis for determination of population frequencies, genetic linkage studies, and association studies relating genotype with phenotypes of interest to answer some of these questions (Bamshad et al., 2003; Rosenberg et al., 2002). Genotypic or phenotypic classification of human populations is important in various epidemiological contexts, such as better understanding disease (Pearson et al., 2003) and drug response (Kirchheiner et al., 2004; Meyer, 2000). The current classification of human populations is broadly based on ethnicity; geographical location, language, or self-reported ancestry. However, such commonly used ethnic labels are inaccurate representations of genetic clusters and do not reflect the underlying genetic makeup (Wilson et al., 2001). The inability to explore such relationships is attributed to the complexity of human demographic history, which gives rise to neither an obvious natural clustering scheme nor an obvious appropriate degree of resolution (Editorial comment, 2001)".

Hence, from the above-mentioned numerous researches, we can see how different scientists are engaged in understanding the physical properties of the Tridoshas and how they work in tandem, to promote health and to understand their role in identifying and rectifying disease states. What is common to all of them is the underlying principle that the Tridoshas are the cornerstone of biological behaviour which has far-reaching consequences for the study of the psychological implications that are implicit and explicit to the present researcher. This is from the medical perspective. But what about the psychological perspective? Is it not possible to use these same principles to understand the psychological basis of behaviour in both the physical and the mental states? This is also a cornerstone of understanding the human psyche and has been quite neglected till date. Though the inherent interdependence of the physical and the psychological is talked of and acted upon in Ayurvedic medical perspective, it has not followed suit in psychology. The Cartesian dichotomy of the body and the mind did a lot to disturb this basic theory and it is only now that the world is realizing the value and the truth of the Ayurvedic principles of Prakriti, its manifestations and combinations.

Delineation of the Tridoshas-Vata, Pitta and Kapha

According to Ayurveda, the human body (the physical entity) is composed of three fundamental categories called Doshas, Dhatus and Malas. The Doshas are three in number, the Dhatus are seven, and the Malas are three. The three Doshas (Tridoshas) are Vata, Pitta and Kapha. Their psychological correlates which play a role in the functioning and behaviour of humans is the Trigunas-Sattva, Rajas and Tamas.

These psychological attributes are not restricted or confined to humans alone, but are also attributed to almost all living beings, including the food we eat, and all other elements in the environment we live in, which are said to have a predominance of one or the other characteristic Guna/Prakriti which gives that matter its unique quality.

The Tridoshas are composed of all the five Mahabhutas, but one or the other is predominant, with the other four are in lesser dominance. There can never be a state when one or the other Mahabhuta is absent totally. All five are essential to sustain life. Proper balance among these three Doshas is essential for good health.

- Vata Dosha is composed of Akasa (ether) and Vayu (air) Mahabhutas.
- Pitta Dosha is composed of Tejas or Agni (fire) and Ap Mahabhutas.
- Kapha Dosha is composed of Ap (water) and Prithvi (earth) Mahabhutas.

When we talk about imbalance of Doshas, we say that a person is Vata, Pitta or Kapha dominated. This does not mean an absence of the other two Doshas, but that the other two Doshas are suppressed compared to the dominant Dosha. This also does not mean that a person who is either of the Dosha dominated is not in good health. That particular dominant Dosha is his natural state of being or Prakriti. It is not ill health.

"Prakriti is specific for each individual. It is said to be determined at the time of conception (in modern terms, by the recombination of zygotic DNA from sperm and ovum) and remains unaltered over the individual's lifetime. Prakriti specific treatment, including prescription of medications, diet, and lifestyle, is a distinctive feature of Ayurveda. We hypothesize that Prakriti has a genetic connotation that could provide a tool for classifying the human population based on broad phenotype clusters".

Each Dosha gives certain characteristic qualities to the person, based on which an individual can be classified as belonging to that particular Dosha type. Charaka and Sushruta recognize seven types or categories into which people can be classified, depending on the dominance of the Doshas in their body.

They are said to belong to a particular Prakriti or constitution as follows:

1. People with dominant Vata Dosha, i.e. Vata Prakriti (or constitution).
2. People with dominant Pitta Dosha/Prakriti.
3. People with dominant Kapha Dosha/Prakriti.
4. People with dominant Vata-Pitta Dosha combination/Prakriti.
5. People with dominant Vata-Kapha Dosha combination/Prakriti.
6. People with dominant Pitta-Kapha Dosha combination/Prakriti.
7. People with balanced Doshas or with Vata-Pitta-Kapha Dosha combination/Prakriti.

This is accepted by all the different schools of Ayurveda, i.e. Charaka, Sushruta, Vagbhata, etc., to name a few. Varahamihira?s Brhat Samhita too has given detailed delineations of the human characteristics.

Delineation of the Trigunas-Sattva, Rajas and Tamas

Prakriti is composed of three Gunas: Sattva (white, knowledge, happiness, pra), Rajas (red , activity, pain, kr) and Tamas (dark, resistance or inertia, confusion, ti). Thus, it is endowed with all the necessary and sufficient powers of production, preservation and dissolution of the phenomenal world. Mainly, it is the material cause of multiplicity.

The three Gunas-Sattva, Rajas and Tamas-also promote different kinds of temperament based on the dominance of one or the other

Gunas. The temperament of a person can be discerned based on the "mode of worship, the type of food consumed and other activities of everyday life".

Sushruta clearly describes the five Mahabhutas as being constituted by the Trigunas. According to him (S.S. III. 1.20.), Akasa is predominant with Sattva, Vayu with Rajas, Agni with Sattva-Rajas, Ap (Jala) with Sattva-Tamas, and Prithvi with Tamas. Inferentially, since both Charaka and Sushruta clearly state that Vata Dosha is a combination of Akasa and Vayu, Pitta Dosha of Agni and Ap and Kapha Dosha of Ap and Prithvi, we can deduce the Gunas that are predominant in each of them.

Hence, Vata Dosha is a combination of Sattva and Rajas Gunas but is referred to as being predominantly Rajasic-as Rajas Guna overtakes or is stronger than the Sattva Guna. Pitta Dosha is said to be more Sattvic in nature, though it has an element of Rajas and Tamas in it. Kapha Dosha is said to be more Tamasic in nature though it has an element of Sattva in it (but no Rajas). Hence, we understand the Doshas in respect of the Gunas exhibited by them due to the relative dominance of one or the other Pancha Mahabhutas that they are made up of. "This Trigunatmaka description of the constitution of Pancha Bhutas is the most applied aspect of philosophical concept of Gunas in the field of science and medicine".

This is invaluable in deducing the behaviour exhibited by individuals depending on the dominance of one or the other Dosha or Guna that is constitutionally present in the person from conception-which is referred to as the particular Prakriti-Guna combination that a person exhibits. This Prakriti-Guna combination is unique to every individual and is not changeable during the course of their lifetime.

Each Guna gives certain characteristic qualities to the person, based on which an individual can be classified as belonging to that particular Guna type. Charaka and Sushruta recognize seven types or categories into which people can be classified, depending on the dominance of the Gunas in their body. They are said to belong to a particular Guna combination, as follows:

1. People with dominant Sattva Guna.
2. People with dominant Rajas Guna.
3. People with dominant Tamas Guna.
4. People with dominant Sattva-Rajas Guna combination.

5. People with dominant Sattva-Tamas Guna combination.
6. People with dominant Rajas-Tamas Guna combination.
7. People with balanced Gunas or with Sattva-Rajas-Tamas Guna combination.

(Charaka and Sushruta Samhitas, Vagbhata?s Ashtanga Hrdaya, and Dhanwantari by Johari and many other books and classical texts have emulated references to these seven types of Doshas and Gunas.)

Krishnan says that Varaha Mihira, an eminent scholar, using the "Guna" theory, presents a sevenfold classification of persons. They are Sattvic, Rajasic, Tamasic, Sattvic-Rajasic, Sattvic-Tamasic, Rajasic-Tamasic, and Sattvic-Rajasic-Tamasic. Quite evidently, the mixed types are recognized too, other than the basic three types of Gunas.

In the Indian psychological literature, Guna theory is already empirically tested and accepted.

"Mental disposition (Sattva) is basically threefold: pure (suddha), violent (Rajasa), and dull (Tamasa), depending on the preva-lence of each of the three Gunas. The first is largely free from defects (specially abnor-malities with respect to speech, thought and bodily behaviour), while the other two are defective or abnormal. The distinction is bet-ween the disease-free (the first type) and the disease-prone types (the other two types). Among the disease-prone types, one is domi-nated by excessive activity prompted by anger and other emotions, while the other is dominated by inactivity due to delusions and confusion.

Each of these has varieties depending upon physical characteristics and psychological tendencies. It is recognized that the mind and the body are interdepen-dent and that there is an impact of the mind on the body and of the body on the mind. There is also a hierarchical notion in describing the pure type as the best (sreshtha), the violent type as middling (madhya) and the dull type as the worst (adhama).

Besides the basic seven types of Prakriti (Vata, Pitta and Kapha and their blends), Ayurveda recognizes 16 types of personalities based on the classical Guna theory. Both Charaka and Sushruta Samhitas have a description of these types. According to them, there are 7 types of Sattva, 6 of Rajas and 3 of Tamas, totaling 16 types of personalities under which all people can be grouped.

The seven types of Sattva are: Brahma Sattva, Mahendra Sattva, Varuna Sattva, Kubera Sattva, Gandharva Sattva, Yama Sattva and Rishi Sattva.

The six types of Rajas Sattva are: Asura Sattva, Rakshasa Sattva, Paisaca Sattva, Sarpa Sattva, Praita Sattva and Sakuna Sattva.

The three types of Tamas Sattva are Pasava Sattva, Matsya Sattva and Vanaspatya Sattva.

Discussion

Keeping the above in the backdrop, the authors wish to develop their arguments on four issues as follows.

Trigunas are the psychological manifestations of the Tridoshas

This sevenfold classification of people with respect to the Gunas is similar to the sevenfold classification of people with respect to the Dosha Prakriti. In fact, it is identical in as much as one is concerned with the body constitution (Doshas = physical = Vata, Pitta and Kapha Prakriti), while the other is concerned with the mental or psychological characteristics exhibited by people with these Doshas (Gunas = psychological = Sattva, Rajas and Tamas Gunas). Taking these two striking classifications one step further, it would not be wrong to say that the physical constitution leads to the corresponding psychological attributes in a person or vice versa as both are interdependent. Indian tradition does not share the Cartesian dichotomy of the body and the mind as is common in western psychological thinking. In fact, the interplay between the mind (Sattva), soul (Atman) and body (Sharira) in a tripod allusion is the cornerstone of Ayruvedic philosophy.

Interaction of Tridosha and Triguna to complement the psyche of man

In the words of Charaka, "The psyche is of three types-Pure, Rajas and Tamasa. The pure is said as devoid of defects due to having beneficial fraction whereas Rajasa and Tamasa are defective because of the fractions of agitation and ignorance respectively. Out of these three types of psyche, each one has got innumerable sub-divisions due to relative degrees and variations in interaction of psyche and body according to species. Body follows psyche and vice versa. Hence some of the types of psyche are described here as illustrations by showing their similarity with some well known symbols". After this, Charaka goes on to describe the 16 personality traits with examples, which has not been quoted here for obvious constraints. Though Charaka has described the 16 personality traits, he has not detailed them as much as he has detailed the biological aspects of personality, namely Vata, Pitta and Kapha Prakritis.

For a further understanding of the psychological aspects of these physical traits, we have to look elsewhere for the delineation.

"There are two basic laws of the Gunas that are crucial in understanding their workings. The first law of the Gunas is 'the law of alternation'. The three Gunas are ever in dynamic inter-action. All three forces remain intertwined, affecting each other in various ways. Rajas and Tamas exist in the field of Sattva, Tamas and Sattva are found in the field of Rajas, and Sattva and Rajas move in the field of Tamas. The essence of the three qualities is their interplay. Rarely is seen pure Tamas, pure Rajas or pure Sattva. There must ever be readiness for the Gunas to change. The second law of the Gunas is 'the law of continuity'. The Gunas tend to hold their particular natures for a certain period once they come into dominance. Substances stabilize on the level of one of the three Gunas. While it is initially is difficult for Tamas to become Rajas, or for Rajas to become Sattva, once they do so they will continue in that same quality".

Understanding the working of Tridosha and Triguna to categorize/ typecast people

The classification of people into types can be noticed in a variety of literature ranging from dramaturgy (where it is restricted to heroes and heroines leading to around 384 varieties or types) to sexual science like Rathisastra or Kamasutra where the authors expound about the classification of men and women on the basis of their physical and psychological characteristics. This shows that typology or categorizing people into different categories is not a new field of enterprise where Indian knowledge systems are concerned. Hence, being able to making use of this pre-existing knowledge base to develop the field further would be an obvious step in the same direction.

Although Ayurveda recognizes the uniqueness of every individual, generalization and classification of people into categories is necessary. To quote Shakespeare, "All men are not alike, clay and clay differs in dignity, whose dust is both alike" (Cymbelline, 11-2) and Plato?s aphorism too is relevant in this context-"It is far more important to know as to what type of a person suffers from a disease rather than what disease the person is suffering from".

According to Frawley, "Yoga examines individuals in terms of their mental/spiritual level according to the three Gunas. Ayurveda looks at individuals in terms of their psychophysical constitution through the three Doshas. Yet Ayurveda also considers the role of the

Gunas as factors of mental health and well-being and yoga considers the Doshas relative to physiological functioning. For a complete ascertainment of the individual nature, both the gunic and doshic natures must be considered.... The Doshas are a biological classification that is horizontal in application with no necessary spiritual implications. A Vata type may be a saint or a sinner; the same is the case with the other two types.

The Gunas are a spiritual classification that is vertical in nature. It has no necessary physical implications. A saint or sinner may be Vata, Pitta or Kapha in body" (pg. 46). Hence, it is necessary to understand and categorize people according to both the Tridosha and the Triguna classification as has been delineated in ancient Indian texts and scriptures. Trying to study people in exclusion of the other will not give a complete picture of the nature of human personality, which is a complex interplay of thoughts, emotions, predispositions and behaviour, both conditioned and unconditioned.

Effects of imbalance of the Tridoshas and Trigunas: Its predictive value

By knowing the inherent qualities of a person, it is easy to categorize a person as belonging to any of these three Doshas. But can all people be categorized into just these three groups knowing how wide a spectrum of differences we can see in them, in each and every aspect, be it the physicality or the psychological tendencies that they exhibit? What about those people who exhibit a combination of two or more Doshas? How and where are they to be represented? At this point of merger, can?t a new group of people be created who exhibit the traits of both the categories that this line is trying to bifurcate? It is not possible that the Doshas are in balance at all times.

How is the imbalance of the Doshas to be understood? How can the imbalance and the resultant state of behaviour and thought processes that are exhibited by this imbalance be predicted? Can this imbalance be brought back into a state of balance? If so, as is dictated by Ayurvedic principles, then how is it to be done? What would be the resultant predictive value of these Tridoshas and Trigunas? How can this and their consequent behaviour be understood? This is not only highly probable but very possible too, as dictated by logic and as stated in the Charaka and Sushruta Samhitas, and also in Vagbhatacharya?s Ashtanga Hrdaya. This viewpoint is expressed by Varaha Mihira in his classification of people too.

"The three Gunas comprise the magnetic field for the soul. One Guna usually predominates and polarizes our mind and life according to its qualities. Souls become Sattvic, Rajasic or Tamasic in nature. However, in the ordinary, unrefined field of human nature, one Guna seldom prevails. After a time the other Gunas must assert themselves. Our lives are an interplay of dullness, distraction and virtue, with shifting currents of good and evil, truth and falsehood.... Only a rare human being can become so totally dominated by one Guna that the other Gunas lose their power. Such extreme types are the hardened criminal or complete Tamasic type, the super achiever or complete Rajasic type, and the selfless saint or complete Sattvic type, but even these types can have their admixtures of the other Gunas. Both Ayurveda and yoga seek to reduce the lower Gunas of Rajas and Tamas. They are factors of mental and physical disease which Ayurveda addresses and the spiritual ignorance that yoga seeks to dispel".

According to Rao, "Plato observed that: "For this is the great error of our day that Physicians separate the Soul from Body.... Ayurveda says that the mind possesses three Gunas (attributes), viz. Satva, Tamo and Rajo (invisible qualities and energies), which are responsible for its activity on the body. Hindu scientists recognized this fact. After their deep study of the mind and its various acts, they grouped the activities of the mind into three categories and coined three generic names for each group as Satvika, Rajasika and Tamasika. Mind acts on the body through its Trigunas (three attributes) and their material states are Pancha Bhutas, which in the physical body constitute bio-chemicals. In other words, the bio-chemicals are the physical agents of Trigunas. Trigunas in their subtle states are energies, qualities of the mind. Mind acts on the body through Trigunas, Pancha Bhutas (the primordial elements which constitute the animate and inanimate objects of the universe) are the physical basis for three Doshas. The three Doshas trigger the endocrine and exocrine glands and specific nerves to release appropriate bio-chemicals (neuro-humors) at appropriate time, which in turn trigger the relevant organs to act accordingly".

"Thus the involvement of the mind has impact on the hormonal balance of the body and its activities.... The Trigunas, which are the qualities of the mind, are responsible for the difference in the moods (attitudes). The Trigunas transform into different combinations of Tanmatras, (which are the subtle physical forms of Trigunas), which form into thought waves and carry them to the target places. (Three

Dhatus/Doshas are the bio-physical factors that govern the various activities of the physical body both in health and ill health, respectively.) There, the Tanmatras, which are subtle, transform into gross form of Pancha Bhutas. These are innate forms of Tridoshas that transform into bio-chemical substances (hormones, etc.) in a rapid succession to play their role in the physiology of the microcosm. There are two kinds of thought waves. One is "sensory thought waves" created by efferent nerve impulses, which derive their stimulation from external sources-sensory organs. These waves are those that move from a particular sensory object toward the mind. The second one is "motor thought waves" created by afferent nerve impulses which derive their stimulation from internal organs/sources that emanate from the mind in response to the sensory thought wave carrying the orders of the mind to the target places of action. Some are created directly from the mind as a consequence of any psychological episode and move toward the target places".

"Mind influences the physiology and pathology of the physical body. This fact was realized by the founding fathers of Ayurveda. Therefore Ayurveda is defined as a philosophy and science of life..." (pg. 40). "It is the Sattva Guna that is responsible for preparing the mind to produce positive thought waves. Sattva Guna tries to bring a balance between the Rajo and Tamo manasika Doshas, the pathological psychic factors, which are finally responsible for the disturbance of the three somatic factors (Vata, Pitta and Kapha). These three somatic factors are responsible for the various body ailments".

Though there is some amount of work that is done in the field of Ayurveda by scientists to establish the scientific validity of the Tridoshas, there is a possibility and a need to empirically test and validate it from the domain of psychology. This would also lead to a better categorizing of people based on the Trigunas, where people know their inherent psychological constitution, modes of behaviour and conduct, which would help them to understand themselves better, leading to better adjustment in both personal and professional lives. The ripple effect of this would be to choose the best people suited for a particular field of enquiry/work, wherein people are satisfied in their chosen professions, giving rise to a more harmonious society. The advantage of developing testing procedures that are in alignment with the laws of nature are evident, to say the least, where they would be applicable the world over, without cultural and racial overtones or biases. The uses and benefits of this exercise are innumerable and far outweigh the difficulties that would be faced in trying to develop a test of such truly global standards and applicability.

Know Yourself: Your Ayurvedic Body Type

Figure: *When you are sitting by a stream of gushing water, absorbed in it, it can be hard to realize this simple fact of life-we are that.*

We are made up of water and the other five elements that exist in nature. This understanding forms the baseline of Ayurveda, a 5000-year-old science of wellness and longevity; a science so precise that when your pulse is examined by an Ayurveda doctor, he/she can tell you not just about the imbalances at the root of existing diseases but can share in elaborate detail specific qualities about your body type, behaviour, and conditions you may be predisposed to.

The science of Ayurveda is all about creating balance-balance between the body, mind, and spirit, and balance between the tridosha (three doshas) that take from the five elements in nature. It does this by first identifying the prakruti or nature of an individual. Secondly, it examines the existing dosha imbalances. Lastly, Ayurveda provides a roadmap to an individual to live a healthy, perfectly balanced life using specific herbs, holistic cleanses and detox treatments, personalized diet that is aligned with one's unique dosha constitution.

Your Ayurvedic body type, or constitution, is at the heart of Ayurveda's approach to well-being. Knowing your constitution allows you to maximize your quality of life, health, and happiness by following the recommendations for food and lifestyle for each constitution.

Ayurveda is a personalized school of medicine where there is no one size fits all when it comes to wellness and treatments. Ayurveda uses an ancient and time tested tool for diagnosis of imbalances in the body called the Nadi Pariksha, or pulse diagnosis.

An Ayurvedic pulse diagnosis with an expert is the best way to recognize one's constitution. It can help determine what your dosha dominance is and what are the current vikritis, or dosha imbalances. Pulse diagnosis in Ayurveda is different and runs much deeper than the Western method of pulse examination. In Ayurveda, it includes examination of an individual's state of body, mind, and spirit as a whole. It meaningfully examines not just the pulse rate, rhythm, and volume but also observes the flow, amplitude, force, and consistency. It is based on the knowledge that symptoms manifest in the pulse before they manifest in the affected part of the body and that severe aggravation of doshas leads to illnesses in the body. For example, the effect of an imbalance in your blood can be detected much earlier in your pulse.

We discuss here general characteristics of body types of each dosha to help familiarize readers with general tendencies. So read on to acquaint yourself with the main constitutions and the self-discovery that is the joy of Ayurveda.

THE GOOD LIFE (For Your Type)

Ayurveda means the science of longevity; it is the science of how to live a long, healthy life. "Ayu" is the life span we spend with the body. The spirit is immortal-it can be with the body or without it, but the union of body, mind and spirit-how long that combination stays, that time span is called ayu. How to live that time happily and in good health is the knowledge of Ayurveda. So how do we live this way? In this respect, Ayurveda says there are four aspects:

- What is good for the body
- What is unhealthy
- What makes us happy
- What makes us sad

It is like driving a car in that once you know the rules of the road, you can drive safely. And it is the same with life also, once you know these four aspects. For that we need to know the body and mind. The body is made of five elements, space, air, fire water and earth. Physiologically, these elements function as three bio-dynamic forces, called vata, pitta and kapha. These are called variously dhatus, substances, dosha, or prakriti, our natural constitution. What is the importance of knowing you Ayurvedic body type? The five elements (Panchamahabhutas) combine to form three basic bio energies, or doshas- kapha,vata and pitta. These three subtle elements govern all our life functions, personality traits and the mind-body complex that define us as individuals. Each of these doshas has specific traits. The pitta dosha is made up of the fire and water element and it primarily governs digestion. The vata dosha is the air element and is the force behind all types of movements in the body. The kapha dosha is the earth element and provides moisture to the skin and lubrication to joints. It is the grounding dosha. Usually in a person, two of three doshas dominate.

VATA

Those who are born with more of the space and air element have a vata constitution. Vata constitution is governed by the features of space and air. Generally, a vata person will be very thin, more talkative, restless; they typically have a lower body weight, dry skin, brittle nails, thin hair, and small, slightly sunken eyes. While walking, their joints may make sounds. In terms of climate, they tend to prefer warm or hot weather; they may have trouble tolerating the cold. They have a hard time gaining weight, so they tend to be thin with a low weight. Vata is located in the abdomen below the navel; including the colon, pelvis, pelvic organs besides thighs, skin, ears, nervous system, and lungs. It is responsible for movement in the body and mind. Sensory impulses, breath, excretion, speech, and pumping of blood are some of its main functions. It also ignites agni, the digestive fire in the body.

Signs of Vata Imbalance

- Dryness and roughness of skin
- Too much weight loss. Emaciation happens.
- Irregular bowel movement or constipation
- Pain in bones, joints
- Flatulence
- Fear and restlessness
- Abnormal pulse rate
- Palpitation
- Preference for hot environment and surroundings

Diseases Caused by Vata Imbalance

Imbalance of this dosha can cause irregularity in functioning of bowel movements, nervous system, disorders in muscles and joints, etc. Here are some of the disorders that vata imbalance can cause:

- Dryness
- Insomnia
- Headaches
- Tinnitus
- Loose teeth
- Facial Paralysis
- Acute stress
- Tonic and Clonic Seizures
- Tremors
- Earache and hearing disorders
- Sciatica
- Stiff legs
- Cramps in calf muscles
- Stiffness in the neck
- Arthritis
- Constipation

Remedies for Balancing Vita

1. Get to bed before 10:oo pm and rise by 6:00 am
2. Maintain a daily routine with regular times for eating, sleeping, and working (dinacharya)
3. Drink warm beverages and eat freshly prepared, warm, whole foods.
4. Eat foods that are naturally sweet, sour, and salty in taste.
5. Use generous amounts of high-quality oils or ghee and warming spices like ginger, black pepper, cinnamon, and cumin in your daily diet
6. Avoid alcohol, caffeinated beverages, and chocolate
7. Incorporate a regular exercise routine into your week
8. Vata-reducing herbs and remedies

PITTA

Next are pitta people, those who are born with hotter constitutions, containing more of the fire element. A pitta person is generally active, good looking, a perfectionist, dynamic, intelligent and also short tempered. They may have leadership qualities, a moderate build, a smart personality, a sharp nose, and their eyes will also be sharp, sometimes offset with a slight pinkish tint. Due to the unfortunate ease with which a pitta person gets imbalanced, hair loss and early greying are common.

They are generally slightly warm to the touch with rosy lips and pink nails with a slight curve.

Though a combination of fire and water, it is more dominant with fire element. It is intensified during summers. The seat of pitta in the body is small intestine, stomach, liver, spleen, gallbladder, blood, sweat glands, sub-cutaneous fat, eyes, and skin.

It is responsible for stability in the body and mind. It regulates body heat, digestion, lightens the appetite, absorption, assimilation, gives vitality, and the ability to understand. It nourishes the body by carrying amino acids and enzymes which are important for digestion of food. It also keeps neurotransmitters and neuropeptides which are responsible for thinking.

It augments understanding and intelligence, if in balance. If out of balance, it gives room for host of negative emotions.

Signs of Pitta Imbalance

- Excessive heat marked by desire for cold things
- Yellow colouration of the skin
- Giddiness
- Weakness
- Reduced sleep
- Increased anger and agitation
- Burning sensation
- Excessive thirst and hunger
- Increased tendency of being a perfectionist
- Bitter taste in the mouth
- Bad breath
- Hot flashes

Diseases Due to Pitta Imbalance

- Peptic ulcers, inflammation of the stomach or esophagus, if the imbalance is allowed to persist for too long
- Skin disorders like eczema, psoriasis

- Fatigue
- Migraine
- Acid Reflux Tendonitis
- Herpes
- Jaundice
- Bad breath
- Conjunctivitis
- Pharyngitis
- Dissatisfaction
- Stomatitis
- Fibromyalgia
- Redness of the skin
- Low blood sugar

Remedies for Balancing Pitta

1. Maintain a daily routine with regular times for eating, sleeping, and working (dinacharya)
2. Use ghee, or clarified butter, in your cooking.
3. Drink 4-5 litres of warm or room temperature water every day
4. Keep company with people who are happy and positive
5. Meditation is the key to the happy mind. It helps controlling emotions like anger, irritability, among others. A few minutes meditation twice a day is recommended. Sahaj Samadhi meditation of the Art of Living helps significantly in managing Pitta aggravation.
6. Moderately difficult yogasanas can pacify Pitta by increasing the blood circulation and detoxifying the body.
7. Spend time in nature-be with plants, walk on the grass, walk by the lakeside, and moon gaze to bring peace to the mind.

KAPHA

They're cheerful all the time! Other qualities include a thick build, thick, dark hair, big eyes with white around, and prominent, shiny, white teeth. The skin may also be thick, moist, and a little cool to the touch. As a personality type, while they tend to accumulate stuff, they also have a sharing streak that moves them to service for society.

***Figure:** Kapha indicates a preponderance of the water and earth element. People with this kapha constitution are generally cool, calm, lazy, cheerful, stocky (if not overweight). If assigned a task, they never complete the task in time. Actually, Ayurveda says that because a kapha person is the least bothered, happiest type of person on the whole planet, the best constitution is kapha.*

Location of Kapha is in bones, muscles, and tendons. It acts as the 'binding agent' to keep the cells together. It keeps the body moist. It lubricates joints, moisturizes the skin, and maintains immunity. In balance, kapha is synonymous to love, calmness, and forgiveness. If out of balance it can be the cause of negative emotions like greed and jealousy. Kapha personalities have good appetite and low digestive ability which makes them put on weight. Kapha personalities live an easy-going life and prefer to maintain the status quo. They are peaceful and balanced. They are sensitive. If they experience injustice with them or others, they tend to slip into depression. Lack of routine, lethargy, no exercise, irregular sleeping time, heavy food, eating frequently, and intake of too much dairy are some of the reasons which can cause the imbalance.

Signs of Kapha Imbalance

- Anorexia
- Drowsiness
- Cough
- Respiratory disorders
- Obesity
- Sweet taste in the mouth
- Goitre

- Indigestion
- Hardening of blood vessels
- Loss of appetite
- Flu
- Sinusitis
- Bronchitis
- Disorders of the joints

Remedies for Kapha Imbalance

1. Foods that are astringent, spicy, and bitter tastes are conducive for keeping kapha under check. Dry and warm food helps too.
2. Keeping the body active is a must for kapha personalities. It ensures that they do not slip into lethargy and inertia.
3. Regular practice of yoga helps keeping the energy high, keeping toxins away and the body active.
4. The controlled and long breath taken during Pranayama keeps the mind calm and increases the health of lungs.
5. Avoid sleep during the day which can increase kapha.

These are the three main Ayurvedic body types, though mixes also appear-pitta-kapha, pitta-vata, vata-kapha, and saamya, one whose constitution contains all of the five elements in equal ratios.

Constitution is what we are born with. When we eat the proper food and follow the lifestyle that suits our Ayurvedic body type, we have better chances of staying fit, healthy and happy for a long time.

Understanding Different Body Types in Ayurveda

Different Ayurvedic Body Types

We see the human body as a complex system of organs, bones, muscles, arteries and veins. But we often overlook how this complex system is interconnected to sustain life. This is where Ayurveda sheds light on different aspects that make up the human body and facilitate various internal functions. According to Ayurveda, the human body is governed by three principal energies, also known as doshas. These doshas are Pitta, Vata and Kapha. Every individual has all three fundamental doshas; however, one dosha is more prominent than the rest. This prominent dosha determines the Ayurvedic body type or constitution, also known as Prakriti.

For instance, a person with a predominant Vata dosha will have a Vata body type. What does that mean? How do these body types differ, and why does any of that even matter. In this blog post, we will discuss Ayurveda body types, what they mean, how they influence your lifestyle, and physical and mental characteristics. Ancient wisdom defines the human body as a conglomeration of water, air, earth, fire, and ether. These 5 elements make up the human body and handle its functioning. However, all the elements must exist proportionally to ensure balance and stability. If this balance is disturbed beyond a certain point, the body may experience discomfort or collapse altogether. Further, Ayurveda groups these five elements into three fundamental energies, hence three body types: Kapha, pitta and Vata.

Vata is the principal energy derived from air and ether elements; Kapha is water and earth; Pitta is fire and water. What is my Ayurveda body type? - you might ask. So, let's understand all three types of body according to Ayurveda to give you some context and clarity.

Kapha Body Type

Kapha is characterized by the binding nature of water and earth. It provides structure, stability, and cohesiveness. Apart from maintaining immunity and hydrating the cells, Kapha is also responsible for moisturizing the skin and lubricating the joints. Kapha is primarily in the lungs, throat, head, connective tissues, ligaments, fatty tissues, and tendons. People with Kapha body types have an easygoing demeanor and a laid-back approach to life. However, their graceful appearance makes up for the qualities they lack. They have the stomach for constructive criticism and rarely get offended. They get attached quickly and cling to things and people for a long time.

Physical Traits of Kapha body type: While Kapha body type is well-developed, it is highly likely to be on the heavier side. Kapha people may have broad chests, fully developed muscles, and thick skin that conceals almost all of their tendons and veins. Because of the predominant Kapha dosha, their skin is naturally oily, and their hair is dark, thick, and wavy. Kapha people have a slow metabolism and eat less than their counterparts. Despite that, Kapha people show commendable stamina and remain centered and optimistic about life.

Mental Traits of Kapha Body Type: Kapha people portray a calm and poised demeanor. It's challenging to provoke them, but they get possessive about things or people they hold close to their hearts. They make peace and forgive easily because they like tranquility and harmony around them. Kapha people may not be quick to comprehend complex concepts, but once they do, the information sticks around for a long time in their heads.

Also read: Kapha Dosha: Everything You Need to Know

Pitta Body Type

Pitta is the fire energy with water as its secondary element. It is the force that drives transformation and governs the body's metabolism and temperature. Pitta is neither stable nor mobile but mobilized through carrier substances like enzymes, organic acids, bile, and hormones. Primarily, pitta lives in the liver, pancreas, small intestines, eyes, and blood. It renders energy and heat to the body and facilitates transformation. For instance, pitta breaks down food molecules and converts them into energy that supports the body and mind.

Physical Traits of Pitta Body Type: Pitta people exhibit medium height with moderate muscle development, and their overall body frame seems to be on the delicate side. People with a pitta body type usually have soft skin and silky hair prone to thinning and premature graying.

Their radiant skin is perfectly complemented by copper or green eyes of medium prominence. Regarding the internal systems, pitta people have good digestion, which also implies strong metabolism. Their slender body frame may make you think otherwise, but they have a relatively enormous appetite with a strong craving for sweet foods.

Mental Traits of Pitta Body Type: Pitta people show excellent concentration power and a sharp mind. They are quick to comprehend complex equations and respond swiftly, making them prominent leaders and decision-makers. People with pitta body type love to explore their competitive side and take on challenges that help them get ahead in life.

Also read: Guide to Pitta Dosha | Symptoms, Home Remedies & Diet

Vata Body Type

Vata dosha corresponds to the air and space elements and governs various biological activities, like breathing, heart pulsations and muscle contractions, while also mobilizing the other two doshas. That is why it is called the energy of movement. Vata imbalance can often mean that the bodily fluids are not being mobilized how they should, which can seriously threaten the organs and the body's functioning. Besides physical symptoms, the Vata imbalance can also affect the mental faculties and lead to confusion, impulsive behaviour, anxiety, mood swings, etc.

Physical Traits of Vata Body Type: Vata people have an underdeveloped body frame. They are slim and slender, and you can see the veins and muscle tendons right through their thin skin. People with a Vata body type often have to deal with dry, cracked skin, especially during winter. Their hair is wavy and sparse, with chiseled jawline, thin eyelashes, and sunken eyes defining their facial characteristics. Vata people may have brittle and rough nails; their hands and feet are cold to the touch, and they often experience irregular sleep patterns or sleep less than their counterparts. People with a Vata-dominant body constitution may also experience digestive concerns, which lead to toxins accumulation in tissues and joints.

Mental Traits of Vata Body Type: Vata people quickly grasp and understand things but struggle to keep the information for a long time. With short-term memory, it may be difficult for Vata people to recount an event from the distant past.

Vata people may lack willpower, confidence and tolerance, but they make up for it with their sharp wits.

Also read: Vata Dosha: Symptoms, Causes and How to Balance High Vata Levels

How to Identify Ayurveda Body Type

How to know your dosha, and why does it matter: Each body type exhibits certain physical, mental, and emotional indicators. Identifying these indicators can lead you to your body type so that you can follow the recommended diet and lifestyle to maintain good health.

Identifying Vata Dosha:

- You have a Vata body type if your skin is dry and chapped.
- If you struggle to gain weight despite eating complete meals, you have a Vata body type.
- You are highly active and talkative but can't memorize information too long. It's a sign that you have a Vata body type.
- Have you ever been told that you sleep with your eyes half open? If so, you could be the data type.

- Sleep is another area where Vata people struggle, which may affect their appetite.
- Vata people are more likely to feel anxious than their counterparts. If this describes your general state of mind, you may be the data type.
- With Vata energies governing your body, it's common to have gastric issues.

Balancing Vata Dosha

Having a Vata body type is far from being virtuous. You may face specific physical and mental challenges, which can be counter-productive. Therefore, Vata people must balance their Vata dosha through dietary and lifestyle interventions. And here are a few pointers to help you:

- Eat small meals at regular intervals to keep your digestive system from acting up and causing gastric troubles.
- Include warm herbs and spices in your meals, such as ginger, cardamom, and pepper.
- Eat sweet fruits like papaya, banana, berries, mangoes, grapes, apples, etc.
- Avoid sour fruits, potatoes, white sugar, lettuce, and raw onion in the salad.
- Eat well-cooked vegetables. Do not eat stale or cold food as it can impair digestion and aggravate Vata in your body.
- Choose hot beverages over cold drinks and drink plenty of water, especially after waking up in the morning.
- Take Dhanwantharam Gulika (Tablets) or perform a self-massage using Dhanwantharam thailam. These herbal formulations contain ingredients like ginger and cardamom, which are suitable for the Vata body type. With nationwide shipping on all orders, you can buy Dhanwantharam thailam and tablets from Kerala Ayurveda.

Identifying Pitta Dosha

Pitta dosha is associated with micro-processes involved in digestion, from the assimilation and absorption of food to the formation of energy and heat. Pitta lives in the liver and regulates various fluids and enzymes that aid digestion.

Following are the signs of a pitta body type:

- Would you describe yourself as medium-built? Do you find it easy to lose or gain weight at your will? If so, you may be a pitta, body type.
- When pitta people get hungry, either make them a sandwich or stay six feet away. Pitta people cannot tolerate thirst or hunger and often become cranky when deprived of food for too long.
- Pitta people are brave. They don't run away from a dangerous situation. Instead, they like to get in the storm's eye and emerge victorious.
- Pitta people do not feel comfortable during warm weather and sweat profusely as the temperature increases.

Balancing Pitta Dosha: If you identify with the traits mentioned above, it is recommended that you follow these lifestyle and dietary suggestions to stay healthy and avoid diseases.

- Set a fixed time for your meals, work, and sleep routine. Try to be in sync with nature.
- Consume at least 1-2 tsp of ghee daily or use it in your cooking. Doing so will help nourish your joints and ligaments.
- Maintain 4 liters of water intake daily. Drink warm water.
- Pitta people are highly likely to get angry or irritated. Meditating 30 minutes daily can help them control their emotions and pacify pitta.
- Pitta people should avoid meat and take eggs in moderation, as these foods can aggravate the pitta.
- It is also recommended to use spices sparingly in cooking.
- You can consider taking herbal remedies from Kerala Ayurveda, such as Alsactil, Amrutharishta (Arishtam), Amruthotharam Kwath, or Amruthotharam Kwath Tablets to ensure your pitta dosha is at its optimum level.

Identifying Kapha Dosha

Kapha people are laid-back and calm. If you couldn't associate yourself with the traits defined under pitta and Vata body types, you will find the following traits relatable.

- Kapha people have fully developed bodies. While they tend to gain weight without trying, losing weight is like climbing Everest.

- They often show a laid-back attitude toward life, but they can endure mentally and physically challenging situations with aplomb.
- Kapha people are blessed with thick, long hair and radiant skin.
- They are good at maintaining their poise; inciting them is difficult.

Balancing Kapha Dosha

- Eat less than what you think will satisfy your appetite or craving.
- Avoid cold drinks and cold food. Plus, Kapha people are not required to drink plenty of water daily.
- Add spices and chili to your cooking as much as you desire or can tolerate.
- Eat fruits like apples, apricots, berries, pomegranates, peaches, and raisins.
- Drink herbal teas with cinnamon or ginger as the primary ingredient.
- Kapha people are prone to cold and nasal discharge. In that case, using Anu thailam or Karpooradi Thailam can help them find relief and avoid chest congestion.

Key Takeaways

- Every human has three principal energies or doshas: Pitta, Vata, and Kapha.
- One out of three doshas is prevalent in every individual, which defines their overall constitution.
- It is crucial to identify whether you have a Pitta, Vata or Kapha body type.
- Based on this knowledge, you can alter your diet and lifestyle to maintain good health and prevent illnesses.
- For additional support in managing your prevalent dosha, you can consider buying herbal supplements and remedies from Kerala Ayurveda.

Ayurveda-balance Between the Mind, Body & Spirit

It is the science of preventive health (take care of health so that disease does not get a chance to get in) and the living habits that check over indulgence in physical senses, going against conscience and natural resistance to the call of the soul (refusal to enjoy the present moment)

Ayurvedic Treatment

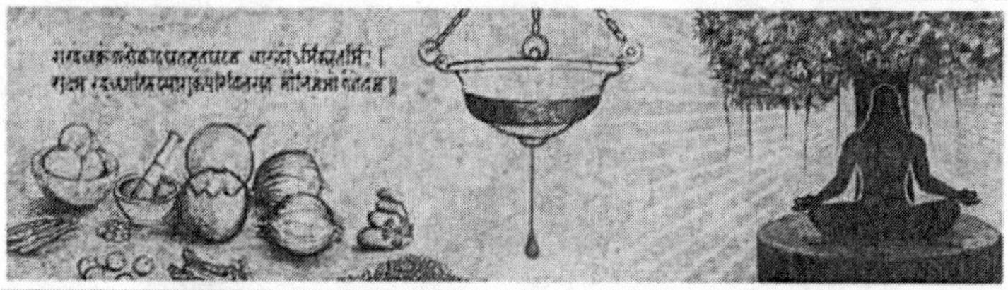

***Figure:** What if when someone is already ill ? It deals with internal medicine (kayachikitsa), surgery (Shalyachikitsa), Treating eye,ear,nose and throat (shalakyachikitsa), Pediatrics, gynecology and obstetrics treatment (kaumarabhritya) and mental health (bhutavidya).*

Body Elements & Constitution (Prakriti)

***Figure:** There are five elements of which the human body is made up of : akasha (ether), Vayu (air), Agni (Fire), Jala (Water) and Prithvi (earth).*

Because of the above five elements, all human beings are constituted with a combination of two or three primary ones. Those are called body humors or Doshas: Kapha, Vata and Pitta. Any person is easy to treat with the identification of his/her category.

Vata category is combination of space and air elements : People are fearful, illogical and insecure. Skin is dry. They have thin hair.

They have dark brown or grey eyes. Vata activates the nervous system, hearing and speech and the persons is a great enthusiast with creativity. However, the state of his mind gets imbalanced easily because of which he gets diseases like insomnia, cramps and constipation.

Figure: *Pitta category is fire element : These people are achievers, intellectual, fiery, angry, judgmental, with clear voice and precise expression. They have soft and fine hair. Eyes are blue, grey and hazel. They are good leaders and warm personality when healthy. Because of emphasis on metabolism and anger, they suffer from acidity, ulcers and rashes and also thinning of hair occurs.*

Kapha category is(water and earth element : They have thick lustrous hair. Eyes are blue or brown. People have great endurance capacity with calm and steady mind. They are capable of forgiveness and intense love. Sometimes they are greedy and possessive. Kapha is the lubricant that keeps the joints working, keeps the body vibrant and balanced with immunity. Too much of it leads to lethargy, congestion, allergies and weight gain.

Nature of Ailments

Figure: *The other type of ailment is clogging or blockage (Ama) for life energy to circulate for vitality. When this is corrected, it produces energy, perfect immunity, physical strength and hence a general sense of bliss which is summarized in Ayurveda in one word called Ojas.*

After the Prakriti is decided, one should know the nature of the diseases(Vikriti). It is imbalance obviously, but there are tow extremes to every imbalance, either deficiency or excess. Those are heavy-light, slow-sharp, cold-hot, unctuous-dry, smooth-rough, solid-liquid, soft-hard, stable-mobile, subtle-gross, and non-slimmy-slimmy. When corrected, Prakriti ororiginal constitution is restored.

These 20 characteristics that with regards to ones basic constitution will decide the treatment. These may be caused by wrong foods causing improper digestion, wrong sleeping habits, improper mindset, anxiety etc.

Some Herbs and Minerals

Malabar nut : bronchitis, asthma, boosting immune systems

Bael : Digestive system

Garlic : lipids and cholesterol

Asparagus : Female reproductive system and lactation

Aloe Vera : Hair and skin treatment

Neem : blood purifier and anti-fungal treatment

Ayurvedic Elements

Ayurveda believes that every human being is a made up of five primary elements. These five primary elements combine and create various physiological functions in the human body.

Ether or Space

Air, Water, Fire, Earth.

These Elements Combine to form Three Doshas- Vata, Pitta and Kapha

Doshas and Dooshyams: Dosha means that which vitiates. Even though they are 'vitiating things ' they become significant for our experience only when they are out of equilibrium. When they are in equilibrium they are transparent and control the functions of the body. Due to unfavourable circumstances equilibrium of the doshas gets altered and this in turn 'vitiates' the 'dhatus' and 'malas' of body.

The 'dhatus' and 'malas' which are 'vitiated' is called 'dooshyas'. Rasa, raktha (blood), mamsa (flesh), medas (fat), asthi (bone), majja (bone marrow), and sukla (sperm) are the seven dhatus. If we examine the body we can see that body contains all these seven dhatus. So they are called deha dhatu.

As doshas act on these dhatus they undergo changes accordingly producing diseases. The doshas also acts on the 'malas' (the waste products from body, motion, urine, sweat, etc.) and produce changes in the state of malas which in turn produce diseases. That is why they are called 'dooshyas'.

Ayurveda believes humans are all made up of unique proportions of Vata, Pitta and Kapha. These ratios of the doshas vary in each individual. Each person has one predominant dosha in their constitution.An imbalance in the doshas is the cause of any disease. Imbalances may be caused by an unhealthy diet, too much or too little mental and physical work, or from the weather, chemicals, or germs.

Doshas

Vata dosha: Ether and air combine to form what is known as the Vata dosha. Vata administers to the principle of movement and is considered the most powerful of all doshas. It controls the very basic body developments such as cell division, heart, respiration, and the mind. Vata can be out of balance by, staying up late at night, or eating before the previous meal is digested. People with vata as their main dosha are thought to be particularly prone to skin, neurological, and mental diseases.

Pitta dosha: Fire and water combine to form the Pitta dosha. Pitta controls the hormones and digestive system. When pitta is out of balance, a person experiences harmful emotions and has physical symptoms such as heartburn. Pitta is upset by, eating spicy or sour food; being angry, tired, or fearful, or spending too much time in the sun. People with a predominantly pitta constitution are vulnerable to heart disease and arthritis.

Kapha dosha: The elements water and earth combine to form the Kapha dosha. Kapha is considered to help keep up strength and immunity and to control growth. A symptom of kapha imbalance is nausea immediately after eating. Kapha is aggravated by, sleeping during the daytime, eating too many sweet foods, and eating and drinking foods and beverages with too much salt and water.Those with a predominant kapha dosha are exposed to diabetes, gallbladder problems, stomach ulcers, and respiratory illnesses.

Dravyas: Dravyas are the 'things' which has got functions and properties. All dravyas are perceived by mind through one or more 'indriyas'(senses). It contains the properties of 'mahabhoothas'(sound, touch, form, taste and, smell). Due to the peculiarities of the combination of 'mahabhoothas', stable dravya itself will show marked differences in characteristics. Hence, dravyas are classified as 'prudhiva', 'aapya', 'aagneya', 'vaayavya', and, 'aakasya'. Since Ayurveda studies about dravya with an aim of the use and application of dravya as food and medicine, the knowledge about the properties like taste, etc., is enough to determine the utility of dravya. The utility of dravya depends on the 'rasa', 'guna', 'veerya', 'vipaka', and 'prabhava'. Of these properties, taste (rasa) plays an important role in Ayurveda because dravya is taken as food or medicine.

RASA: There are six rasas madhura (sweet), amla (acidic), lavana (salty), thikta (pungent), katu, and kashaya. Dravyas taken as food or medicine can correct the imbalance of doshas. This is due to to the gunas. The gunas of food or medicine increases the dosha which has the same guna. It was found that madhura, amla, and lavana rasa decrease vatha while all other rasas increase it. Similarly, thikta, katu, and kashaya rasa decrease kapha while all other rasas increase kapha. Kashaya, thikta, madhura rasas decrease pitha while the other rasas increase it. Rasas in dravya are present by virtue of the 'panchabhootas'contained in the dravya. The six rasas are formed as follows.

Madhura: Due to the increased presence of 'pruthvi' and 'jala'

Amla: Due to the increased presence of 'agni'

Lavana: Due to the increased presence of 'jala' & 'agni'

Thikta: Due to the increased presence of 'akasa' & 'vayu'

Katu: Due to the increased presence of 'agni' & 'vayu'

Kashaya: Due to the increased presence of 'pruthvi' &'vayu'

Guna: Another property which is inherent is called guna. There are twenty gunas as given below.

Guru (heavy): laghu (light)

Mandam (slow): theekshanam (fast)

Seetham (cold): ushanam (hot)

Snigdha (oily): rooksha (rough)

Sleshmam: gharam

Sandram: dravam

Sookshmam (micro): sthoolam (macro)

Visadam: pichilam

Sthiram (static)- chalam (mobile)

Mrudu (soft)- katinam (hard)

Veeryam: Dravyas has veeryam, the potency to manifest work. It is classified into two namely Ushnaveeryam and Seethaveeryam. Actually these two are gunas which present in abundant and hence behave differently.

Vipaka: A rasa of dravyam after it has undergone digestion get transformed into three rasas called 'vipaka' of that rasa. Madhura and lavana becomes madhura, amla becomes amla itself, and katu and kashaya becomes katu after digestion by Jataragni. Knowledge of vipaka is needed in understanding physiological changes.

Prabhava: Is the power of dravyam to manifest work in its unique way. When rasa, guna, veerya, and vipaka in a substance is found same as in another substance, but in action the two substances differ it is said that the change is due to 'prabhava' of dravyam. 'danthi' is having the same rasa, vipaka, veerya and guna of 'chithraka'. But 'danthi' produces 'virechana' while 'chithraka' don't. So the action of 'virechana' found in 'danthi' is due to its prabhava. A person is said to be in Arogya when the doshas in his constitution is in balanced state. When they are in an imbalanced state his state is called as roga. Diagnosis of roga is done by darsanam,sparsanam (touching), and prasnam (questioning). An Ayurvedic Expert with the help of the above methods determines the Prakruti of the patient. Ayurveda shows that the path to optimal health is different for each person depending on their prakruti.

A disease will manifest in different constitutions in different ways. An individual with a predominatly vata prakruti will experience symptoms different from a pitta or kapha predominant person even when all of them are suffering from the same disease. Thus Ayurveda gives us a model to look at each individual as a unique combination of the tridoshas and provide treatment that specifically address a persons health challenges.It can suggest specific lifestyles and nutritional guidelines to assist the individual in reducing the doshas. Thus it is a guide to action for good health.

Ayuerveda is a pure holistic treatment in sync with nature. It is health, not disease, specific and takes into account the patient's entire individuality - body, mind and spirit before treatment. Ayurveda is the Veda of Ayus. Ayus means 'naturally diminishing'. Veda means informing (about something). Ayurveda is the science, which informs about the ways and measures to be adopted for sustaining and extending Ayus. It discusses about Anayushya and Ayushya. Those, which contribute towards health and long span of life, is Ayushya and which act against this is anayushya.

Every individual wants to live a healthy, long life. In order to achieve this he has to follow certain discipline in all walks of life. Ayurveda deals with all these in detail.

The effect and changes produced by various substances used as food and medicines on body in Arogya (health) and Anarogya (unhealth) demonstrates the power of methods and medicines used in Ayurveda. In order to estimate the 'guna' and 'karma' of these substances (Dravya), and to evaluate the effects and changes on body certain hypothesis was formed. They are the 'theories of' Panchabhoothas and thridoshas'.

Man, by nature is a complex being of physical, biological, mental and spiritual factors. He is the subject matter of Ayurveda and in him alone knowledge, delusion, pleasure, pain, birth, death, and love of self are co-existent. To establish the equilibrium between human nature and his environment in a comprehensive manner, Ayurveda has developed the necessary principles and practices.

Everything that is subject to human experience has evolved from the 'avyaktha prakruti' (fundamental cause). "Prakruti" can only be inferred and can't be perceived directly. It becomes active only by the presence of 'purusha'.

Prakruti has the quality 'satwa','raja', and 'thama'. These factors interact with 'purusha' {desa(space), kala(time)} to form the five "bhootha thanmatras". This interaction of both 'purusha' and 'prakruti' is the first step in the process of evolution. These panchabhoothas are called akasa (sky), vayu (air), agni (fire), jala (water), and pruthvi (earth). Of these five 'akasa' is the subtlest, and 'pruthvi' the heaviest. During the transformation process the 'bhoothas' which evolved later acquires the qualities of the previous 'bhootha'. The qualities of akasa, vayu, agni, jala, and pruthvi are sound, touch, form, taste, and smell respectively.

In the consequent 'pancheekarana prakriya' these most subtle and indivisible thanmatras successively undergo specific changes to form the 'mahabhoothas'which are in the grosser plane. 'Mahabhoothas' are the basic elements with which the universe is made. Everything in the universe, including all biological organisms, is made up of these 'pancha Mahabhoothas. So also our body.

Ancient Acharyas have classified the human body (sareera) as "sthoola (macro) sareera" and "sookshma (micro) sareera". The "sthoola sareera deha (body)" is made of 'dosha','dhatu', and 'malas'. When we examine the 'deha' we can find a process of production, maintenance, and destruction in progress always, there by continued existence is taking place. This happens under the influence of a power classified into three - productive power, sustaining power, and destructive power. These three-fold powers are termed as " Vatha, Pitha, and Kapha" respectively, which are called 'Doshas'.

Like all things in the world, the body is also made of 'Pancha Bhoothas'. The doshas exist all over the body. That means they have a relation with the basic constituents - Pancha Bhoothas - of the body. When this was examined carefully it was found that the basic " thridosha theory " was evolved from the "Pancha Bhootha theory". The union of 'Vayu' and ' Akasa' resulted in the 'Vatha' force that of 'Pruthvi' and 'Up' resulted in the formation of 'Kapha' force, and from 'Agni' the 'Pitha' force originated.

Ayurvedic science's premise is that the health of the soul is primary, and everything else revolves around that ultimate state of well-being. Because it has a clear conception of consciousness, intellect, mind, and body, understanding them to be distinct hierarchical realities which evolve from the supreme consciousness to individual consciousness on down, this science is well-equipped to care for all states of disease. Physical, mental, emotional, social, and environmental diseases are all within its scope.

On the level of physical health, which is the primary if not exclusive concern of allopathy, ayurvedic scientists were at least as competent as modern allopaths in dealing with any ailment, including the necessity of surgical operations, which were done under herbal anesthetic. I mention this only because the accomplishments in the allopathic surgical field are touted as some of the greatest medical achievements of our time. Ayurvedic surgical insights are recorded in the Shushruta Samhita (1000 B.C.). Any number of modern-day operations, from routine hernia removals to complex organ transplants are mentioned therein. These, however, were not the pride of Ayurvedic treatments. They were last resort measures that were necessary only a fraction of the time in comparison to our modern medical analysis. This was so because of other advances in ayurvedic treatments and the world view that such holistic treatments are part of-one in which nonviolence is held as an esteemed virtute to be cultivated by all.

The Vedic rishis divided sentient beings into two broad categories: "moving"- humans, animals, birds, aquatics, etc.-and "non-moving," which included plants, and stones. This prevented such misconceptions as the "animal-metabolism" theory of Hippocrates, and the serious Descartian miscalculation that animals were little more than machines. The rishis understood the nature of consciousness and biological life processes in such a thorough way that not only could every substance produced by the animal, mineral, and plant kingdom be included in the materia medica, but also it allowed for the development of branches of ayurvedic medicine, which include the treatment of disease in animals and plants. The sensitivity of the rishis was such that they discouraged not only the exploitation of the animal kingdom, but the exploitation of the plant and mineral kingdoms as well, thus preventing the type of environmental crisis that Western science has brought upon us.

The basic psychosomatic life processes are delineated as vata, pitta, and kapha, or tridosha, provide the overall conceptual framework upon which to build a complete understanding of the living world. The doshadhatus are: 1) vata, which involves the breath or vital airs; 2) pitta, the bodily fires; and 3) kapha, which involves the bodily fluids. These were translated into English hundreds of years ago as wind, bile, and mucous. These three psycho-biological complexes are present in every living being, and health is said to be a perfect balance of all three.

The tridosha are the basic building blocks of life, and they make up the hierarchical complex called saptadhatu, or the seven tissues: 1) food nutrients, 2) blood, 3) flesh, 4) fat and connecting tissues, 5) bone, 6) bone marrow and cerebro-spinal fluid, and 7) semen or ovum. Besides doshadhatu and saptadhatu, a third dhatu: rasadhatu is described, the system of rasas or tastes. The rasas, which are six in number, are derived from foods and the environment. They nourish the bodily tissues in different ways and form the basis for ayurvedic dietetics and herbology. These six tastes-sweet, sour, salty, pungent, bitter, and astringent-determine the nutritional value of foods and the medicinal effects of herbs, which are considered concentrated foods. These three systems-doshadhatu, saptadhatu, and rasadhatu are foundational to all ayurvedic understanding. The tridosha framework, which determines the individual constitution of each and every person, causes the medical practitioner to not only deal with every patient as a unique individual, but every disease as a unique disturbance.

All these systems are understood within the conception of the triguna, which views the phenomenal world in terms of its three principal modes of influence: sattva (clarity), rajas (passion), and tamas (darkness). These trimodal influences-the five gross elements, ether (space), air, fire, water, and earth-and the subtle elements of mind, intellect, and material ego comprise our biological and psychic bodies, and the entire world of material experience.

If there is any conceptual framework in allopathy from which its successes arise, it is the simplistic idea that all life is reducible to biochemical and ultimately molecular processes. This is opposed to ayurvedas acceptance of a hierarchical structure of realities culminating in the divine.

Although allopathy's view is well formed, it has come about as a result of experimentation; it does not rest on a secure foundation of a fixed conceptual framework, but formulates concepts to serve the conclusions of ongoing experimentation. While ayurvedic understanding works from a broad base down to specifics, allopathy works backwards, coming up from the collection of data and phenomenon from which larger conclusions are then drawn-a clearly speculative, inferior approach.

The problem here is twofold: one, a view based solely on experimentally derived data is one that is subject to change when new and even contradictory data arises through subsequent experimentation, which is endless in this system.

This unstable structure can totter at any time, and thus it would be difficult to build a stable society upon it. Entire schools of medical education and funding for all sorts of projects in a particular direction would be risky ventures. Everything could change in the instance that conflicting verifiable data arises. Although it seems laudable theoretically to experiment, go forward, and be prepared to change direction at any time, it is highly impractical on a societal level.

This brings us to the second problem, which is that consistent data does arise regularly, challenging the existing paradigm. But due to the fact that there is so much at stake, it is often ignored, or experimentation loses its objectivity inasmuch as it continues with a view to produce only data that conforms with the existing world view. In other words speculation, which is what modern medicine is seeded in, invariably lends to loss of integrity. Ironically, it is often billed as the noble pursuit of truth.

No doubt experimentation is a valid means of acquiring relative knowledge, but it must be conducted within a larger framework which includes descending knowledge in order that it not degenerate into self-deception. Experimentation conducted within the ayurvedic tradition either rejects or accepts evidence based on whether it is or is not contradictory to descending knowledge, the spiritual world view.

The intuitive or divine origin of the ayurvedic tradition opposes the blind prodding of dead matter that makes up experimental Western medicine. While experimentation is an important part of pramana, in the ayurvedic tradition it is carried on within a larger conceptual framework based upon descending knowledge.

Again, Western medicine is just a collection of identified systems, symptoms, and results lacking any guidance from higher intelligence. The ayurvedic tradition descends from higher intelligence, and is not subject, at least from the start, to the faults of conditioned human reason. The allopathic approach is much more akin to the superstitious medicine of uncivilized peoples than is the ayurvedic tradition, although modern medicine men would have it seem otherwise. Here the unbiased will have to ask themselves: "Is there perfect knowledge?" If the answer is "no," then we may as well stop there. But Western thinking assumes that there is perfect knowledge to which we can evolve, while the questionable means of evolution involves the utilization of imperfect instruments and human frailties. Vedic science also admits to perfect knowledge, but being that it is perfect, that knowledge is considered superior to mankind, and thus human society can attain it only if it chooses to reveal itself. Although the knowledge of the ayurvedic tradition is basically secular, dealing with the phenomenal world, the conception of the material world is one that descends from the spiritual plane.

Allopathy's rational methodology, it must be remembered, arose as a reaction to irrational European reliance on incantations and superstition that could be considered pre-rational spiritual sentiments, or a vitiated form of the rational spirituality of ancient India. It is an overreaction to unscientific medicine and pseudo-spirituality, neither of which are elements of ayurvedic teachings. It sprang not from the spiritual platform, but the speculative mental fabric of "religious" men of the time. Although the founding fathers of the new European era of reason "believed in God," their spiritual premise was so weak that they could not foresee that the new concepts they introduced would develop into the greatest nemesis of their ill-conceived spirituality.

Not so for rational Vedic spirituality, however, which even today is having an impact on many of the world's greatest scientific minds, as is its subsidiary, the ayurvedic teachings.

Such teachings are paradigmatically different from the neo-Aristotelean paradigm reigning in Europe before the reactionary advent of modern medicine. While modern medicine's votaries sought to secure an experimentally testable method to replace ad hoc medicine, ayurvedic vaidyas (physicians) were employing their own scientific, experimentally testable methodology and divine insight within the dhatudosha framework.

Although modern medicine is credited with "successfully" treating infectious disease, it may really only have succeeded in causing what is now called chronic disease, which in turn it does not know how to treat. Because it arises as a reaction to another form of ignorance, it is only a half-ruth at best. Reactionary solutions are never complete solutions. A Hegelian synthesis has yet to appear to balance the antithetical movement of modern medicine and science. Many persons in the West are now attempting to resurrect Eastern healing systems and interface them with allopathy in such a synthesis. Eastern medicine is foundationally different from modern medicine, which makes such a synthesis almost impossible. Of the two foundations, the structural composition of conventional medical knowledge in the West rests on an enormous yet flimsy infrastructure of experimental achievements. Thus it lacks the comprehensive aura of true medical wisdom.

Ayurvedic Body Types: Doshas and their Characteristics

Home | Blog Details

Ayurvedic Body Types: Doshas and their Characteristics

Ayurveda is an ancient Indian science of medicine that has been practiced for thousands of years. According to Ayurveda, every individual is unique and has a specific body type, which is determined by the doshas present in their body. The three doshas are Vata, Pitta, and Kapha. Each dosha has its own unique characteristics, and understanding them is essential for maintaining a healthy body and mind. In this article, we will explore the different Ayurvedic body types, their characteristics, and the appropriate diet for each body type.

What are Ayurvedic Body Types

Figure: *Ayurvedic body types, also known as doshas, are the three fundamental energies that govern the functioning of the body and mind. These energies are known as Vata, Pitta, and Kapha, and they are present in varying degrees in every individual. The balance of these doshas determines an individual's body type.*

Vata Body Type

The Vata body type is characterized by qualities such as lightness, dryness, and coldness. People with a dominant Vata dosha tend to be thin and have a fast metabolism. They are usually creative, energetic, and spontaneous but can also be anxious and have trouble sleeping. Vata body types benefit from warm, nourishing foods that help to ground them and calm their nervous system. Foods such as cooked grains, root vegetables, and warm soups are ideal for this body type.

Pitta Body Type

The Pitta body type is characterized by qualities such as heat, intensity, and sharpness. People with a dominant Pitta dosha tend to have a medium build, a strong appetite, and a high metabolism. They are usually intelligent, ambitious, and have a strong will but can also be irritable and prone to inflammation. Pitta body types benefit from foods that are cooling and calming, such as fresh fruits and vegetables, whole grains, and lean proteins.

Kapha Body Type

The Kapha body type is characterized by qualities such as heaviness, oiliness, and coldness. People with a dominant Kapha dosha tend to have a heavier build, a slower metabolism, and a calm disposition. They are usually loving, nurturing, and patient but can also be prone to lethargy and weight gain. Kapha body types benefit from foods that are light and dry, such as raw fruits and vegetables, whole grains, and lean proteins.

Vata, Pitta & Kapha Body Type Diet

Figure: *The Vata Pitta, & Kapha Body Type is a way of eating that is tailored to an individual's specific dosha. It focuses on foods that balance the doshas and promote optimal health and well-being.*

Each dosha has its own unique characteristics and requires a specific diet to maintain balance and promote optimal health. The ayurvedic body type diet is not a one-size-fits-all approach and is personalized to meet the needs of each individual.

Here are the dietary recommendations for Vata, Pitta & Kapha Body Type:

Vata Body Type Diet: The vata body type is characterized by the elements of air and space, which make them prone to digestive issues and anxiety. To balance their dosha, vata Body Type individuals should follow a diet that is warm, nourishing, and grounding.

Foods to include in Vata Body Type Diet:

1. Warm, cooked meals
2. Moist and oily foods such as ghee and coconut oil
3. Sweet, sour, and salty tastes

4. Nuts and seeds
5. Cooked vegetables such as carrots, beets, and sweet potatoes

Foods to avoid in Vata Body Type Diet:

1. Cold and raw foods
2. Dry and light foods such as crackers and rice cakes
3. Bitter and astringent tastes
4. Carbonated drinks and caffeine
5. Cold and dry air-conditioned environments

Pitta Body Type Diet: The pitta body type is characterized by the elements of fire and water, which make them prone to inflammation and digestive issues. To balance their dosha, pitta Body Type individuals should follow a diet that is cooling, hydrating, and soothing.

Foods to include In Pitta Body Type Diet:

1. Cooling and hydrating foods such as cucumber and melons
2. Sweet, bitter, and astringent tastes
3. Dairy products such as milk and ghee
4. Whole grains such as basmati rice and quinoa
5. Sweet and juicy fruits such as grapes and mangoes

Foods to avoid In Pitta Body Type Diet:

1. Spicy and acidic foods
2. Fried and greasy foods
3. Alcohol and caffeine
4. Sour and salty tastes
5. Hot and humid environments

Kapha Body Type Diet: The kapha body type is characterized by the elements of water and earth, which make them prone to weight gain and respiratory issues. To balance their dosha, kapha Body Type individuals should follow a diet that is light, dry, and stimulating.

Foods to include In Kapha Body Type Diet:

1. Light and dry foods such as popcorn and crackers
2. Pungent, bitter, and astringent tastes
3. Fruits such as apples and pears
4. Vegetables such as leafy greens and sprouts
5. Spices such as ginger, black pepper, and turmeric

Foods to avoid In Kapha Body Type Diet:

1. Sweet, sour, and salty tastes
2. Heavy and oily foods
3. Dairy products and red meat

It is important to note that the Ayurvedic body type diet is not a substitute for medical treatment and should be used in conjunction with a healthcare professional's advice.

Ayurvedic Body Types and Exercise

Figure: *In addition to diet, exercise is also an important factor in maintaining a healthy body and mind. Each ayurvedic body type requires a different type of exercise to maintain balance.*

Here are some exercise recommendations for each body type:

Vata Body Type Exercise

1. Gentle, calming exercises such as yoga and tai chi
2. Walking and hiking
3. Swimming and water aerobics

Pitta Body Type Exercise

1. Cooling exercises such as swimming and water sports
2. Moderate-intensity exercises such as biking and hiking
3. Yoga and meditation to promote relaxation

Kapha Body Type Exercise

1. High-intensity exercises such as running and aerobics
2. Strength training and weightlifting
3. Dynamic yoga and other energetic activities

In conclusion, understanding your Ayurvedic body type can help you make informed decisions about your diet and exercise routine. Each dosha has its own unique characteristics, and by balancing these energies, you can achieve optimal health and well-being. By following the ayurvedic body type diet and exercise recommendations, you can maintain balance and harmony in your body and mind.

Personalized Health with Ayurvedic Body Types: A Guide to Understanding Doshas

Ayurveda is founded on the belief that the world is made up of five elements and a combination of each element results in three doshas known as the vata, kapha and pitta. These three play a vital role in a person's overall physiological, mental and emotional health. While understanding doshas: ayurvedic body types and personalized health, the Ayurveda practitioner will look into the person's Kapha, Vata and Pitta ratio that will define the optimal health of the person.Now let's take a detailed look into it.

Understanding Dosha's: Vata, Kapha and Pitta

Here is a general overview of each dosha.

Vata

Our Ayurveda college in Kerala experts points out that vata mostly consists of two elements, air and space. They are generally characterized as cold, light, dry and rough. Those with predominant vata doshas are known for their thin, energetic, and creative nature. These people's moods are known for being influenced by various factors including the weather, people around them and food.

Ayurveda suggests that a vata-dominant individual should follow a regular daily routine, regulate stress through meditation and other relaxing activities, and maintain a warm body temperature by avoiding cold weather and consuming warm foods and liquids for best health.

Diet for Vata Dosha: Since Vata is a cold and chilly dosha, ayurveda suggests warm, nourishing foods with a somewhat thick texture, as well as extra butter and fat, help to balance it. You can choose foods with salty, sour, and sweet flavours, as well as foods that are relaxing and pleasant. Vatas-dominated people can include cream, butter, warm soups, stews, hot cereals, freshly baked bread, and raw nuts in their diet.

Kapha: When it comes to Kapha Dosha, Water and earth are the primary components that combine for it. It absorbs the qualities of each of these elements: the earth's solidity, steadiness, and firmness, as well as water's free movement, and cooling characteristics.

Diet for Kapha Dosha

Warm, light, and dry food is preferred, as are cooked light meals and they are ideal for people with dominant Kapha Dosha. Kaphas thrive on minimally cooked or fresh fruits and vegetables. Try dry cooking methods (baking, broiling, grilling, sautéing) to moist cooking methods such as steaming, boiling, or poaching.

Pitta: The pitta dosha is based on fire and water and is known for controlling the metabolism of the body. People with dominant Pitta Dosha have stronger appetites and digestion. Ayurveda points out that anger, emotional strain, excessive alcohol, meat, sugar and white flour will throw the dosha out of balance. Because they are hot-headed, they can handle the cold better. They are aggressive and impatient by nature, as well as intelligent.

Diet for Pitta Dosha: Cool or warm dishes with relatively heavy textures, rather than blazing hot foods are better for pitta. Bitter, sweet, and astringent flavours are preferred. Salads, milk, and ice cream are examples of cold, refreshing foods to eat during the summer or hot weather. Pitta is soothed by herbal tea, particularly mint or liquorice root tea.

Exercise and Lifestyle for Each Doshas

Your Ayurvedic practitioner will recommend exercise according to your dosha type. Exercise and lifestyle choices cannot go unmentioned in the blog 'Understanding Doshas: Ayurvedic Body Types and Personalized Health'.

Vata: People with vata-dominant doshas should include activities such as cycling, running and walking in their lifestyle. They can also include activities like yoga and Thai chi etc.

Pitta: People with pitta dominant dosha should be focusing on cardio and weight-resistant exercise. Any kind of physical activity is beneficial for this group

Kapha: Swimming, long-distance walking, trampolining, and a leisurely jog are all terrific possibilities. Visiting a sauna after exercise is also excellent for a Kapha type since it allows them to sweat out any stored toxins while also raising their internal body temperature.

Ayurveda promotes whole-body healing starting from physical, mental, and emotional well-being. Yoga, meditation, mindful eating, sleep hygiene, spending time alone and with others, and managing your work-life balance are all examples of such practices recommended by Ayurveda practitioners.

It is especially recommended to establish a daily routine that incorporates these healthy lifestyle practices. A regular regimen is also recommended to keep you in touch with the elements and promote optimum health in Ayurveda. Our experts at the School of Ayurveda and Panchakarma, the top Ayurveda Institute in Kerala can provide you with more details about the holistic practices mentioned in the blog.

A study found that vata dominant has dificulty sleeping while kapha-dominant people tend to oversleep. So incorporating mindfulness, and meditation can help you out with balancing your doshas.

Chapter 3

Exploring the Mind in Ayurveda

Introduction

Exploring the Mind in Ayurveda involves understanding the intricate relationship between the mind and body and recognizing the vital role of mental health in overall well-being. In Ayurvedic philosophy, the mind is considered a powerful force that significantly influences physical health and emotional balance. Ayurveda views the mind as an integral part of the holistic system of health, with mental well-being being essential for maintaining harmony and equilibrium in the body.

Ayurveda identifies three mental qualities or gunas known as Sattva, Rajas, and Tamas, which influence mental states and behaviours. Sattva represents purity, clarity, and harmony and is associated with qualities such as love, compassion, and tranquility. Rajas represents activity, passion, and desire and is associated with qualities such as ambition, restlessness, and agitation. Tamas represents inertia, darkness, and stagnation and is associated with qualities such as lethargy, ignorance, and depression.

According to Ayurveda, imbalances in the gunas can lead to disturbances in mental health and well-being. For example, an excess of Rajas may result in anxiety, stress, and irritability, while an excess of Tamas may lead to depression, lethargy, and apathy. Cultivating Sattva, on the other hand, promotes mental clarity, emotional balance, and spiritual growth.

Ayurveda offers a variety of practices to support mental health and well-being, including meditation, mindfulness, and yoga. These practices are designed to calm the mind, reduce stress, and promote inner peace and harmony. Meditation involves focusing the mind and cultivating awareness through techniques such as breath awareness, mantra repetition, and visualization. Mindfulness involves paying attention to the present moment with openness, curiosity, and acceptance. Yoga combines physical postures, breathwork, and meditation to integrate mind, body, and spirit.

Ayurveda also emphasizes the importance of maintaining a healthy lifestyle to support mental health. This includes following a balanced diet, getting regular exercise, and getting adequate rest and sleep. Ayurvedic herbs and supplements may also be used to support mental well-being, such as Brahmi, Ashwagandha, and Jatamansi, which are known for their calming and rejuvenating properties.

In conclusion, exploring the mind in Ayurveda involves recognizing the interconnectedness of mental and physical health and adopting practices that promote balance, harmony, and well-being on all levels. By cultivating Sattva, practicing meditation and mindfulness, and adopting a healthy lifestyle, individuals can support their mental health and cultivate inner peace and happiness.

Ayurveda and the Mind

A Great Inner Adventure Into the Dimensions of Consciousness

Ayurveda has an integral view of the mind, physical body, and immortal Self. The body is a crystallization of the deep-seated mental tendencies (from previous lives). Body, mind and spirit are one.

Most physical diseases are due to external factors like wrong diet, and exposure to pathogens. Most mental diseases arise from inner factors like wrong use of senses, and the accumulation of negative emotions.

Our way of life breeds unhappiness. Ayurveda teaches harmony with nature and how to live in a state of balance. This requires changing how we live, think and perceive. We understand our own nature for our own happiness and well-being, and understand others for harmonious social interaction.

This is our third week of exploring Ayurveda: our doshas (elements and constitution), practices to balance our doshas and this week, our mind. Reference book Ayurveda and the Mind: the Healing of Consciousness, by Dr David Frawley. What does Ayurveda say about this by our doshas. Remember that most people are a balance of 2 or even 3 doshas, and we all have some qualities of each.

People with high vata have minds that are quick and agile, and they are talkative and informed. When not balanced, their mind wanders, they can lack determination, and be spaced out and absent minded. They tend to feel fear and anxiety. They are also creative, social, and are good communicators.

People with high pitta have minds that are intelligent, perceptive, discriminating, and sharp. They have systematic, probing minds. They can also be opinionated, self-righteous, prone to anger, and may lack compassion.

Mind-Body Connection in Ayurveda: Cultivating Mental Clarity and Emotional Balance

Ayurvedic doctor in Hyderabad Draws from the holistic approach of Ayurvedic medicine, this study investigates how various factors, including doshas and specific techniques, can impact mental well-being.

By examining Ayurvedic practices that aim to calm the mind and manage stress, as well as nourish the emotional body, this article aims to provide evidence-based insights into harnessing meditation and yoga for emotional balance. The findings presented here contribute to a deeper understanding of Ayurveda's potential in promoting overall wellness.

1. The Ayurvedic Approach to Mind-Body Wellness The ayurvedic treatment for stress and anxiety in Hyderabad is to approach mind-body wellness focuses on cultivating mental clarity and emotional balance through a combination of dietary modifications, ayurvedic supplements, and lifestyle practices. Ayurveda, an ancient Indian system of medicine, believes that the mind and body are interconnected and that imbalances in one can affect the other. To enhance mental clarity, Ayurvedic herbs such as Brahmi (Bacopa monnieri) and Shankhpushpi (Convolvulus pluricaulis) are recommended. These herbs have been traditionally used to improve cognitive function and memory. Additionally, Ayurvedic lifestyle practices like yoga, meditation, and pranayama (breathing exercises) can help reduce stress levels and promote emotional balance. These practices aim to calm the mind, release emotional tension, and restore inner harmony.
2. Understanding the Doshas and Their Impact on Mental Clarity Understanding the doshas and their impact on mental clarity

involves examining the relationship between certain bodily functions and cognitive processes. According to Ayurveda, an ancient Indian system of medicine, there are three doshas - Vata, Pitta, and Kapha - that govern various aspects of our physical and mental well-being. Each dosha represents a unique combination of elements and is responsible for specific physiological functions. When these doshas are in balance, it promotes optimal mental clarity and emotional balance. However, imbalances in the doshas can lead to mental disturbances such as anxiety or depression. Ayurvedic remedies aim to restore this balance by identifying individual constitutional types and providing personalized treatments including dietary modifications, herbal supplements, lifestyle changes, meditation practices, and body therapies.

3. Ayurvedic Techniques for Calming the Mind and Managing Stress Ayurvedic techniques for calming the mind and managing stress involve implementing various holistic approaches. These include dietary modifications, herbal supplements, lifestyle changes, meditation practices, and body therapies. Breathing exercises are one of the fundamental practices in Ayurveda that can help relieve stress and promote mental clarity. Controlled breathing techniques, such as diaphragmatic breathing or alternate nostril breathing, have been shown to activate the parasympathetic nervous system. This leads to a relaxation response in the body. Additionally, Ayurveda utilizes several herbal remedies for anxiety management. Adaptogenic herbs like ashwagandha and Brahmi have been traditionally used in Ayurveda to support healthy stress responses and promote emotional balance. These herbs are believed to nourish the nervous system and enhance resilience to stressful situations. Incorporating these holistic approaches into daily life can help individuals cultivate mental clarity and emotional well-being.

4. Nourishing the Emotional Body Through Ayurvedic Practices Nourishing the emotional body through Ayurvedic practices involves implementing various holistic approaches that support healthy stress responses and promote well-being. Ayurveda, an ancient Indian system of medicine, recognizes the intimate relationship between the mind and body. To nourish the emotional body, Ayurveda emphasizes self-care rituals and the

use of healing herbs. Self-care rituals can include daily meditation, yoga, or pranayama (breathing exercises) to calm the mind and reduce stress. Additionally, incorporating specific healing herbs into one's diet can further support emotional balance. Ayurvedic doctor in Hyderabad also deals with mental diseases, Ashwagandha is often used in Ayurvedic medicine for its adaptogenic properties that help manage stress and anxiety. Similarly, Brahmi is known for its ability to enhance cognitive function and promote a sense of tranquility.

5. Harnessing the Power of Meditation and Yoga for Emotional Balance Research indicates that the practice of meditation and yoga can have a positive impact on emotional well-being by promoting relaxation, reducing stress, and enhancing self-awareness. Breathing exercises are an integral part of these practices, as they help create a sense of calm and balance in the body. By focusing on deep, slow breaths, individuals can activate the parasympathetic nervous system, which is responsible for relaxation responses in the body. Mindfulness involves bringing one's attention to the present moment without judgment or attachment. This practice helps individuals become more aware of their thoughts, emotions, and bodily sensations, allowing them to respond to challenges with greater clarity and equanimity. Through regular meditation and yoga practices that incorporate breathing exercises and mindfulness techniques, individuals can cultivate emotional balance and mental clarity in their lives.

The Spiritual Lens of Ayurveda

If you prefer to use the spiritual lens to study the balance between our mind, body, and spirit, understand that Ayur, Sanskrit for life, is the union of the physical body, senses, mind, and spirit. It is known by dhatri, that which sustains, jivita, that which is life, nityaga, that which is in continuum, and Anubandha, that which is interdependent or that which acts as a link between the past life and the future life.

Our mind, body, and spirit are connected to the laws of nature. The practice of meditation helps to get in touch with the Self. The seat of intelligence is the Self as per nature. It is the key to knowing oneself. Knowing your own body and then taking it even a step further, your mind is the way to be attuned to your spirit.

Taking Care of Our Mental Health Through Ayurveda

Many of us realize the role that rest plays in our lives, and how important it is for recovery and balance.

Now, let's take a look at different Ayurvedic tools that you can apply to your daily life to create a calm alignment for your body, mind, and soul. It is surprisingly easier to take care of our bodies than it is our minds! Different fields of medicine deal with diets, lifestyle changes, and exercise routines to ensure that the human body continues to function at an optimum level. However, it is easy to let mental health take the backseat, but it can also prove to be the most dangerous one!

When we eat warm and fresh food, we are not only feeding our body but also nourishing it. Similarly, kind words and generous deeds bring kindness in return while harsh words breed anger and resentment.

To ensure that we take care of our mental health and in turn our spiritual health, we must first understand what makes up the mind and how it connects to our soul.

The Three Aspects of the Mind

The three aspects of the mind can help us in understanding how the Atma or spirit, mind, and body are connected to each other and in turn the higher self.

Dhi: The ability to learn & acquire knowledge. It is a Sanskrit word that translates to understanding, reflection, or intellect. In the context of our discussion, it means the mind's ability to learn or acquire knowledge.

Dhriti: The ability to process and retain information. Is a Sanskrit word that means "to act with determination." It also means the quality of discernment, of knowing right from wrong. Dhriti is about getting in touch with your inner self and discerning whether a particular course of action or decision is right or wrong.

Smriti: The ability to recall or remember. Smriti is recollection in Sanskrit. Good memory can be seen in different aspects. It might be the knowledge of cause and effect or seeing similarity or even contrast. It could also contribute to high concentration powers, or the ability to practice a particular task for long hours. Attaining or acquiring information of the metaphysical kind and the ability to communicate an event or a story effectively so that someone else can comprehend the ongoing works is also the work of good smriti.

Smriti is impaired when there is an excess of rajas and tamas. Smriti or memory is the remembrance of things that are directly perceived, heard, or experienced earlier. One of the most complex processes carried out by the brain, memory is the one where information is encoded, stored, and retrieved. It has a prominent role in the perception of knowledge.

Smriti is more closely related to Buddhi (intellect) and Manas (mind). Memory is said to be the result of the collective action of Atma, Manas, and Buddhi. It is the recreation of past experiences by the synchronous firing of neurons that were involved in the original experience. Manas play an important role in the process of retention of knowledge and it also coordinates the external environment with the brain through the different Gyanendriyas or sense organs.

The capacity to multitask has been heralded as a sign of productivity. However, since we only have one mind, it can only connect with one sensory organ at a time. It is precisely why information from multiple sensory organs cannot be processed and translated to the Atma all at once.

Perceiving Your True Self

If you don't clean the mirror in your house for some time, it will be covered in dust, and eventually, you will not be able to see your own self. Similarly, if your mind is disconnected from your soul, you will be unable to perceive your own true self.

According to Ayurveda, the mind is an irreplaceable part of life. It impacts the overall health of the body and soul. Increasingly, we've begun to observe that there is a rise in psychosomatic diseases because of high levels of stress. Emotional balance is perturbed wherein Dhi, Dhriti, Smriti are not functioning at an optimal level. When there is such an imbalance between the three pillars, the balance should only be restored with non-pharmacological treatment.

A simple quick-fix mentality will not suffice when it comes to lifestyle disorders. So we must understand how to better catch minor imbalances when they arise. The easiest way to do this is through present moment awareness. When we are aligned with the true nature of our being, we can live a life full of purpose, intention, and happiness.

Established in Yoga, O winner of wealth,

Perform actions having abandoned

Attachment and having become balanced in

Success and failure, for balance of mind is
Called Yoga.
(Bhagavad-Gita, II, 48)

The Openness of Mind

Mind is the frontier of science; it is also the foundation of science. Without mind, science does not exist, although the universe that science studies does. Empirical science is based on experience and observation; scientific theories are products of our intellect; scientific research is a purposive human enterprise, an expression of our capacity to wonder, our aspiration to know, our urge to control. One cannot properly analyze the structure of science without examining the nature of the human mind. Conversely, systematic investigation of mind must include an account for the presuppositions of science. Thus the science of mind is also an inquiry into its own foundations and conditions of possibility.

Self-criticism is crucial for the interpretations of cognitive science. More than in other sciences, here philosophers are prone to confuse science with scientism, the technique worship that reaps it profit by abusing the name of science. To see the significance of cognitive science properly, we must recognize a fact tacitly denied by most models of the closed mind controlled by mind designers: Science is a human enterprise without divine power. Scientists are not gods or godlike mind designers but ordinary men and women. Research is not a miracle but a mundane activity not qualitatively different from any other profession. Scientists and folks in the street think about different things, but they think in the same general ways, and their thinking shares the general characteristics and structures of the human mind. These characteristics, which I summarily call mind's openness to the world, are the topics of my analysis, because they provide a big picture of mind.

Mind Engaged In and Open To The World

Cartesianism has been under attack for centuries. Its notion of the closed mind controlled by mind designers persists partly because it is the easiest mental model. It can dominate cognitive science also because here artifacts-computers, connectionist networks, dynamical systems-become the paradigms of mind, so that computation displaces meaning and understanding. Artificial mind can do without body or world because it is a kept system. Its flesh and blood human designers and users, working in the physical and social world, take care of meanings. Whenever people are the paradigms of mental beings, embodiment and engagement become essential, although their theoretical representations pose great difficulty. Embodiment and engagement are different issues, as an embodied mind is not necessarily incompatible with solipsism. Philosopher Charles Taylor (1985) provided a clear analysis of engaged agents, emphasizing their autonomy, understanding, and concern with significance.

Therefore engagement is different from AI's situated cognition with its emphasis on interactive behaviours evaluated by mind designers. Decades before the cognitive revolution, continental phenomenologists developed sophisticated analyses of the embodied and engaged human existence. Many psychologists also emphasized environmental influences. Now, discontent is noticeable within cognitive science, as some scientists contend that computationalism and behaviourism alike have no place in the truly mental. More and more, embodiment and engagement become key words in the literature (Kirshner and Whitson 1997; Hurley 1998). The literature is diverse and multicultural. Researchers with different agendas opt for different forms of embodiment and engagement.

Developmental Theories

Several scientists with biological orientations maintain that an organism's mental abilities depend on their history of acquisition. This history is embodied because organisms must cope physically in their living environments in both growth and organic evolution. Among these theories is the "genetic epistemology" of developmental psychologist Jean Piaget. Drawing on his extensive empirical work with infants and children, Piaget proposed that newborns come equipped with sensorimotor organs and limbs but no cognitive ability. They have the notion neither of objects nor of self; they fuse their environment with their own motions and are unable to conceive a world distinct from and independent of themselves.

"It is precisely when the subject is most self-centered that he knows himself the least, and it is to the extent that he discovers himself that he places himself in the universe and constructs it by virtue of that fact."The process of self-discovery occurs as infantile subjects continually interact with their environment through perception and action. They gradually develop concepts, assimilate the environment to the most suitable ones, and accommodate the concepts to events and effects of their actions. Through several stages of sensorimotor development in the first two years of life babies construct increasingly elaborate notions of objects, causes, space, and time; in short, notions of a permanent world existing independent of their perception and action. Simultaneously, as they discover the external world, they discover themselves as distinct from other objects. "Acquiring possession of the object as such is on a par with the acquisition of self-perception," Piaget (1954:x) wrote."This organization of reality occurs, as we shall see, to the extent that the self is freed from itself by finding itself and so assigns itself a place as a thing among things, an event among events."

Piaget contributed to not only psychology but philosophy. His influence peaked in the 1970s but remains strong among developmental psychologists, although some of his doctrines have been challenged. Recent experiments showed that infants a few months old already have some appreciation of rigidity and continuity of motion.

They are a long way from grasping the full concepts of objects, but by noticing some differences, they are not as cognitively impoverished as Piaget described. Despite disagreement regarding the age when infants form satisfactory concepts of self and object and the possible contribution of innate mental structures, two of Piaget's points are widely accepted. For infants to acquire a sense of self, they must be able to differentiate themselves clearly from their environment and recognize their independence. And to develop the mental differentiation, sensorimotor exercises are indispensable. Development occurs as the babies open themselves to the world (Meltzoff and Moore 1995; Bertenthal 1996).

Existential Phenomenology

Phenomenology was founded by Edmund Husserl at the beginning of the twentieth century. Developed and modified by many philosophers, it flourished for several decades and is still influential in continental Europe. Husserl's (1913) phenomenology has a strong idealistic strand. To study the fundamental structures of mind and intentionality, he maintained, we must abandon the cultural world permeated with scientific notions and return to examine the lived world, the world of immediate experiences. By systematically comparing variations of experiences, we can discard arbitrary changes and extract invariant features as the objects that we experience. This much most people agree. Husserl also prescribed a phenomenological reduction that abandons our "natural attitude" and adopts the equivalent of what cognitive scientists call methodological solipsism. In our natural attitude, our perception and thinking are mostly directed at things in the world. Phenomenological reduction "brackets" the things and the world so that its attention can focus on pure mental acts and analyze their structures. Husserl found consciousness where cognitive scientists find computation. Nevertheless, their minds share the fate of being deprived of the world. It is no surprise that Husserl's best students refused to agree.

Existential phenomenologists, notably Martin Heidegger (1926) and Maurice Merleau-Ponty (1945), adopted many of Husserl's ideas but rejected his phenomenological reduction. Contrary to Husserl, who still engaged in Cartesian meditation, Heidegger abolished the whole Cartesian scheme with its worldless subject inside and unintelligible things outside. He scorned the notion of a mind inside the "cabinet of consciousness" and refused even to talk about consciousness, which he took to be something hiding inside. When Kant, critical of the Cartesian framework but not totally extricated from it, presented a proof for the existence of the external world as a refutation of idealism, he wrote (1781:34): "It still remains a scandal to philosophy and to human reason in general... that the existence of things outside us must be accepted merely on faith, and that if anyone thinks good to doubt their existence, we are unable to counter his doubts by any satisfactory proof." Heidegger (1926:205) retorted: "The 'scandal of philosophy' is not that this proof has yet to be given, but that such proofs are expected and attempted again and again." Those who gladly accept Dr. Johnson's kicking a stone as a satisfactory refutation of idealism would agree with Heidegger. Why would anyone in his right mind need philosophical proofs to believe that external things exist? Being open to the world is the essential and most obvious characteristic of our mentality. It is impossible to characterize mental properties adequately without invoking the world with which our mind is inextricably concerned. This is Heidegger's point.

The scandal of philosophy is far from over, as we saw in the representation theory of mind and the debate between internalism and externalism.The big problem in cognitive science is the meaning of representation in mental representations, which signify the relation between closed mind and the world. Kant's proof for the existence of the external world is a heroic attempt to answer a similar question. The question persists, as do efforts to answer it. Heidegger argued that the scandal lies in the question itself; it is precisely the formulation of the question in such ways that makes it insolvable. The two-part formulation assumes that mind can exist as a closed entity on its own; that it can think meaningfully without regard for things outside; that only as a second thought does it worry about the existence of things. Under this assumption, philosophers first posit mind and universe as two entities independent of each other and ask how they can be related. It is perhaps the most insidious form of dualism. What it puts asunder, no power can unite. Heidegger held that this dualist picture, which is the source of skepticism and solipsism, grossly distorts our being, Dasein (being-there), as Dasein is radically and essentially being-in-the-world. Merleau-Ponty (1945:xi) illustrated: "There is no inner man, man is in the world, and only in the world does he know himself." Mind does not and cannot exist without its world, for the intelligibility of the world is its essential feature. Thus it requires neither proof of nor bridge to the outer world because it has no inner-outer dichotomy to start with.

Human being is essentially being-in-the-world, which is different from situated cognition discussed in the preceding section. The in in being-in-the-world is not merely the in as a tree grows in its ecosystem, and the world is not merely an environment as the warm ocean was the environment for the first life on Earth. Any thing, animate or not, has its environment with which it interacts causally. Human beings too have their environment in this sense, but their world goes beyond it. Our world is not merely a blind causal force but is intelligible and meaningful to us. Things in it exist in the original Greek sense, which means "to stand out from." Because things are significant and useful for us, our being-in the world is not merely physical occupancy but also care, involvement, and understanding with certain states of mind. Only because we are in the universe in this peculiar sense can we turn the blind environment into a meaningful world that we can choose to trash or preserve. Heidegger set himself the task of analyzing the meaning of our being-in-the-world.

The primary meaning of our being, he argued, resides not in theoretical and scientific thinking but in our everyday handing of things and being with other people. Imagine yourself driving a car, negotiating the sharp turns, enjoying the scenery, listening to music on the radio, musing about the friend you are going to visit. The car handles so well you are almost oblivious of it; it is so integrated into your activity it has become a part of you, so to speak. All things-your friend, the car, the music, the road, the scenery-are interrelated and constitute your world with its primary meaning, a living meaning. Everything is significant and contributes to your purposive activity, but the significance is tacit and not explicitly articulated. The car is something you maneuver to keep on the road that leads to your friend. The car, the road, and your friend are handy. They relate to each other, and together they constitute the world of primary significance. If the car breaks down, however, it ceases to be handy equipment and becomes a mere thing present to you.

Then you switch to the theoretical attitude and try to figure out what is wrong with the thing and what to do with it. In doing so, your world acquires a secondary significance. According to Heidegger, the theoretical attitude is a common mode of being human, albeit a secondary and derived mode. When you switch to the theoretical attitude, you abstract from many cares and concerns that you are normally involved in, focus your attention on a few things, and make them stand out by themselves as things in space and time. You trade the richness of wider experience for the clear and refined vision of a few objects. The world to which your mind is open is thereby narrowed and impoverished, but it is not closed off. It is still meaningful to you. You still stand firmly in the world, your judgment is still objective or about objects, your understanding is still influenced by your background knowledge and cultural heritage, although the influence is correspondingly weakened by your abstraction from other concerns and your striving for intersubjective agreement. In this sense, theoretical reason is a general aspect of mind whose functions pervade our daily activity: perceiving, cognizing, understanding, and thinking. We exercise our theoretical reason whenever we devise a tool, explain an event, classify an object, or report a perceptual experience as simple as "there's a chair in the corner."

Usually, the functions of theoretical reason are small in scope and so embedded in our daily routines they are hardly noticeable. When something goes wrong to disrupt a smooth routine, however, they come to the fore to deal with the problem. Science refines, develops, systematizes, and applies in large scale this theoretical attitude that everyone is capable of on smaller scales. It sees a simplified world more clearly from a vantage point, not an alien world from God's position. Illiterate street vendors can make change correctly without knowing formal arithmetic. This is an example of know-how. Heidegger maintained that such know-how and practice, by which we deal with things concernfully in our everyday life, constitute the primary intelligibility of our being-in-the-world. One can make this tacit intelligibility more explicit by interpretation and articulate it by verbalization, such as specifically recognizing the thing one is using to be a hammer or describing it in words. We achieve supreme explicitness in scientific reasoning. However, no matter how far scientific articulation is developed, it can never exhaust all the primary significance of our everyday world. It always takes for granted something that is tacitly understood in the primary intelligibility of the world that continues to function as the indispensable background to all our scientific knowledge.

I basically agree with Heidegger; my model of mind as the intelligibility of objects follows from his meaning of beings. Heidegger's phenomenological analysis, although profound, is famous for its obscurity. His word-twisting terminology alone would alienate most English readers. Therefore I critically borrow only major ideas from him. For explication I keep to the theoretical approach familiar to scientists and illustrate mental phenomena in the general framework of complexity theories.

Phenomenology made an impact on cognitive science when Hubert Dreyfus (1972) used it to launch a scathing criticism of AI. This earned him the eternal wrath of much of the AI community, but it produced some positive results. Some AI researchers, such as Winograd and Flores (1986), examined their professional practice from an existential phenom-enological viewpoint. Reading their book, Clancey (1994) said he was struck by the idea that "I realized that I don't have any patterns, associations, or preferences stored in my mind."When recently AI turn to dynamical systems and situated cognition, some engineers found themselves repeating what they hated Dreyfus for saying, even when they had little sympathy with phenomenology. In explaining his approach of "intelligence without representation," Brooks (1999:97) wrote: "In some circles much credence is given to Heidegger as one who understood the dynamics of existence. Our approach has certain similarities to work inspired by this German philosopher (e.g.), but our work was not so inspired. It is based purely on engineering consideration." It is encouraging that phenomenology and the engineering of intelligent robots, whose concerns and styles of reasoning cannot be more different from each other, converge on a similar conclusion. The Cartesian Trojan horse with its intermediary mental representations is untenable. Outside AI, other cognitive scientists are trying to bring phenomenology to bear on their respective areas of investigation (Petitot et al. 1999).

Mind's Eastern Embodiment

Heidegger's analysis addressed all general aspects of Dasein. Merleau-Ponty's argument for the primacy of perception offered a detailed phenomenological analysis of how the structures of perception depend on our body and the perceived world. As concrete as their descriptions of living experiences are, they are theoretical and involve general concepts such as spatiality and sexuality. They are philosophical theories whose topics are pragmatic and life experiences. This is a fatal flaw, according to Francisco Varela, Evan Thompson, and Eleanor Rosch.

Varela et al. (1991) insisted that phenomenology breaks down because Husserl, Heidegger, and Meleau-Ponty reflected on pragmatic matters theoretically, and the theories themselves lacked a pragmatic dimension. Theoretical reason cannot overcome the rift between science and experience. Varela and company asked: "But if we turn away from reason, if reason is no longer taken as the method for knowing the mind, what can be used instead" They found nothing useful in Western philosophy and science. Consequently they turned to the East, to the mindfulness meditation of Madhyamika Buddhism.

Mindfulness meditation is a practice in which the meditator's mind comes into the presence of itself so that it gains insight into its own nature and functioning. According to Buddhism, one finds no self in meditation but only five aggregates: forms, feelings, perceptions, dispositions, and consciousness. This selfless state of being is the technical meaning of mindfulness. Meditators find that our ordinary state, in which we pursue our selfish goals, are not mindful. Varela et al. (1991) identified human experience and embodiment with mindfulness, as the meditation brings one's mind and body together. Western theoretical reflection, including phenomenology, is disembodied, because it is not mindful and leaves out the presence of mind itself.

I wholeheartedly support the effort to expand the intellectual horizon beyond Western philosophy and thinking, and I hope that meditation can become a useful method in cognitive science. However, I am skeptical that the peculiar sense of embodiment attained in mindfulness meditation is compatible with openness to the world. As Varela and Jonathan Shear (1999) point out, mediation is similar to

Husserl's phenomenological reduction and the introspective method used in early experimental psychology and abandoned later. All three strive to gain "the view from within." All three have problems relating to the world.

Varela, Thompson, and Rosch rightly emphasized the importance of practice, but they were too restrictive in their range of practices. Meditation is a practice. So are all our mundane activities, from taking a bath to writing computer programs. They are not as conspicuous as meditation because they are not as esoteric, but their mundane nature makes them more, not less, illuminating about mind. Mindfulness is a special state in which one achieves tranquility by detaching oneself from selfish yearnings and the buzzing events in the world.

It may be superior to ordinary mental states where one is confounded and exhausted by chasing after desires and happenings. Even so, it cannot displace everyday mentality as the basic topic for the science of mind, because everyday mentality is what most of us are most of the time. Most activities of meditators, and all activities of nonmeditators, are not mindful. Our everyday state of being does not have to be the best. Heidegger called it fallen and inauthentic, but nevertheless maintained that it is the most important for understanding mind. I agree. At issue is scientific investigation of natural mental states, not value legislation or conversion of people. Therefore I stick to a more ordinary sense of embodiment, in which all our mundane mental activities, unmindful as they are, are embodied. It is the embodiment that Merleau-Ponty described most concretely.

Explanations and Experiences of Mind

Unlike Varela, Thompson, and Rosch, I refuse to turn away from reason and theorizing. Reasoning is both an essential mental ability that an adequate science of mind must account for and an indispensable process for the practice of scientific research. For neither is it sufficient; there is much more to mind than rationality, and science also needs circumspection and intuitive judgment. However, it is necessary for both, including gaining knowledge about mind. I think that Varela et al.'s abandonment of reason is based on a confusion between the practice of theorizing and the topic of theories, between experiences and explanations of mind. The five aggregates are theoretical descriptions of what meditators experience in practice. Their general status is not different from theoretical descriptions of structures of our ordinary experiences offered by phenomenologists.

Human abstract thinking or theorizing is a fully embodied practice, complete with the sense of frustration, feeling of headache, and other factors that Heidegger called "mood." These pragmatic factors are usually not included in topics that scientists or philosophers think about, but this does not imply that the topics are necessarily disembodied. Suppose you are writing a paper on backache and your back aches while you work. It suffices that your paper includes adequate descriptions of the general causes or characteristics of backache; descriptions of your own discomfort while producing the paper would be beside the point. Heidegger gave extended descriptions of the embodied pragmatics of theoretical thinking. Varela and company wrongly dismissed it as disembodied and merely theoretical.

There is a difference between existential knowledge and theoretical knowledge of mental states. Consider philosopher Frank Jackson's (1982) story about Mary who is confined to a black and white room and sees the world only through a black and white television. Being a brilliant scientist, Mary has learned everything there is to know about colour vision, from light to reflectance spectra to retinal excitation to the working of the visual cortex. Now suppose she is released from the room and sees the colourful world for the first time in her life. Does she learn anything new? Jackson answered obviously yes. Behavioural and eliminativist philosophers answer obviously no. They are talking about two kinds of knowledge. Mary does not acquire any more theoretical knowledge by her visual experience. If her theoretical knowledge is adequate, she should have known all along, by measuring the light in her room, that she was not seeing colour. Nevertheless, she does gain existential knowledge of colour vision. I think more than a few people would gladly trade the knowledge on paper for the knowledge in life. Mary's existential knowledge will make her a better painter and a better scientist of vision, because science is theoretical but not merely theoretical.

By the very conscious nature of mind, a person in a mental state is spontaneously aware of its contents. The awareness can be regarded as a kind of knowledge, as people say they know they are in pain or they know their own minds. This is existential knowledge of mental states that we acquire by being in the states and possess as subjects of experiences. Embodied, immediate, prevalent, intelligible, but often poorly articulated, existential knowledge is distinct from the theoretical knowledge in which mental states occur as objects. It is rather data for theoretical explanations of mind. Mindfulness meditators gain existential knowledge for a special kind of experience by disciplining their states of mind. Meditation provides data in addition to our ordinary experiences but cannot supplant them.

I understand theoretical in the modest sense of the theoretical attitude described by Heidegger. Much if not all of epistemology is concerned with theoretical knowledge, also known as objective knowledge, as it is about the objects that we know through perception and inference. Science develops the theoretical attitude and produces highly systematic theoretical knowledge. Scientists exercise their refined theoretical reason, partially detach themselves from most value judgments, inspect systematically certain classes of phenomena, carefully assess information gathered in perception and experiment, and think in highly conceptualized and symbolized forms. Theorizing is a mental practice. In investigating mind, however, scientists regard mental beings and states as objects, thus they seldom if at all consider explicitly the existential knowledge that they themselves are immediately conscious of as theorizing subjects. Such considerations of themselves would be at best superfluous in a scientific theory. Suffice that a theory of mind describes mental beings capable of existential knowledge generally.

Following custom, by knowledge of mind without qualification I refer to theoretical knowledge. Therefore to know about a mental state is different from to be in that mental state. Theoretical knowing is a peculiar mental state that is distinct from the mental state that happens to be the object of theoretical knowledge. Having theoretical knowledge about a mental state does not imply that we are in that mental state or that we can transport ourselves into it. One can learn the causes and symptoms of pain without ever being in pain. The science of mind provides general knowledge about mental states, but it does not put us into the states to experience their phenomenal fullness.

To be in a certain mental state is always a concrete and particular event. A state of a complex being typically has a staggering number of facets, all of which are relevant to its particularity. When I am in a particular mental state, I experience the full richness of its facets, although perhaps hazily. The concrete details constitute the phenomenal consciousness of my state of being. Phenomenal consciousness has low degree of conceptualization, because conceptualization usually abstracts from particularity and fullness of details. Therefore phenomenal consciousness is inarticulate and difficult to communicate. Imagine yourself standing at the rim of the Grand Canyon and seeing the colourful landscape. Now try to describe your phenomenal visual experience. Even if you are good with words you will find your account falling short of your experience. Verbal description is perhaps the least abstract operation of theoretical reason. More particular details will be discarded when science seeks general principles in higher abstraction.

Yo u are in a different mental state when you are enjoying the sight of the Grand Canyon than when you are wracking your brain to find the words for it. Thinking is a specific mental process complete with its own phenomenal feelings such as frustration. In communicating our thoughts linguistically, we abstract from most aspects of our phenomenal consciousness and articulate only certain salient aspects in the propositional form. Thus the propositional content, although important as knowledge, does not exhaust all the features of a mental state.

I agree with Varela et al. that theoretical knowledge invariably leaves out many details of phenomenal consciousness. Theoretical representations of complex phenomena invariably abstract, generalize, universalize, idealize, and approximate. In extracting the salient regularities of wide classes of complex states, representing them in words and symbols, and seeking general principles, we blur or discard many particular details, regarding them as irrelevant to theoretical understanding. When we apply generalizing and idealizing theoretical reason to our own states of being, the difference between concrete and abstract, between particular and general, becomes glaring.

Theoretical reason is much broader and more versatile than logical inference because it is inalienable from objective experience, whereas logic abstracts further from the relation to the physical world. Nevertheless, it is only one mode of our mental capacity. Therefore we must be realistic about what science using theoretical reason can tell us about mind with its great variety of modes. With its penchant for abstraction and its emphasis on general principles, science would probably never capture the full richness of particular living experiences. In this respect it may be inferior to the arts and literature. Despite the limitation, however, I am more sanguine about theoretical reason than Varela et al. I think that to a certain degree of abstraction science can give embodied activities a proper place in its theoretical representations and explanations, even if it cannot fill in all their details.

A Rigid Notion of Embodiment

Adopting some arguments of Varela et al. but not following them into Buddhism, George Lakoff and Mark Johnson (1999:20,77) advocated a specifically rigid notion of embodiment:"An embodied concept is a neural structure that is actually part of, or makes use of, the sensorimotor system of our brain. Much of conceptual inference is, therefore, sensorimotor inference." They claimed that our thoughts are mostly based on a few hundred "primary metaphors," examples of which are important is big, bad is stinky, and control is up.

These metaphors are embodied in the specific sense of being determined by the peculiarities of our sensorimotor organs and hard-wired in our brains. "Our brains are structured so as to project activation patterns from sensorimotor areas to higher cortical areas. These constitute what we have called 'primary metaphors.' Projections of this kind allow us to conceptualize abstract concepts on the basis of inferential patterns used in the sensorimotor processes that are directly tied to the body."

This is a highly specific notion of embodiment in which the peculiarities of our limbs and sensory organs determine most of our thoughts. Our sensorimotor equipment does contribute to our thinking. The case of colour is a case in point; the systems of colour words in various languages share a general pattern that conforms to the characteristics of the photoreceptors in our eyes. However, this is the best case; apart from it Lakoff and Johnson offered few other examples. I reject their narrow notion of embodiment, because I doubt that scientific evidence exists for the general brain structures that they allege; they give no reference. Sensorimotor areas in the brain do project to areas for higher cognitive functions. However, I know of no evidence that the projections preserve entire activation patterns that are recognizable as sensorimotor inferences or metaphors such as "control is up."

Lakoff and Johnson demand a lot from the embodiment of mind. They stipulate strong and rigid sensorimotor restrictions and contributions, where sensorimotor inference dominates abstract inference. Our sensory and motor organs are highly specific and thus impose very narrow constraints on the range of inference. The neural structures in our brain are far more complex and hence far more versatile. Our eyes are sensitive only to visible lights, but we can think of the entire electromagnetic spectrum from gamma ray through ultraviolet and infrared to radio wave. Such thinking is not metaphorical but theoretical. We can develop science because our minds can transcend the specific limitations of our sensorimotor organs.

Lakoff and Johnson base much of their theory on the strength of metaphors. Metaphors are important to our thinking, both in enrichment and heuristic, but their roles should not be overstated. Lakoff and Johnson present several basic schema onto which a great variety of phenomena can be mapped and take this to be the evidence for metaphorical thinking. Because the schemata are couched in sensorimotor terms, they conclude that all mapped phenomena are conceived as sensorimotor metaphors. I contend that the same mapping can be interpreted in a different, non-metaphoric way that undermines their thesis.

Sciences have many examples in which a certain mathematical structure is applicable to many phenomena that are widely disparate. Riemanian geometry, for example, can describe anything ranging from space time to colours. Such application is possible because all phenomena involved share a certain structure that is captured by the mathematics. They are isomorphic as far as that particular structure is concerned, and therefore can be mapped from one to the other. To recognize isomorphism is a powerful cognitive capacity.

Once we see that two phenomena are isomorphic, we can transfer our knowledge about one to the other. Unfortunately, isomorphism is usually not apparent and escapes most people. Metaphors are helpful because they bring together two isomorphic or partly isomorphic phenomena, so that people can pattern a strange phenomenon after a familiar one. However, metaphors usually fail to bring to relief the iso-morphic structure, therefore they are often misleading and not susceptible to further generalization.

Theories supersede metaphors by bringing out isomorphic structures explicitly. Using theoretical reason, we discern and clearly articulate the structure hidden in a familiar phenomenon, which enables us to see the structure more readily in strange phenomena. This power of generalization is the secret of the success of science. In theoretical sciences, the discerned structure is often articulated in mathematical terms that are applicable to other areas. Mathematics is not necessary, however. General concepts such as space, time, and causality express general structures that are hidden in all physical phenomena, including our sensorimotor behaviours.

Once we grant the possibility of abstraction and theoretical reasoning, the schemata and mapping of Lakoff and Johnson prove only that much of our theoretical reasoning concerns physical factors and we recognize that our body shares many general features with other physical systems.

They fail to prove that we conceive of other physical systems as metaphoric extensions of our body. If we discard theoretical reasoning, we have to rewrite not only all Western philosophy as metaphoric, as Lakoff and Johnson trumpet, but all theoretical science beginning with physics. Concepts such as time and causality are indispensable in physics. If they are metaphoric, we end up with metaphorical physics.

The success of science is evidence enough that we are capable of theoretical reasoning. Granted that we need not adopt Lakoff and Johnson's specifically rigid sense of embodiment where our mind is totally structured by our specific sensorimotor organs. We need only a more flexible sense of embodiment where mind is structure by the general features of physical objects. I propose this flexible sense of embodiment, lay out its general structures, and present ample evidence.

Ayurveda and the Mind-Body Connection

Have you ever wondered just how much impact your state of mind has on your health This has long been debated, and is somewhat difficult to study empirically. But the short answer, at least according to Ayurveda, is that the mind has a very powerful influence on our overall health and well-being. Ayurveda defines health not only as an absence of disease, but as a completely holistic level of vitality throughout all facets of our lives. As a result, the Ayurvedic approach to treating any single aspect of our health begins with taking into account the whole of who we are-body, mind, and spirit.

Similarly, the Ayurvedic tradition recognizes that any of these three aspects of self-body, mind, or spirit-can either support or undermine our well-being, making the mind one of three equally influential players in our overall health.

Ayurveda considers even minor disturbances in the mind to be deeply influential, with the potential to compromise the quality of our lives, and to cause any number of diseases-physical and otherwise.

Thankfully, Ayurveda also provides us with a very elegant and insightful perspective on the mind, and on the art of fostering its health-a thriving state of mental, emotional, and even spiritual well-being. With this goal in mind, Ayurveda offers a number of practical and powerfully effective tools for balancing common disturbances of the mental and emotional realm.

Whether you are interested in fine-tuning the habits of your mind, strengthening your mental acuity, or simply cultivating a more calm and peaceful emotional state, you've come to the right place.

We will begin by exploring the Ayurvedic perspective on the mind and conclude with links to several useful resources geared toward supporting you in cultivating vibrant mental and emotional health.

The Big Picture

According to Ayurveda, the body is a crystallization of the mind. So just as impaired agni and indigestion are at the root of all diseases, the mind also plays a critical role in our overall health. In fact, mental ama (toxins) and unresolved emotions can lead to disease in very concrete ways.

For example, unresolved anger can accumulate in the liver and impair its functioning, unprocessed grief can disturb the lungs, and chronic anxiety can upset the health of the colon. Beyond these, there are countless other ways that imbalances in the mind can manifest as physical disease.

When it comes down to it, the mind is incredibly influential and has a very direct and potent impact on our overall health and well-being-making the channel of the mind genuinely worthy of our sincere care and attention.

Ultimately, our focused efforts to support the channel of the mind can't help but ripple out to positively impact every cell, tissue, and subtle pathway throughout our mind-body ecology.

The Channel of the Mind

According to Ayurveda, substances and energies move throughout the body via distinct channels-both physical and energetic-known as srotamsi. Remarkably, one of the primary channels named in the Ayurvedic tradition is the channel of the mind, known in Sanskrit as mano vaha srotas.

The fact that there is a channel of the mind at all tells us how important a role the mind plays in our overall health and longevity. And the more we explore the particulars of this channel, the more we will see how significant and influential it actually is.

But before we delve into the Ayurvedic perspective, let's examine our own personal and cultural preconceptions for a moment. Briefly reflect on this idea of "mind." What are your natural associations with it? And where in the body do you imagine the mind resides?

Here in the West, most of us think immediately of the head. Our culture tends to associate the mind with the brain itself, and so we are naturally inclined to envision the "mind" residing within the confines of the cranium. But in no way does Ayurveda subscribe to these same limitations.

Instead, the Ayurvedic tradition defines the mind far more broadly. Ayurveda's map of the mind quite elegantly reveals its significance in the broader landscape of who we are-both in terms of its level of importance, and also in terms of its vast field of influence on our overall mind-body ecology.

Ayurveda's Map of the Mind

For each of the major srotamsi, Ayurveda describes a root (mula), a pathway through the body (marga), and an opening (mukha). These aspects of each channel serve to orient us to its prominent locations in the body, illuminate important influences upon it, and inform our approach when it comes time to restore balance.

The Root of the Mind

In general, the root of each channel is seen as the developmental center, or point of origin, for that particular srotas. As such, it tends to hold a unique significance for the channel system as a whole. Think back to where you first imagined the mind might be located in the body-very likely the brain.

Now, consider this: according to Ayurveda, mano vaha stortas is rooted-not in the brain-but in the heart. Let me say that one more time.

The channel of the mind is rooted in the heart. It is also located in the ten great vessels, but we'll get to that in a moment. So as soon as we begin to explore the channel system of the mind, Ayurveda asks us to get out of our heads and step into our hearts.

This is incredibly significant because the Vedic sciences of Ayurveda, Yoga, and Tantra all view the heart as a critically important energetic hub in the body-a meaningful intersection of a diverse range of physical and energetic pathways.

Picture a wagon wheel with the heart at the center, each spoke representing a different system, channel, or substance that either originates from, resides within, or passes through the heart.

For example, of the thirteen srotamsi present in both men and women, three of them are rooted in the heart. This is notable because it is actually rather unusual for the physical location of distinct channels to overlap at all. Incidentally, the three channels rooted there also happen to permeate the entire physical body-which is also rare.

So we are beginning to get a sense of the heart as the powerhouse organ and energy center that it is. The heart is intimately connected to every cell and tissue throughout the body, three different times, through three distinct channels. No other organ in the Ayurvedic srotamsi shares that level of integration with the entire body.

The heart center is also said to be the very seat of our emotional experience, home to our purest form of self. And of course, the heart chakra (anahata chakra) is associated with our capacity for unconditional love.

As the root of the mind, all of these energies that are associated with the heart take on a newfound significance. In truth, Ayurveda invites us to adopt a fundamentally expanded view of the mind as a whole-one that includes the heart and its connection to the entire body.

The Ten Great Vessels

The fact that the mind is also rooted in the ten great vessels (an important set of subtle energetic pathways that inform the subtle body) is a testament to the profound level of influence that subtle energies have upon the mind. While this is a vast and meaningful topic, we will keep our exploration brief.

For now, it is important to understand that of the ten great vessels, the three that are considered most influential are the solar, lunar, and central channels-ida, pingala, and sushumna.

These nadis, or subtle energy channels, travel from the base of the spine to the crown of the head, intersecting at each of the seven chakras, and are said to carry the flow of prana, or life force. These subtle channels establish an important relationship between prana, the subtle body, the heart, and the mind.

Interestingly, when we practice pranayama (yogic breathing exercises), ida, pingala, and sushumna are among those pathways that are most profoundly activated, cleansed, and balanced. This is why pranayama so powerfully supports our psycho-spiritual health.

As we can see, mano vaha srotas extends far beyond the boundaries of the brain and the rational mind. In fact, as we continue to explore the Ayurvedic map of the mind, this channel's immense field of influence only expands further.

The Pathway of the Mind

According to Ayurveda, the pathway, or physical location, of mano vaha srotas is the entire body, making it the most overtly all-encompassing srotas of them all. The mind quite literally affects and is affected by every cell and tissue throughout the body-meaning that there is a direct and undeniable relationship between the mind and our overall health and vitality. And this field of influence travels in both directions. In other words, while the mind certainly influences physical matter, our physical health also affects our state of mind. In this way, our every experience has the potential to either support or disturb our overall state of balance-in both the body and the mind.

Doorways to the Mind

The channel system of the mind also has a number of important openings (mukhas) to the exterior of the body. These doorways significantly influence the channel of the mind, and, when necessary, can be used strategically to help restore balance to mano vaha srotas.

First among these openings are the five sense organs-the eyes, ears, nose, tongue, and skin. When it comes to our mental and psycho-spiritual health, the sense organs-as well as the sensory input they receive on a daily basis-play a major role.

For better or worse, we tend to align energetically with the qualities of our day-to-day sensory experience. For instance, if we are exposed to a great deal of trauma, our systems develop a natural and familiar association with that energetic pattern-and begin to anticipate its recurrence.

On the other hand, if we are routinely surrounded by loving, inspiring relationships, our systems naturally tend to orient toward hope and possibility. Of course, each of us has a unique degree of sensitivity to these influences. For some, simply watching or listening to a disturbing news broadcast can cause a noticeable shift in the tendencies of the mind. Others are less sensitive and may not notice much of a shift at all when exposed to the same sensory input.

But for all of us, changing the overall quality of our sensory experience can radically alter our state of mind. If we are serious about inviting vibrant health and balance into the channel of the mind, the quality of our sensory input is a vitally important consideration.

Another important doorway to the mind is found in the marmani-a set of precise energy points on the surface of the skin that are connected to deeper, more subtle energetic pathways throughout the body.

Each marma point offers a powerful access point for shifting the energy within the channel of the mind and working with these points can be an effective means of restoring balance to mano vaha srotas.

Sattva, Rajas, and Tamas: Ayurveda names three maha gunas (universal attributes or qualities of consciousness)-sattva, rajas, and tamas-that are especially pertinent to this conversation. Though these qualities are very subtle, they are present in our food, our experiences, and our overall state of consciousness.

Together, sattva, rajas, and tamas are said to give rise to all phenomena in nature, and they have a profound influence on the subtle body and the mind.

- Sattva engenders equilibrium, clarity, light, intelligence, compassion, insight, and wisdom.
- Rajas ignites kinetic energy, movement, passion, and the ability to act.
- Tamas is responsible for inertia, darkness, heaviness, slowness, sleep, and decay.

Over the course of our lives, there is a natural place for all three of these energies. For example, tamas supports restful sleep, rajas engenders decisiveness and excitement in our lives, and sattva supports clarity of mind.

But when it comes to our evolving psycho-spiritual health, the Vedic sciences reflect a clear preference for sattva, because it is directly aligned with the qualities of liberation and enlightenment. Conversely, most mental imbalances can be attributed to an imbalance in rajas or tamas-usually an excess in one or both of these energies.

Mental Constitution

Just as each of us is born with a unique ratio of vata, pitta, and kapha in our constitution, we are also born with a distinctive proportion of sattva, rajas, and tamas. The relationship between the three becomes an individual baseline for what Ayurveda calls manas prakriti-the mental constitution.

Unlike our physical constitution, which is established at conception and considered fixed from that point onward, the mental constitution can change and evolve over time. This reflects our capacity, with practice, to develop more sattvic states of consciousness throughout our lives.

Of course, manas prakriti can also change for the worse, especially if we consistently make poor lifestyle choices and surround ourselves with negativity. This is where Ayurveda's map of the mind becomes an incredibly useful tool. It helps us to see where to direct our attention in order to support the evolution of consciousness-to encourage thriving mental and emotional health.

As we have already discovered, some of the most effective tools in this realm include welcoming the heart center into the conversation, monitoring the quality of the sensory input we receive daily, being mindful of the quality of our relationships, working with the marma points, and engaging with practices that help to activate and balance the subtle pathways of the mind-pranayama, yoga, meditation, and prayer.

The Mind and the Three Doshas

As we move toward understanding more specific imbalances and how to address them, the three doshas provide an important context for our exploration.Much like the three maha gunas, the three doshas each have an important role to play in our overall health.

When provoked, each of them tends to cause a specific range of imbalances that can manifest either in the physical body or in the more subtle realms. As a result, vata, pitta, and kapha each have a particular flavor of influence on the mind, emotions, and overall consciousness, and each of them can either support or undermine our overall health-it all depends on whether or not they are in balance.

Vata and the Mind

Vata dosha, which governs the nervous system and the mind, is primarily made up of the air and ether elements. Not coincidentally, the mind is also primarily composed of the air and ether elements, making it especially susceptible to vata imbalances. When in balance, vata is generally associated with creativity, intuition, clairvoyance, the capacity to connect with the subtle realms, profound spiritual understanding, and a natural sense of expansiveness.

Vata imbalances, on the other hand, typically manifest as a certain instability, agitation, or hypersensitivity in the mind, and often involve excess rajas as well.

Aggravated vata can cause rapid changes in mood, fear, anxiety, contraction, a sense of being scattered, a lack of direction, spaciness, ungroundedness, excessive speed in thoughts and words, and a sense of loneliness or isolation.

Excess vata also tends to draw us out of our bodies and can leave us feeling somewhat disassociated or disembodied, disturbing our sense of security and belonging to the material world.

Aggravations of vata in mano vaha srotas are often the result of overexertion, overworking, stress, trying to attend to too many things all at once, times of travel or transition, overstimulation (e.g., lights, crowds, technology, etc.), loud noises, loud music, stimulants such as nicotine, caffeine, and recreational drugs, and excessive exercise or sexual activity. Vata can also be elevated in the mind as a result of a vata-provoking diet, which may include too many dry, light, and rough foods like raw vegetables, crackers, dried fruits, and the like.

Pitta and the Mind

Pitta dosha, which governs insight and intellect, is primarily made up of the fire and water elements. Pitta is closely associated with the gray matter of the brain and has a very important connection with the mind as a whole. Healthy pitta is generally associated with courage, confidence, will power, intelligence, leadership, a sense of vision, acceptance, contentment, satisfaction, enthusiasm, cooperation, and the capacity to surrender. But when pitta, which is closely related to a number of rajasic qualities, accumulates in excess, it tends to cause aggravation in the mind. For example-anger, irritability, frustration, impatience, resentment, envy, judgment, criticism, a rigid attachment to one's personal beliefs, excessive ambition, and a ruthless desire for power.

Disturbances of pitta and rajas in mano vaha srotas are often caused by excess heat and upward moving energy in the body, imbalances in the liver, periods of intense focus or ambition, as well as a tendency to disregard the needs of one's body in favour of achieving one's goals. Pitta can also be elevated in the mind as a result of a pitta-provoking diet, which may include too many hot, spicy, sour, oily, or fried foods.

Kapha and the Mind

Kapha dosha, which governs structure and lubrication in the body, is primarily made up of the water and earth elements. Kapha is closely associated with the white matter of the brain and is strongly connected to our capacity for memory. Healthy kapha is generally associated with love, compassion, patience, groundedness, loyalty, steadiness, endurance, and an overarching sense of ease in one's life.

But as the densest of the doshas, kapha can bring the heavy qualities of tamas to the mind, causing lethargy, complacency, laziness, depression, stubbornness, attachment, greed, emotional possessiveness, and a tendency to hoard material possessions.

Aggravations of kapha and tamas in mano vaha srotas are often caused by an overly sedentary lifestyle, a lack of stimulation or interest in one's life, inadequate exercise, a sluggish digestive fire, and an excess of downward moving energy in the body. Excess kapha in the mind can also be triggered by a kapha-provoking diet-too many foods that are heavy, dense, or cold, like cheese, ice cream, and fried foods.

Correcting Imbalances of the Mind

The Ayurvedic tradition is a holistic approach to health and healing. As such, disturbances of the mind must be understood from a broad perspective that includes our physical, mental, emotional, and even spiritual health. Restoring balance to the channel of the mind can involve a diverse array of therapeutic strategies, and it is certainly ideal to seek the guidance of a trained Ayurvedic practitioner to guide you in your journey. That said, there are a number of common imbalances that are worth exploring collectively. We hope that the links below will help to further inform your journey towards vibrant mental, emotional, and physical health. Feel free to pick and choose the resources that will best serve you in this moment, and come back to these guides as often as you need.

The Importance of our Mind-Body Connection

Figure: *Our body and mind are inextricably linked. That's something which Western medicine is only just beginning to understand and accept, but it's been at the heart of Ayurveda from the very beginning -- more than three thousand years ago.*

Balancing our mind, body constitution (prakriti), and life forces (doshas) is what Ayurvedic medicine is all about. Everything is interconnected.

Throughout the next few blogs, I'm going to take a closer look at what that means so you'll hopefully gain a much greater understanding of how vitally important the mind-body connection is in your own life.

The Three Aspects of Self

What are the three aspects of Self Body, mind, and spirit. All three are equally essential to our health and well-being. If any one of them is disturbed, it can open the doorway to sickness and dis-ease.

How can the mind negatively impact the body Think of it like this.

Our body is the vehicle we inhabit, and if we take good care of its mechanics, it should remain strong and vital for the whole of our life. But a vehicle needs a driver, and if the driver is unhealthy and doesn't focus on the road ahead, very bad things can happen. The vehicle can become slow and unreliable and eventually break down, or it might crash and suffer catastrophic damage.

Our mind is the driver of our body. In the same way that our body can accumulate toxins (ama) that will eventually lead to physical illness, our mind can also accumulate ama, leading to the same result.

Take a condition like anxiety. When we're anxious about something, it puts our nerves on edge. We might feel sick in our stomach, develop a headache, start to shake. If our anxiety becomes chronic (i.e. longterm),those symptoms will inevitably grow worse, turning into skin rashes or ulcers or something much more severe.

Unresolved emotions like anger or grief can do that as well. They fester inside the mind, spill out into the body, and eventually manifest into disease. Every cell, tissue, and physical and energetic pathway in our body is positively or negatively affected by our emotional state and the state of our mind. That's why a calmer, peaceful, clearer mind is crucial to achieving and maintaining a healthier, stronger, more capable body.

Where is Your Mind Situated?

Not where you might think it is!In Ayurveda, the mind is a channel; in Sanskrit, it's called 'mano vaha srotas'. The mano vaha srotas isn't in the head; it's rooted in the heart and the 'ten great vessels' that channel subtle energy throughout the body.

No other organ connects with the body as wholly as the mind. That's one of the reasons why, when we practise pranayama breathing to calm and cleanse our mind, we're also simultaneously calming and cleansing the organs, tissues and cells in our physical body. Beyond that, we're extending our mind into the universal consciousness, but I'll write more about that in my next blog. Just as the mind directly influences the body, the body directly influences the mind.

One of the easiest ways to explain this is by thinking about our five senses - sight, hearing, smell, taste, and touch. Every second of every day, even while we sleep, our five senses are physically processing everything that goes on around us. Everything they experience is input into our mind, and our mind responds accordingly, and often un(or sub)consciously.

There are also energy points on our skin called 'marmani' that are connected to the pathways in our body and can be used to restore balance in our mano vaha srotas.

The difference between our mental and physical constitution

According to Ayurveda, our physical constitution (i.e. our unique balance of Vata, Pitta, and Kapha) is fixed from the moment we are conceived. However, our mental constitution (called the 'manas prakriti') is fluid, and it can change (for better or for worse) as our diet, lifestyle, and mental attitudes change. As we get older, if we consistently make better decisions about our health, emotions and the company we keep, our manas prakriti grows stronger. If we make poor decisions, it grows weaker, just like the doshas that govern our body.

In a similar way to our five senses, our doshas can have an effect on our manas prakriti too. A Vata imbalance can cause mood changes, loss of focus, and anxiety. A Pitta imbalance can cause excessive negative emotions like anger, jealousy, and irritability. A Kapha imbalance can cause laziness, depression, and selfishness.

I'll go into more detail about those in a future blog. How to strengthen the mind-body connection As I mentioned at the beginning, it's all about balancing your three aspects of Self.

- Follow a healthy lifestyle (diet, exercise, sleep, and rest)
- Regularly practice a technique that will help you calm and relax your mind, like pranayama, meditation, yoga, or mantra
- When negative emotions arise, find a strategy for dealing with them. (I'll talk about that in a future blog too, but if you need my help in the meantime, please get in touch.)
- Treat yourself, everyone, and everything around you with kindness and compassion.

Until next time, to your enduring health and happiness in Ayurveda.

Mind Types in Ayurveda

The doshas in Ayurveda - Vata, Pitta and Kapha represent the body types. In the same way, mind types in Ayurveda are based on the principle of gunas. Gunas are the qualities that constitute our psychological makeup. The three gunas are:

1. Sattva (peace, tolerance and harmony)
2. Tamasa (ambition, spontaneity and passion)
3. Rajasa (sloth, inertia and ignorance)

The ultimate state of mind out of all the mind types in Ayurveda, as is evident above, is the Sattvic state of mind. In Ayurveda, it is believed that one must always strive to achieve this state of mind. While difficult, it is definitely possible by trying one's best to channelize Sattvic impulses as opposed to the other two types. Those who have a predominantly Sattvic nature are tolerant, generous, and giving. They are also more spiritually inclined than others. In order to contribute towards emphasizing Sattvic qualities, it is better to consume food that is neither heavily spiced nor too sweet i.e. simple and nutritious food.

Figure: *The ancient principles of Ayurveda believe that the mind and body both need to be in harmony in order to achieve overall good health. We all have different temperaments, body types, mindsets and interests and the beauty of Ayurveda is that it recognizes this. Treatments and diagnoses are made on the basis of an individual person's particular body and mind type.*

The Tamasa guna has the qualities of idleness, fear and lethargy and hence most people should make efforts to reduce this guna as far as possible. The Tamasic state of mind is often depressed, with little or no spirituality or motivation to work and be active. Junk food constitutes a big part of their diet,and also sleep heavily. They tend to avoid any work that taxes the body or brain.

Finally, those who have predominantly the Rajasic guna seek control and are extremely dynamic in nature. They are brave and often very ambitious as well, however they are also prone to being sometimes rude, arrogant or jealous. Their sleeping patterns are usually disturbed, and their diet consists of strong and excessive flavours like spice, caffeine, and stimulants.

The stages of mental healing include moving from mental lethargy to motivation and action through the breaking up of Tamas, and developing Rajas. The next step would be to calm Rajas emotions, and gradually develop Sattvic tendencies through changes in your diet, other daily habits and developing the mind. It is important to remember, however, that all three gunas have their place and so all of us are made of all three gunas. For the mind types in Ayurveda, the right balance will help. Our Ayurvedic healing therapies take all three gunas as well as the doshas into consideration in order to provide you the most holistic solution to your health and well-being.

The Mind: According to Ayurveda

The mind is considered the launchpad between the senses and the soul. It is an extraordinary organ that controls both sense-related and functional activities of the body. It has unique characteristics to correlate with every emotion of life - happiness, fear, anger, shame, contempt, disgust, guilt, distress, interest, surprise, and joy.

A person's mind depends on three qualities like sattva, rajas, and tamas in which one's character is modulated. An uncertain proportion of these qualities and a dynamic imbalance of doshas may upset the mental balance. Marma Training in Kerala finds a natural solution to fight negative elements and thereby relieves sleep deprivation, stomach-related issues, and mood swings, hence improving quality of life.

The Origins of Mental Illness

Mental illness occurs due to any sort of brain damage, Stressful life situations, and chronic medical conditions that may lead to various forms of mental health disorders such as OCD, depression, mania, PTSD, and psychosis. Hence, mental illness comes under a vast category in which its unauthenticated behaviour affects emotion, thinking ability, and attitude.Ayurveda College in Kerala sets a customized treatment approach to stabilize the imbalance of doshas that cause mental illness through herbal massage, nasal breathing, meditation, and yoga practices.

Why is Ayurvedic Prevention for Mental Disorders Important?

Ayurveda's approach to treating any ailments does not include the treatment of any single disease alone. Ayurveda follows a therapeutic regime to remove toxins that inhibit the natural energy flow in the body. Ayurveda prevention of mental disorders aims at the relaxation of Ojas to pacify the conscious mind for better mental and physical health. Ayurveda practitioners conduct a detailed analysis of a patient with respect to their medical history, lifestyle pattern, and diet regime and recommend an effective therapeutic solution to improve their cognitive abilities.

Certain herbal medications along with their purificatory treatments address the underlying root cause of the mental disorder and are able to find an effective solution for the cause of mental illnesses such as Stress, Migraines, Dementia, Mood swings, Emotional disturbance, and insomnia. Ayurveda seeks realistic behaviour of physical and mental health through holistic light to recognize their actual self for mental nourishment. This systematic technique of mindfulness nourishes the brain cells to achieve positive signals that trigger good thoughts, observations, concerns, feelings, and opinions.

Ayurvedic Tips for Enhancing Mental Health

Ayurvedic management of mental health brings both Agni and doshas in balance and enhances a sense of good contentment and well-being.

Following a healthy lifestyle with a nutritious diet can relieve signs of mental disorders to a great extent. Also, Ayurveda treatment can calm or relax your body tone in the natural way of the detoxification process.

Diet and Lifestyle Modifications for Mental Health Paying attention to what you eat and when you eat are inevitable factors one could consider for good mental strength. Ensure we follow a strong brain-healthy diet and healthy lifestyle routine to support better mental emotions. Here is a list of healthy eating tips for the betterment of mental strength.

- Stay hydrated to flush out toxins in your body
- Avoid high levels of processed food such as fried chips, sugar-filled snacks, and soft drinks.
- Practice leisure time apart from a busy work schedule
- Eat seasonal fruits and veggies
- Enhances the intake of healthy fats for appropriate brain functioning
- Chew well for better digestion
- Exercise regularly
- Have a sound sleep
- Make a good social connection with friends and family
- Always consume freshly prepared warm foodstuff
- Consume food that contains omega-3 fats which are present in oily fish like tuna, salmon, mackerel, perch, herring, and sardines.

Ayurveda Therapies for Enhancing Mental Health

The application of medicated herbs with personalized therapies can calm and relax the mind, body, and soul. Ashwagandha is one such magical herb to improve cortisol levels and thereby increases the proper functioning of brain cells. Brahmi can accelerate positive impact on memory, concentration, and intelligence and helps to reduce the signs of negative emotions in mental health. Turmeric can improve blood circulation and helps to prevent the brain cells from developing mental disorders.

Virechana is a type of panchakarma therapy in which bitter purgative herbs are introduced to induce vomiting and thereby cleansing of the body takes place to relieve the stress associated with mental disorders. Shirodhara is the Ayurveda technique of pouring medicated oil onto the center of the forehead and is effective in people who suffer from insomnia, sleep disorders, anxiety, depression, and other forms of mental disorders. Satvavajaya chikilsa induces positive thoughts regarding self-awareness, family, and social responsibilities. This therapy is effective in treating mental disorders that are caused due to emotional disturbances.

Ayurvedic Approach to Mental Health

Ayurveda is a holistic science that 'acknowledges the mind-body correlation. Its definition of health as Swasthya (being centered in the self) includes equilibrium of:

- Doshas (energy principals)
- Digestive and metabolic fire
- Tissues
- Excretions
- A blissful state of spirit, sense organs and mind

Ayurvedic methods of mental health (Manas Shastra) management focus on prevention, gentle intervention and do not stigmatize mental health.

We all go through cycles of feeling lethargic, productive and restless, light, alert and blissful. Ayurveda enumerates three attributes of the mind to summarize these qualities: Tamas (heaviness), Rajas (activity and restlessness) and Sattva (pure, clear, happy quality of the mind). We need Tamas to rest and Rajas to act, but when they go out of balance, psychological issues like depression, loss of focus and extreme aggression result. Sattva endows us with good mental health, happiness, wisdom and the ability to do our 100%. To enhance mental health, you can follow practices to improve Sattva.

Similarly, you need to attend to the Doshas, or fundamental energy principals. The Doshas known as Vata, Pitta and Kapha combine to form your unique Ayurvedic constitution, and when they are balanced, the mind is pleasant and tranquil. We tend to be dominant on one or two Doshas. Vata personality people tend to be creative and imaginative; Pitta, intellectual and motivated and Kapha, nurturing and loving.

An imbalance in the Doshas impacts the mind; Vata imbalance leads to restlessness, fear and anxiety, Pitta manifests as anger and irritability and Kapha as lethargy and depression. The converse is true; when the mind is in a state of imbalance, the Doshas can go out of balance like a sudden shock that leads to Vata imbalance.

If you consult with an Ayurvedic practitioner, every intake assesses mental wellbeing. The consultation delves into physical, physiological, psychological and genetic history. Overall Dosha imbalances are corrected through palliative measures like herbs and modifications in lifestyle and nutrition; as well as cleansing with therapies like Abhyanga (self massage) and Shirodhara (pouring warm medicated oil on the forehead) or Panchakarma (a detailed and powerful, therapeutic detoxification).

Spiritual therapies like prayer, mantras and chanting based on your belief system, psycho-behaviour therapy and mental hygiene practices are advised. Ayurveda relies heavily on Yoga, Meditation, Pranayama and Marma to enhance mental health. These are well researched techniques; a Harvard Study demonstrated that just 8 weeks of meditation can change the grey matter of the brain and another recommended Yoga for COVID-19 anxiety!

Mental health is boosted by strengthening immunity which is correlated with Ojas or vitality (and vice versa). Ojas is the essence of all the bodily tissues and the ultimate resort of both our nutrition and our genetic inborn strength. Depleted Ojas impacts mental health and psychological factors like grief or anxiety could trigger a depletion in Ojas and immune resistance.

Ten Ayurvedic Tips for Enhancing Mental Health

1. Increase Sattva and Practice Self Care At the onset of the pandemic, Vaidya. Karthik Krishnan, Senior Medical Officer

at Kerala Ayurveda Ltd, India recommended ways to improve Sattva and asserted that the fastest route to do so is Yoga or stretching, Pranayama and meditation.

- Yoga: Find an experienced yoga practitioner online or try some stretches based on your physical ability and personal preference.
- Breathwork: Nadishodhan (alternate nostril breathing) and deep breathing or abdominal breathing) are calming and grounding.
- Meditation: Try a guided meditation, spend a few minutes internalizing with eyes closed or learn a practice of meditation
- Follow a routine, getting enough exercise and having a healthy, fresh nutritious diet.
- Practice self care by reading, journing, taking online courses to enhance skills, stay creative and engaged, be kind to yourself and take a break when necessary.

2. Balance Agni and Doshas To bring both mind and body in balance and enhance a sense of contentment and wellbeing.

Vaidya. Jayarajan Kodikannath, Chief Ayurvedic Consultant at Kerala Ayurveda advises to:

- Follow personal and seasonal balancing of Doshas
- 'Take a deep breath' - internalizing and balance are key in navigating this time.
- Get enough sleep and exercise and sticking to a routine.
- Eat well, planning ahead to prevent succumbing to food cravings (with healthy snacks like nuts, seeds and raisins instead of candy) and taking breaks.

Knowledge of one's Prakriti, Vikrati, Ayurvedic guidelines for good health that include the three pillars of health, Nutrition (Aahar), Sleep (Nidra) and balanced Lifestyle (Vihar) and following Dinacharya (daily regimen) and Ritucharya (seasonal regimen) guidelines help in Ayurvedic management of mental health. Seek an Ayurvedic consultation to find out more.

3. Try a cleanse! When the Agni or digestive and metabolic fire is hampered, Ama or toxins build up and are a cause of all physical and mental ailments. These toxins can be endogenous, environmental and psychological and you have to be careful about toxic news, relationships and psychological inputs. Cleansing lends clarity, helps get rid of Ama, restores health

and wellbeing and prevents future recurrence of diseases. Our Fall Rejuvenation program officially starts later this year, though our Vaidyas are available for one-on-one online consultations and can support you with a personalized program that is seasonally appropriate anytime.

4. Have a nourishing diet Nutritional psychology and psychiatry are buzzwords now but the food mood connection has always been acknowledged by Ayurveda. We recommend warm, easy to digest fresh food and using seasonally appropriate spices and herbs like turmeric, cumin, black pepper, ginger, Tulsi, cardamom and coriander. Favour plenty of fruits and vegetables, whole grains, good fats and try to incorporate the six tastes or Shadrasa in your diet. Avoid processed, cold and raw foods as much as possible. Make sure to hydrate enough in-between meals.
5. Get adequate sleep Studies have shown that inadequate sleep can impair cognition, focus, increase sadness and anxiety and impact immunity; the Dinacharya practices of Ayurveda that promote sleep are corroborated by the science of circadian rhythms. Guidelines to follow include:
   - It's best to sleep before 10pm Kapha time (unless you have an imbalance);
   - Take a media break a few hours before sleeping
   - Eat 2-3 hours before hitting the bed
   - Have a soothing nighttime ritual (you could apply oil under your feet, but make sure to wear socks to avoid slipping if you get up!).
   - Get adequate sleep; the dinacharya practises of Ayurveda are corroborated by the science of circadian rhythms. Try to avoid day time sleep which increases Kapha or lethargy.

6. Maintain a balanced lifestyle These are basic but so effective when practiced for mind and body harmony. Eat at regular mealtimes and ensure that staying or working from home doesn't disrupt your routines. Make time to follow your hygiene practices - they help you stay healthy and "feel right." Get some exercise each day and spend time in nature which is grounding and relaxing.
7. Stay distanced - but socially connected Ayurveda pays attention to one's connection with family and community, and studies have shown nurturing relationships improves longevity and mental health. If you need more connection, try Seva or volunteering online which has many physical and mental health benefits like reducing hypertension and depression, besides providing a social connection and intellectual stimulation. Your spiritual life is also a great source of support and always with you.

8. Avoid overstimulation of senses Schedule breaks during your work or school day to breathe, rest your eyes, internalize or go for a nature walk. Media breaks minimize digital overload and also help you to be more mindful. We perceive the world through our sensory organs and taking care of them is part of a healthy Dinacharya that protects our mental health. Soothe the sense organs/senses in the following ways:

- Eyes/Visual - Akshi Tarpana, Colour Therapy, periodically resting the eyes and doing eye exercises
- Nose/Smell/Respiration - Nasya, Net Pot, steam inhalation and Aromatherapy with essential oils
- Skin/Tactile - Abhyanga, Shirodhara and Marma. These practices go much beyond soothing the tactile sense and are employed in many therapeutic ways.

- Ears/Hearing - Karna Poorna (medicated oil in the ears), Chanting and Soothing music
- Tongue/Taste - Tongue cleaning, having nourishing food at regular meal times, herbal teas, avoiding overeating

9. Attend to immunity and Ojas Systemic prophylaxis or prevention focuses on overall health. Rasayana. rejuvenating therapies are a specialty of Ayurveda to boost immunity and involve immunomodulatory herbs and a nourishing diet with dairy, ghee and honey, practices like silence, internalization, self-care and Achara Rasayana.

Local prophylaxis or prevention measures include:

- Pratimarsa Nasya (application of one or two drops of oil like sesame oil in the nostrils)
- Steam inhalation
- Gargling with a herbal decoction,
- Having hot food
- Drinking warm water and herbal teas

You can also try herbs and formulations that boost immunity. Rasayana herbs, specifically Medhya Rasayanas or brain tonics are immunomodulatory, rejuvenating herbs and adaptogens that help with mental health and boost immunity. These include Guduchi or Amruth, Brahmi, Yashtimadhu, Amalaki, Ashwagandha, Holy Basil, Guggulu, Brahmi Ghrita, Kalyanaka Ghrita, Chyawanprash and Manasamitra Vatakam. Many of the herbs in clinical trials for COVID-19 work simultaneously on mental health and immunity. To purchase herbs from Kerala Ayurveda, learn more here.

If you prefer to take your herbs in the form of tea, here's a recipe for the herbal tea Ayush Kwath, the immune boosting tea suggested by the Indian Ministry of Ayush (which governs traditional Medicines).

10. Try a self-massage! Try a self massage or therapies like Nasya, Abhyanga and Shirodhara (at an Ayurvedic facility if you're comfortable, if it is available and allowed in your county). Some therapies include:

- Nasya - Nasya involves application of warm medicated oils or herbal remedies in the nostrils in a therapeutic manner and studies have shown it has a calming effect on the mind, improves clarity and enhances memory. You could start a Pratimarsha or daily Nasya with 1-2 drops of Anu Taila, Sesame oil or ghee.

- Shirodhara or continuous pouring of warm, medicated oil on the forehead is traditionally used for anxiety, insomnia and PTSD.
- Abhyanga - therapeutic massages with regular oils like sesame or coconut oils or medicated oils.

Other individualized therapies like Shirolepa, Takradhara and Shirobasti as prescribed by the Ayurvedic practitioner.

Special Circumstances: For caregivers, patients that are self-quarantined, people with comorbidities who may be anxious, or those who have a sick family member far away or someone close who may have passed away this could be a very hard time. Self-care is of paramount importance; make sure to nourish yourself and stay connected, increase Sattva, rejuvenate Ojas and attend to Vata Dosha with warmth and grounding. Especially if there is a death in the family, Ayurveda does believe in the journey of the soul towards evolution and peace; we are sorry for your loss. Do bless those that have passed and honor their contribution in your life.

Ayurveda Based Advocacy for Mental Health

To promote mental health and prevent illness, there is a need to create such living conditions and environment that support mental health and allow people to adopt and maintain healthy lifestyle. The intake of healthy 'Ahara' as per the rules prescribed and adhering to the principles of 'Dinacharya', 'Ritucharya' , 'Sadvritta' & 'Achara Rasayana' are the fundamental entities which play a pivotal role in attaining positive mental health. Ayurveda has description of many single drugs and formulations for Psychiatric illnesses like Brahma Rasayanam, Brahmi Ghrita, Kalyankaghritam, Mahakalyanaghirtam, Maha Panchgavya Ghrita, Sarasvata Churna etc

The concept of Dhatusamyata, is also relevant here. It is a state of equilibrium of dhatus, where the word Dhatu stands for Dosha, Dhatu and Mala. It is also the main objective of Ayurveda. The characteristics enumerated under Dhatusamyata encompass the equilibrium state of physical and mental wellbeing and may be considered as the subjective markers for 'Vikaropashamana' (alleviation of disease) is as follows

- Alleviation of pain
- Appearance of normal voice and complexion
- Nourishment of the body

- Increase in the strength
- Appetite during the meal time
- Proper digestion of the food taken
- Getting sleep at appropriate time and waking up without fatigue
- Absence of morbid dreams
- Proper elimination of flatus, urine, stool, and semen
- Unimpaired state of the mind, intellect, and senses
- Absence of any type of diseases

General line of treatment of Unmada in Ayurveda

Ayurveda approach Unmada in a holistic approach with due importance to the logic based pharmacotherapy, Panchakarma interventions and psychotherapy in the form of spiritual and psychological interventions.

Daiva -vyapashraya Chikitsa (Spiritual therapy): Ayurveda considers individuals as part of the supreme conscience and the role of spirituality has been explained in detail in various contexts. Logical use of Mantra, Aushadhi, Mani (wearing gems), Bali (auspicious offerings), Upahara (gifts to deserving people), Homa(oblations), Niyama (observance of scriptural rules), Prayashchitta (atonement), Upavasa (fasting), Svastyayana (chanting of auspicious hymns), Pranipatagamana (obeisance to the Gods, going to pilgrimage),etc are aimed at boosting the self confidence and mental strength to the individuals.

Satvavajaya Chikitsa: Satvavajaya Chikitsa literally means controlling the mind, in such a way that it is not acted upon by various stressors making it prone to Prajnaparadha. Acharya Charaka, defines Satvavajaya as withdrawal of mind from unwholesome objects. It includes

- Mano nigraha: regulating mind/subjugating mind from unwholesome interactions
- Dhee-dhairyaatmadi vijnanam: It is providing a deeper level of understanding which helps ultimately in better control of mind.

Charaka also explains the utility of replacing negative emotions with that of positive emotions that is beneficial to psyche. Thus

Satvavajaya encompasses various aspects that deal with mind - its physiology, morphology, morbidity and also management of Psychological as well as Psychosomatic diseases.

Yuktivyapashraya Chikitsa: This includes treatment through logical use of medicines and modification of Ahara and Vihara to suit the needs of the person.

The patient should be encouraged to follow proper dietary regimen, follow rules of Sadvrita, to use Medhya Rasayana (medicines that boost psyche) and Doshahara Ousadha (medicines) to control the imbalanced mind. Medicines usually prescribed for Unmada.

Single drugs:

- Brahmi(Bacopa monnieri)
- Sankhapushpi(Convolvulus pluricalis)
- Yastimadhu(Glycyrrhyza glabra)
- Jyotishmati(Celastrus paniculatus)
- Kushmanda(Benincasa hispida)
- Vacha(Acorus calamus)
- Rasona(Allium sativum)
- Shatavari (Asparagus racemosus)

Other preparations

- Ashwagandharishta
- Saraswatharishta
- Saraswatha churna
- Manasamitra gutika
- Dhanvantara Ghrita
- Panchgavya Ghrita
- Brahmi Ghrita
- Mahakalyanaka Ghrita
- Chetasa Ghrita
- Mahapaishachika Ghrita
- Lashunadya Ghrita
- Mahachetasa Ghrita etc

Panchakarma sodhana procedures are also mentioned to be done, as per the Dosha vitiation.

Role of Diet in Mental Health and Illness

Diet is said to be basis of life, strength, complexion, Ojas, growth and development, perspicuity of Indriyas, happiness, clarity of voice, lustre, pleasure, increase of Dhatus, intellect, health etc. According to Chhandogya Upanishad, the food inside the body is divided into 3 parts: Sthoola, Madhyama & Anu bhaga which nourish Purisha, Mamsa & Mana respectively, which means the subtle and abstract part of the Anna is Mana. "Annamayam hi soumya manah" is a popular quote from Chandogyopanishad, which means the mind is the essence of food we take. Just as when curd is churned up, the butter which is the finest part gather up, the finest part of food rise up and nourishes Manas.

Since Vedic era, food has been given the prime importance. Three categories of Ahara are described in Bhagvad Geeta (17/8, 9, 10) are Sattvika, Rajasika & Tamasika.

Sattvika persons prefers food which increases life span, nourishes Satva, keeps body healthy, increases happiness and prosperity, which are pleasing and full of nutrients, unctuous in nature, providing stability and conducive for the heart and soul. Those persons who take foods which are very pungent, sour, salty, very hot, very sharp in taste, excessively dry, which causes burning sensation, and foods which causes sadness, depression and various diseases are Rajasika persons and thus such foods can be categorized as Rajasika. Food that is not freshly cooked, unhygienic food or food which is devoid of nutrients, foul smelling, stale, mixed with pollutants, dust etc. and left over food comes under the Tamasika food and which is appreciated and practiced by Tamasika persons.

Habit of taking Ahara which is non-Satvika i.e. Rajasika or Tamasika (continuously for a long time) causes some sort of mental disturbances and later on causes serious mental illnesses like Unmada and Apasmara. Satvika ahara not only consists of food with proper nutrition but also it indicates the rules of taking food should be followed. for eg. Ashtaaharavidhi Visheshayatana (Charaka), Dwadashashan Pravicharana (Susruta).

In the treatment aspect also, specific food along with health-conducive routines/regimens plays an important role along with medicines. Somatic or psychic food plays an important role as a preventive factor, causative factor and as a curative factor. Proper diet helps a healthy person to stay healthy/improve it and prevent illness.

In the diseased, it helps in easy recovery, not obstructing the action of medicine and regain lost vigor. The importance of food is studied in all contemporary medical systems but the study regarding the food that influence causation and treatment of psychiatric diseases is comparatively new in modern medicine, called as 'Nutritional Psychiatry' and lots of studies are coming in this filed, but Ayurveda owns clear and scientific concepts in this regard. The influence of digestive system on the emotional aspects of human beings is another domain of related study in modern research. Gut is considered as the second brain due to the intrinsic neuronal networks. The age old medical system, Ayurveda elaborated the same concepts eons before.

Importance of Pathya

Pathya Sevana is one of the most important supportive pillars for the successful management of the diseases. The proper use of diet also prevents the diseases and also helps in preventing the recurrence. "Pathyam patho anapetam yadyachoktam manasa priyam | |"

The Ahara and Vihaara which is beneficial and nutritional to the body and also give the happiness to the mind is known as Pathya and opposite to that is known as Apathya. Wholesome food and regimen agreeable to mind and senses promote Tushti (mental satisfaction), Urja (mental strength) and Sukha(happiness) as a result of which disease gets diminished.

Unwholesome food may not produce disease immediately, but becomes harmful depending on the nature of the locality, time, combination, potency, frequency of intake and quantity. So its effect can be negligible or gruesome depending upon where the person resides, the season prevailing, the associated Doshas and Dhatus, the seat of affliction and the quantity taken. When a person constantly takes unwholesome diet, the body becomes saturated with vitiated Doshas and become susceptible to serious diseases. It is also described that the persons with the habit of taking unwholesome diet and with poor mental strength become susceptible to physical and mental diseases.

These various nidanas described in Ayurvedic texts which are responsible for psychiatric disorders can be grouped under sub categories like Aharaja, Viharaja, Mansika Bhava, Agantuja etc. Though Nidana causing direct harm to mental health are the main etiological agents, beside this Ahara and Vihara also have an equal impact.

Pathya Ahara in Mental Illness

The foods with the qualities like colour, smell, taste and touch can be pleasing to the sense organs and conducive to the health if taken in accordance to the rules is the very life of living beings. If proper, it kindles the digestive fire, promote mental as well as physical strength, complexion, and strength of tissue elements and is pleasing to the senses, otherwise they are harmful.

The Pathyas mentioned in Unmada & Apasmara prakarana of Yoga Ratnakara and Bhaishajya Ratnavali includes:

- Sakavarga [vegetables], Patola [snake guard], Bramhi [Bacopa monnieri [Linn] Pennell], Shobhanjanam [Moringa olifera], Kakamaci [Solanum nigrum Linn], Vastuka [Chenopodium album Linn.], Tanduliyaka [Amarantlus viridis Linn.].
- Dhanyavarga [cereals/pulses]: Raktha/Aruna-Sali [red rice], Godhuma/Yava [Wheat/barley], Mudga [green gram].
- Phalavarga [fruits]: draksa [grapes], Panasa [jack fruit], Matulunga [Citrus medica Linn], Narikela [coconut], Kapittha [wood apple], Kusmanda [ash gourd], Dhatri [gooseberry], haritaki [terminalia chebula]
- Gorasavarga [Milk and Milk products]: Ksira [Milk], Navanita [Butter], Ghrta [Ghee]
- Paniyavarga [drinks/beverages]: Gangambu [Rain water], Madya [Alcohol], Rasala, Kulmasatarpana [Gruel of Kulmasa].
- Mutravarga* [categories of urine]: Kharamutram [urine of donkey], ashvamutram [urine of horse]
- Mamsa varga [Categories of Meat]: Koorma maamsa [Meat of tortoise]

Nootropics is a newly emerging branch of modern research which study drugs, supplements and other substances that may improve cognitive functions, memory, creativity, motivation etc. Botanical nootropics are described in Ayurveda, which are considered as Medhya, Buddhi vardhaka, Smritikara etc. Some of the fruits and vegetables having these properties are Sesame seeds, Ash gourd, Garlic, Pomegranate, black jeera, coconut etc which can be included in the diet.

Apathya Ahara in Mental Illness

The Apathyas mentioned in Unmada & Apasmara Prakarana of Yoga Ratnakara and Bhaishajya Ratnavali include, over indulgence in meat, fish, alcohol, sex, incompatible, heavy, hot and stale food articles, suppression of sleep, hunger, thirst, and natural urges, excessive exercise, excessive strain, leafy vegetables, bitter food items, bimbi, and rude acts, which are not in accordance with prescribed ethical code of conduct. It is also necessary to consider the different food related aetiological aspects of Unmada before suggesting the diet. In Unmada Prakarana of Charaka Samhita, it is mentioned that a person with a strong mind who does not indulge in meat and wine, who eats only healthy foods, remain clean internally and externally does not affected by either "Nija" or "Agantuja Unmada".

Role of Viharas in Mental Health and Illness

'Vihara' means the activities of daily life in accordance with the societal, economical and cultural norms of any person and Ayurvedic classics have described the healthy routines to be followed in Day time (Dina Charya), in Night time (Ratri Charya), and according to the seasonal variations (Ritu Charya) and codes of conduct (Sadvritha & Achara Rasayana). Resorting to these helps in prevention of diseases of body and mind

Pathya Viharas in Mental Illness: The healthy behavioural patterns to be followed by a person as an individual and a social being include Pathya Vihara, among which Sadvritha and Achara Rasayana that have influence on the mental wellbeing are worth mentioning.

Sadvrittha (Code of conduct): Sadvritta deals about the positive codes & conducts and morals & values which when followed transform the person belief system, cognitive framework and perceptive ability strengthening his state of positive mental health/ Satva. Following this, helps the person in preventing Prajnaparadha and thereby preventing disease.

Achara Rasayana: Achara Rasayana is a form of Rasayana [means to provide excellence of tissue elements] wherein practices of Sadvritta and habitual intake of natural products [Milk & Ghrita] will bring about excellence of Dhatus/ tissue elements as well as Satva/Positive mental health. It is based on principle of conditioning showing the interrelation & interdependence of mind & body - 'Psycho-neuro-immunology'. Neurological research has identified over fifty neurotransmitters in the brain, several of which are related to mental health problems - Dopamine, Serotonin, Norepinephrine, and GABA (Gamma Amino Butyric Acid). Too much or too little of these neurotransmitters are now felt to produce psychiatric conditions such as schizophrenia, depression, bipolar disorder, obsessive-compulsive disorder, and ADHD Achara Rasayana emphasizes the conduct of an individual in social settings. Since, human beings are social animals; definitely their social image and social reputation have an enormous effect on their mental status.

Exercise and the Brain

Exercise helps memory and thinking through both direct and indirect means. The benefits of exercise come directly from its ability to reduce insulin resistance, reduce inflammation, and stimulate the release of growth factors-chemicals in the brain that affect the health of brain cells, the growth of new blood vessels in the brain, and even the abundance and survival of new brain cells. Indirectly, exercise improves mood and sleep, and reduces stress and anxiety. Problems in these areas frequently cause or contribute to cognitive impairment.

Many studies have suggested that the parts of the brain that control thinking and memory (the prefrontal cortex and medial temporal cortex) have greater volume in people who exercise versus people who don't Exercise affects the brain on multiple fronts. It increases heart rate, which pumps more oxygen to the brain. It also aids the bodily release of a plethora of hormones, all of which participate in aiding and providing a nourishing environment for the growth of brain cells.

Exercise stimulates the brain plasticity by stimulating growth of new connections between cells in a wide array of important cortical areas of the brain. From a behavioural perspective, the same antidepressant-like effects associated with "runner's high" found in humans is associated with a drop in stress hormones

Yoga and Mental Health

The literal meaning of Yoga is 'to join', that is joining of Mind and Body. Yoga advocates that every life form is interconnected and united the eight limbed path of yoga includes: Yama (moral codes), niyama (self-discipline), asana (postures), pranyama (breath practices promoting life force), pratyahara (sensory transcendence), dharana (concentration), dhyana (meditation) and samadhi (state of bliss).

The application of yoga as a therapeutic intervention began early in the twentieth century, taking advantage of the various psycho-physiological benefits of the component practices. The physical exercises (Asanas) may increase patient's physical flexibility, coordination, and strength, while the breathing practices and meditation may calm and focus the mind to develop greater awareness and diminish anxiety, and thus results in higher quality of life. Other beneficial effects include, a reduction of distress, blood pressure, and improvements in resilience, mood, and metabolic regulation. It has been found in many researches that yoga have positive effects on mild depression and sleep problems, and it improves the symptoms of psychiatric disorders like schizophrenia and ADHD among patients using medication. Some studies even suggested that yoga might affect the body in ways similar to antidepressants and psychotherapy. For instance, yoga may influence brain chemicals known as neurotransmitters (boosting levels of feel-good agents like serotonin), lower inflammation, reduce oxidative stress and produce a healthier balance of lipids and growth factors - just as other forms of exercise do.

Ayurvedic Treatment for Mental Disorders

There are three pillars - A nutritious diet, proper sleep, and a balanced lifestyle which are the underpinnings of good health. The gut-brain axis is a new branch of neuroscience that recognizes the connection between mental health and the gut microbiome. Managing digestive and metabolic fire is the first step in achieving dosha balance for mental and physical wellness in Ayurveda.

Follow a seasonal and daily routine: align with natural cycles; fall can be a stressful period due to Vata imbalance, and winter can be depressing due to Kapha imbalance. Abhyanga (self-massage), Nasya (oil or herb application in the nostrils), or Shirodhara (pouring heated medicated oil on the forehead), and a full Panchakarma treatment can help to relieve mental illnesses.

Ayurvedic Medicine for Mental Disorder

Let's discuss a few Ayurveda herbs that help in treatment for mental illness-

Ashwagandha: Indian Ginseng is the common name for Ashwagandha. Adaptogens are compounds found in the plant that assist the body cope with stress. It also helps to increase brain function and cortisol levels while also lowering blood sugar levels. It improves your mood by promoting healthy brain activity, which eventually reduces mood swings. This aids in the prevention of depression, anxiety and is one of the best ayurvedic medicine for mental health.

Brahmi: Brahmi is an effective herb in the treatment of mental illnesses as well as coping with everyday tensions. Bacosides, a biochemical found in Brahmi, aids in the regeneration of brain tissues, improving memory, focus, and intelligence. Brahmi helps reduce stress and mild anxiety by targeting cortisol, also known as the "stress hormone." The plant also helps to alleviate Alzheimer's symptoms.

Guduchi: Giloy is another name for Guduchi. It means "something which protects the body from ailments" in Sanskrit. It aids in the treatment of depression, as well as stress management and memory enhancement.

Haridra: Turmeric is used in a variety of dishes and home cures. The spice has anti-inflammatory benefits as well as antioxidant capabilities. Turmeric includes curcumin, which aids in blood flow and so helps to avoid heart disease. It also aids in the enhancement of the brain-derived neurotrophic factor (BDNF), which protects against mental illnesses such as depression, Alzheimer's disease, and other mental health issues.

Mandukaparni: Mandukaparni is a fragrant Indian plant that has been shown to improve mental alertness and memory. The herb can be used daily to improve memory. Mandukaparni supports the immune system by increasing and regulating it and taking two capsules twice a day will help you get rid of brain fog.

Ayurveda for Mental Health: A Holistic Approach to Well-Being

In the hustle and bustle of our modern lives, mental health has become an increasingly prevalent concern. Ayurveda, an ancient system of healing that originated in India, offers a holistic approach to mental well-being. At Ayur Healthcare in Parramatta, Sydney, we are pioneers in classical Ayurveda in Australia, dedicated to providing compassionate care and guidance on your journey towards improved health and well-being.

Understanding Mental Health Issues

Mental health issues encompass a wide range of conditions, from anxiety and depression to stress and insomnia. In Ayurveda, these are often linked to imbalances in the three doshas-Vata, Pitta, and Kapha-which govern various physiological and psychological functions in the body.

Causes of Mental Health Issues According to Ayurveda: According to Ayurveda, mental health issues arise from an imbalance in the doshas, which can be influenced by factors such as diet, lifestyle, and environmental stressors. Understanding the root cause is crucial for effective Ayurvedic intervention.

Ayurveda's Role in Mental Health: Ayurveda provides a comprehensive approach to mental health, addressing the mind, body, and spirit. Ayurvedic practitioners focus on restoring doshic balance through personalised treatment plans that may include dietary modifications, lifestyle changes, herbal remedies, and therapeutic practices.

Ayurvedic Treatment Options for Mental Health

Diet and Lifestyle Modifications

In Ayurveda, diet and lifestyle play a pivotal role in maintaining mental equilibrium.

Certain foods and drinks are recommended, while bad habits and excessive stimulants are to be avoided. Additionally, incorporating specific exercises into your routine can have a positive impact on mental well-being.

Ayurvedic Herbal Remedies for Mental Health: Ayurvedic herbal remedies, tailored to individual doshic imbalances, are often prescribed to support mental health. These herbal formulations work synergistically to address the root causes of mental health issues without causing harmful side effects.

Ayurvedic Therapies for Mental Health: Ayurvedic therapies such as Panchakarma detox, Abhyanga (oil massage), and Shirodhara (oil pouring on the forehead) can be highly beneficial in promoting mental relaxation and rejuvenation. These therapies aim to balance the doshas and enhance overall well-being.

Prevention: A Holistic Approach Preventing mental health issues involves adopting a holistic lifestyle that aligns with Ayurvedic principles. This includes maintaining a balanced diet, engaging in regular exercise, practicing mindfulness, and managing stress effectively.

Why Ayur Healthcare: Ayur Healthcare stands out as a pioneer in classical Ayurveda in Australia. Our practitioners, trained in traditional Ayurvedic wisdom, provide personalised care to address the unique needs of each individual.

The Importance of Ayurvedic Consultation

Before embarking on any Ayurvedic treatment, it is crucial to undergo a thorough consultation with our experienced Ayurvedic practitioners.

This ensures a tailored approach, considering your unique constitution and addressing the specific imbalances contributing to your mental health issues.

Conclusion: Ayurveda, with its holistic approach to mental health, provides a path towards lasting well-being. At Ayur Healthcare in Parramatta, Sydney, we invite you to explore the ancient wisdom of Ayurveda for a balanced and harmonious life.

Embrace the transformative power of Ayurveda and embark on a journey towards optimal mental health.

Chapter 4

Nurturing the Soul in Ayurveda

Introduction

Nurturing the Soul in Ayurveda involves recognizing the deeper dimensions of human existence and cultivating spiritual well-being in addition to physical and mental health. In Ayurvedic philosophy, the soul, or Atman, is considered the essence of individual consciousness and the source of inner wisdom and enlightenment. Nurturing the soul is seen as essential for achieving true happiness, fulfillment, and self-realization.

Ayurveda emphasizes the interconnectedness of body, mind, and soul and recognizes that spiritual health plays a crucial role in overall well-being. Practices for nurturing the soul in Ayurveda are designed to promote inner peace, harmony, and spiritual growth. These practices encompass a variety of techniques and disciplines aimed at connecting with the divine essence within and aligning with the universal consciousness.

One of the primary ways to nurture the soul in Ayurveda is through the practice of meditation. Meditation involves turning inward and cultivating a state of deep relaxation, awareness, and inner stillness. By quieting the mind and connecting with the inner self, individuals can access a deeper level of consciousness and experience a sense of peace, clarity, and spiritual awakening.

Ayurveda also emphasizes the importance of living in harmony with the natural rhythms and cycles of the universe. This involves attuning oneself to the changing seasons, cycles of day and night, and phases of the moon. By aligning with the natural order of the cosmos, individuals can cultivate a sense of connection, balance, and unity with the world around them.

Another important aspect of nurturing the soul in Ayurveda is practicing self-awareness and self-reflection. This involves examining one's thoughts, emotions, and actions with honesty and openness and identifying areas for growth and transformation. By cultivating self-awareness, individuals can deepen their understanding of themselves and their place in the world and develop greater compassion, empathy, and wisdom. Ayurveda also emphasizes the importance of living a life of purpose and meaning. This involves aligning one's actions and intentions with higher principles and values and serving others with love and compassion.

By living in accordance with dharma, or righteous living, individuals can experience a sense of fulfillment, purpose, and spiritual fulfillment. In conclusion, nurturing the soul in Ayurveda involves recognizing the deeper dimensions of human existence and cultivating spiritual well-being in addition to physical and mental health. By practicing meditation, living in harmony with nature, cultivating self-awareness, and living a life of purpose and meaning, individuals can nurture their souls and experience greater peace, joy, and fulfillment in life.

Soothing the Soul: Ayurvedic Strategies for Stress Reduction

Are you feeling overwhelmed and in need of some relief? Get ready to free your mind, nurture your soul, and find the tranquility you deserve.

Ayurveda: The Basics

To understand Ayurveda, familiarize yourself with its fundamental principles. Ayurvedic principles are the guiding philosophy behind this ancient system of holistic healing. With the knowledge of Ayurveda at the core of our focused Ayurvedic treatment in CV Raman Nagar, transform your health. Ayurveda views the body, mind, and spirit as interconnected and seeks to restore balance and harmony within them. It recognizes that each individual requires personalized care as each one is unique.

Ayurveda emphasizes the importance of prevention and self-care through practices like meditation, yoga, and dietary adjustments. It promotes using natural remedies derived from herbs, minerals, and oils to support overall well-being. By embracing Ayurvedic principles, you can embark on self-discovery and self-healing. This holistic approach empowers you to take charge of your health and find freedom from imbalances and ailments. Ayurvedic clinic in Kalyan Nagar offers a comprehensive framework for nurturing your body, mind, and soul, allowing you to live a vibrant and fulfilling life.

Identifying Your Dosha: A Key to Stress Reduction

Unlock effective stress reduction in Ayurveda by understanding your dosha. We offer personalized Ayurvedic treatments for stress management in Bangalore that are tailored to your unique constitution. Your dosha, or mind-body constitution, determines how you respond to stress and what strategies will work best for you. Vata, Pitta, and Kapha are three types of dosha. Each dosha type has its unique characteristics and tendencies. Vata types are prone to anxiety and worry; Pitta types tend to be perfectionists and easily get angry; and Kapha types are more prone to lethargy and depression. By identifying your dosha type, you can tailor stress reduction techniques that specifically address your needs.

For Vata types, grounding activities like yoga and meditation can help calm their restless minds. Pitta types benefit from cooling practices like swimming or aromatherapy. Kapha types thrive on energizing activities like hiking or dancing. Knowing your dosha type allows you to choose the most effective stress reduction techniques, bringing you closer to a state of balance and freedom from stress. If you're seeking relief from stress, consult with the best Ayurvedic doctors in Bangalore.

Ayurvedic Herbs and Remedies for Calming the Mind

Once you have identified your dosha type, you can explore the use of various Ayurvedic herbs and remedies to calm your mind and reduce stress. Ayurvedic clinic in Kalyan Nagar offers a wealth of natural remedies for stress relief, specifically targeting anxiety. One potent herb is Ashwagandha, known for its ability to ease nervousness and promote a sense of calm. Brahmi, another powerful herb, helps to improve cognitive function and reduce anxiety. Jatamansi, also known as Indian valerian, is effective in calming the mind and promoting restful sleep.

These herbs can be consumed in the form of tinctures, teas, or capsules. Additionally, incorporating calming practices such as meditation, deep breathing exercises, and gentle yoga into your daily routine can further enhance the soothing effects of these Ayurvedic remedies. Remember, finding balance and serenity is within your reach, and Ayurveda is here to support your journey towards a tranquil mind.

Mindfulness Practices to Cultivate Inner Peace

Cultivating mindfulness is essential for cultivating inner peace. Experience Ayurvedic stress management in Bangalore, Mindfulness techniques and meditation techniques are powerful tools that can help you find a sense of calm and tranquility amidst the chaos of daily life. Mindfulness involves being fully present and observing your thoughts and emotions in the moment without expressing judgment.

It allows you to develop a deeper understanding of yourself and your experiences, leading to increased self-awareness and a greater sense of inner peace. Meditation techniques, such as focused breathing or loving-kindness meditation, can help you cultivate mindfulness and create a peaceful state of mind. Embrace a sense of freedom and inner peace through regular mindfulness practice as part of our Ayurvedic stress management approach.

Lifestyle Adjustments for Long-Term Stress Management

To effectively manage long-term stress, it is important to make lifestyle adjustments that support your overall well-being and promote a sense of calm and balance. By adopting holistic approaches, you can create a foundation for long-lasting ayurvedic stress management in Bangalore. One key lifestyle adjustment is to incorporate regular meditation techniques into your daily routine.

Meditation helps reduce anxiety, calm the mind, and improve overall mental well-being. For this, get a quiet and comfortable space to sit, close your eyes, and focus on your breath. Without making any judgment, let your thoughts come and go.

Another important lifestyle adjustment is to prioritize self-care activities that bring you joy and relaxation. Engage in activities such as yoga, walking in nature, or spending quality time with loved ones. Taking time for yourself and engaging in activities that nourish your soul can significantly reduce long-term stress and promote a healthier, more balanced life.

The Role Of Ayurveda In Nurturing Mental Peace And Resilience

Today with this fast-paced, stressful world; where mental problems like depression and worry are rampant, Ayurveda, this old Indian approach to medicine shares relevant thoughts on how to foster a state of inner calm and strength. Such philosophy and practice that have been around for nearly 5000 years could offer us a way out today.

Understanding Mental Health In Ayurveda:

Mental health and body health are closely linked in Ayurveda. Mind and body is seen as a single entity, where an imbalance in any of them can result in health problems.

It follows from Ayurvedic teachings that there are three main Doshas governing our body and mind viz- Vata ,Pitta and Kapha . Balance among these three dosha leads to stress free mood or mental disturbance.

Balancing The Doshas: Ayurveda presents various specific approaches aimed at bringing the doshas into harmony and fostering inner stability. Such as change of diet, alteration in lifestyle and herbs that assist in regaining balance. One example is the association of Vata with anxiety and fear or Pitta with anger and irritability. You will be able to reduce mental turmoil by finding out the dosha that dominates you and making some changes.

Mind-Body Practices: Mind-body approaches such as yoga, meditation are in essence recommended by ayurveda for promotion of peaceful mental calmness and strength. The techniques relax the mind, relieve stress and promote mental peacefulness. Daily yoga and meditations could form part of good mental health strategies.

Diet And Nutrition: Diet and nutrition are particularly important in Ayurveda. Satvik foods are those that consist of pure fresh fruit, vegetables and whole grains that are beneficial in rejuvenating the body, mind and soul. Mental equilibrium can be maintained by adopting mentally stimulating, not dull, food in your daily diet.

Stress Management: Another vital stress relief strategy available in Ayurveda is Pranayama, a technique of breath regulation, as well as Abhyanga, which involves self-massage using warm oil. Such techniques help reduce stress and develop a strong mind as they are relaxing.

Personalized Approaches: By understanding your dosha, embracing mind-body practices, and making dietary and lifestyle adjustments, you can nurture mental peace and resilience, creating a harmonious balance in your modern life.

Balancing Kapha Dosha and Nurturing Your Body and Soul

Vasant Ritu, also known as the spring season, is a time of renewal and rejuvenation in Ayurveda. As the cold winter months give way to warmer weather, our bodies are ready for a fresh start. In this blog post, we will explore the significance of Vasant Ritu in Ayurvedic practices and how to best take care of your body during this season.

Understand the Dominant Dosha: Kapha

In Ayurveda, each season is associated with a dominant dosha or energy. During Vasant Ritu (spring season), Kapha dosha is the most dominant. This dosha is associated with earth and water elements and governs stability, growth, and nourishment in our bodies. When Kapha dosha is in balance, it promotes a healthy immune system, strong digestion, and stable energy levels. However, when Kapha dosha is out of balance, it can lead to sluggishness, congestion, and weight gain.

Balance Kapha Dosha with Ayurvedic Diet

One of the best ways to balance Kapha dosha during Vasant Ritu is through diet. Incorporate foods that are light, warm, and dry to balance Kapha dosha. Avoid heavy, oily, and cold foods as they increase Kapha dosha. Try adding spices like ginger, turmeric, and cumin to your diet to aid in digestion. It is also important to stay hydrated by drinking warm water, herbal teas, and soups throughout the day.

Detoxify and Cleanse with Ayurvedic Practices

Vasant Ritu is the perfect time to cleanse and detoxify your body. Consider a comprehensive cleansing program like Panchakarma, which includes dietary changes, herbal remedies, and massage therapy. Panchakarma is a holistic detoxification method that helps to remove toxins from the body, improve digestion, and enhance overall well-being. Other Ayurvedic cleansing practices like oil pulling, tongue scraping, and dry brushing can also be helpful in removing toxins from the body.

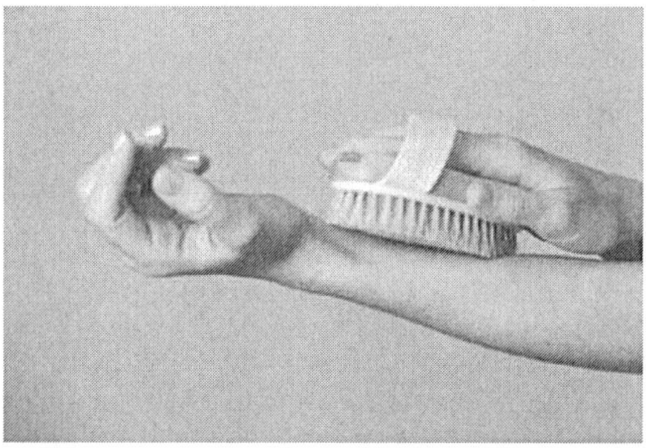

Engage in Physical Activity

Regular exercise and physical activity are essential during Vasant Ritu. Kapha dosha tends to create a sense of sluggishness and lethargy, so it is important to stay active to stimulate the body and balance Kapha dosha. Yoga, brisk walking, and other aerobic activities are recommended to promote circulation, boost metabolism, and improve overall energy levels.

Use Ayurvedic Herbs and Spices

Incorporating Ayurvedic herbs and spices into your daily routine can support overall health and well-being during Vasant Ritu.

Ashwagandha is a powerful adaptogen that helps to reduce stress and boost immunity. Triphala is a blend of three fruits that supports healthy digestion and elimination. Tulsi (holy basil) is a potent antioxidant that supports the respiratory system and reduces inflammation. These herbs and spices can be taken as supplements or added to teas and meals to enhance their health benefits.

Practice Self-Care

Vasant Ritu is a time to nurture your body and soul. Incorporate self-care practices like massage, meditation, and aromatherapy into your daily routine to promote relaxation and rejuvenation. Abhyanga (self-massage with warm oil) is a traditional Ayurvedic practice that helps to calm the nervous system, improve circulation, and nourish the skin.

Meditation and deep breathing exercises can also be helpful in reducing stress and promoting mental clarity. Aromatherapy with essential oils like lavender, peppermint, and eucalyptus can help to reduce congestion and promote a sense of calm and balance.

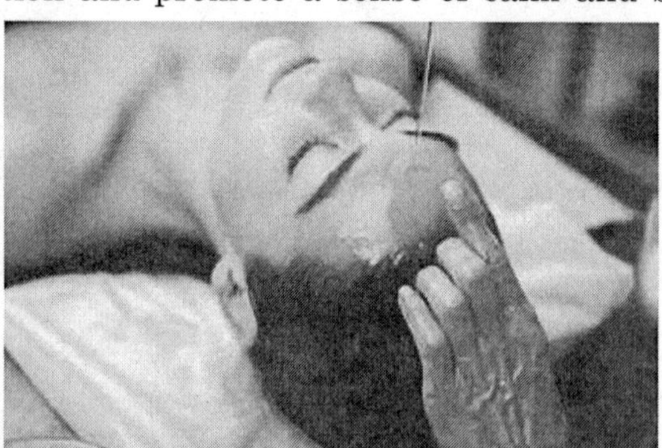

By following this ultimate Ayurvedic guide, you can balance Kapha dosha, detoxify and cleanse your body, engage in physical activity, and practice self-care to support your body's natural ability to heal and thrive during this season of new growth and nourishment.

How Ayurveda's Yogic Diet Can Nourish The Body and Soul

The Yogic Diet, rooted in Indian culture, combines Sattvic foods, non-violence (Ahimsa), moderation, and prana to promote holistic well-being, mindfulness, and spirituality.

Indian cuisine is renowned for its diversity, flavours, and cultural significance. At the heart of this culinary tradition lies a concept deeply rooted in Indian culture and philosophy: the Yogic Diet. This dietary philosophy not only nourishes the body but also nurtures the soul, aligning with the principles of yoga and Ayurveda to promote holistic well-being.

Understanding the Yogic Diet

The Yogic Diet is more than just a list of permitted and forbidden foods; it's a way of life. It draws inspiration from ancient Indian texts like the Vedas, Upanishads, and Ayurvedic scriptures. This diet aims to maintain a balance between body and mind, promoting physical health and mental clarity, which are essential for spiritual growth.

Figure: *Key Principles of the Yogic Diet*

1. Sattvic Foods: At the core of the Yogic Diet are Sattvic foods-those that are pure, light, and promote mental clarity. These

include fresh fruits, vegetables, nuts, seeds, whole grains, and dairy products like milk and ghee. Sattvic foods are believed to have a calming effect on the mind and are therefore favoured by yogis.

2. Ahimsa (Non-violence): Ahimsa is a fundamental principle in yoga philosophy, emphasising non-violence and compassion. This extends to diet, encouraging a vegetarian or vegan lifestyle. Avoiding harm to animals and promoting ethical eating is an integral aspect of the Yogic Diet.
3. Moderation: Portion control and mindful eating are crucial aspects of the Yogic Diet. Overeating is discouraged, as it can lead to physical discomfort and hinder one's spiritual practice. Eating in moderation helps maintain a balanced and healthy body.
4. Prana: Prana, often described as the life force or vital energy, is a central concept in yoga. The Yogic Diet emphasises foods that are high in prana, such as fresh fruits and vegetables, which are believed to enhance vitality and clarity of thought.

The Yogic Diet and Ayurveda

The Yogic Diet shares a close relationship with Ayurveda, India's traditional system of medicine. Ayurveda categorises individuals into three doshas-Vata, Pitta, and Kapha-based on their physical and mental constitution. The Yogic Diet can be tailored to suit these doshas, ensuring a personalised approach to nutrition. For instance, a Vata-dominant individual may benefit from grounding, warm, and nourishing foods, while a Pitta-dominant person might thrive on cooling and calming options.

Yogic Diet in Practice

Now, let's delve into how the Yogic Diet is put into practice within Indian cuisine:

1. Fresh and Seasonal Produce: The Yogic Diet emphasises the consumption of fresh, seasonal fruits and vegetables. These foods are considered highly Sattvic and provide essential nutrients without unnecessary additives or preservatives.
2. Whole Grains: Whole grains like brown rice, quinoa, and millet are staples in the Yogic Diet. They are a rich source of fibre, vitamins, and minerals, providing sustained energy and promoting digestive health.

3. Legumes and Pulses: Lentils, chickpeas, and mung beans are excellent sources of plant-based protein in the Yogic Diet. They are also highly digestible, making them a valuable addition to vegetarian diets.
4. Dairy and Ghee: Dairy products like milk, yoghurt, and ghee are consumed in moderation, as they are believed to be pure and nourishing. Ghee, in particular, is revered for its healing properties and is used in various dishes.
5. Nuts and Seeds: Almonds, walnuts, sunflower seeds, and other nuts and seeds are rich in healthy fats and protein. They are often included in Yogic Diet recipes, providing essential nutrients and energy.
6. Herbs and Spices: Ayurvedic herbs and spices like turmeric, ginger, and cumin are commonly used to enhance the flavour and health benefits of Yogic Diet dishes. They have anti-inflammatory and digestive properties.
7. Hydration: Water is considered a vital element in the Yogic Diet. Herbal teas and infusions, such as tulsi (holy basil) tea, are also popular for their calming and detoxifying effects.
8. Fasting: Periodic fasting, such as Ekadashi fasting, is observed by many yogis as a way to purify the body and mind. During these fasts, individuals often consume fruits, milk, and light meals.

The Spiritual Significance

Beyond nourishing the body, the Yogic Diet is deeply intertwined with spiritual growth and mindfulness. It encourages individuals to develop self-control, discipline, and an awareness of their dietary choices. By adopting a Yogic Diet, practitioners aim to purify the physical body and create an optimal environment for spiritual awakening.

The Yogic Diet is a testament to the profound connection between food, spirituality, and overall well-being in Indian culture. It underscores the idea that what we eat not only affects our physical health but also plays a pivotal role in nurturing our inner selves. In a world where dietary choices can be overwhelming, the Yogic Diet serves as a holistic guide to living a balanced and harmonious life, where the body and soul are in alignment with the principles of yoga and Ayurveda.

Ayurvedic Diet and Nutrition: Nourishing the Body, Mind, and Soul

The Core of Ayurvedic Philosophy

The Three Doshas: Vata, Pitta, and Kapha: At the heart of Ayurvedic philosophy lie the three doshas: Vata, Pitta, and Kapha. These doshas, shaped by the elements of air, fire, water, earth, and ether, form distinct constitutions within individuals. Recognizing one's predominant dosha becomes pivotal in crafting a diet that fosters equilibrium and well-being. Understanding the interplay of these doshas unveils a personalized approach to nourishment, aligning the body and mind in pursuit of optimal health.

The Role of Agni: The Role of Agni in Ayurveda holds paramount significance. Often referred to as the "digestive fire," Agni governs the intricate process of digestion and metabolism within the body. This vital force not only breaks down food into its essential nutrients but also ensures their efficient absorption and assimilation. In Ayurvedic philosophy, Agni is regarded as a transformative energy that converts ingested substances into nourishment, providing sustenance to every cell and tissue.

A well-functioning Agni not only supports physical health but also maintains mental clarity and emotional equilibrium. When Agni is balanced, toxins are efficiently eliminated, preventing the accumulation of ama (undigested waste) in the body. Nevertheless, when Agni is out of balance, it can cause problems like digestion troubles, tiredness, and even emotional unease.

To achieve overall wellness, Ayurveda highlights the importance of taking care of Agni by eating mindfully, choosing appropriate foods, and following a lifestyle that aligns with the body's natural patterns. By tending to the "digestive fire," individuals pave the way for optimal health, vitality, and overall harmony.

The Ayurvedic Diet: A Holistic Approach

Eating According to Dosha: In the intricate tapestry of Ayurveda, the Ayurvedic diet stands as a vibrant thread woven to honor the uniqueness of each individual. This dietary philosophy recognizes that our bodies and constitutions are distinct, implying that our nutritional requirements vary accordingly. This profound understanding prompts Ayurveda to categorize foods based on their inherent qualities and their impact on the doshas the dynamic forces that shape our being.

For instance, when seeking to balance Vata dosha, which embodies the elements of air and ether, the Ayurvedic diet suggests incorporating warming foods. These choices help ground Vata's airy nature, providing stability and nourishment. On the other hand, for Pitta dosha, characterized by fire and water elements, the focus is on cooling foods that soothe and temper Pitta's fiery disposition.

The Six Tastes: At the heart of Ayurvedic eating knowledge lies the idea of the six tastes. These tastes - sweet, sour, salty, bitter, pungent, and astringent - have distinct qualities and contribute to our health. Ayurveda suggests having all six tastes in each meal for a balanced and enjoyable experience, catering to various nutritional requirements.

The sweet taste, found in nourishing foods like grains and fruits, offers comfort and nourishment. Sour foods, such as citrus fruits and fermented items, stimulate digestion and invigorate the senses. Salty foods, when consumed mindfully, provide necessary minerals and enhance the overall dining experience. Bitter foods, like leafy greens and herbs, support detoxification and aid digestion. Pungent flavors, found in spices, kindle the digestive fire and awaken the senses. Lastly, the astringent taste, present in foods like legumes and certain vegetables, contributes to balance and contraction.

By weaving these six tastes into our meals, we embark on a culinary journey that caters to our holistic well-being. Ayurvedic knowledge helps us respect our bodies, know our dosha balance, and welcome the array of tastes nature provides.

In simple terms, the Ayurvedic diet isn't just rules; it's an opportunity to create balance with our bodies, nature, and our core selves. Through mindful consumption, conscious choices, and an appreciation for the six tastes, we align with the rhythms of life and nurture ourselves on a profound level.

Nourishing the Mind and Soul

The Mind-Gut Connection: In the intricate landscape of Ayurveda, the profound connection between the mind and the gut is a cornerstone. Ayurvedic philosophy recognizes that a serene mind has a profound influence on digestion, and conversely, optimal digestion fosters mental clarity. This symbiotic relationship underscores the importance of cultivating a tranquil mental state for overall well-being.

Meditation and Mindful Eating Practices: Central to Ayurvedic living is mindfulness, in both meditation and eating. Meditation, a strong method for calming the mind, encourages relaxation and lessens stress, a main factor in digestive issues. Mindful eating, too, is pivotal. Engaging our senses during meals enhances the digestive process, allowing the body to extract maximum nourishment from the food we consume.

Food as Prana: Ayurveda's wisdom extends beyond the physical to embrace the spiritual and energetic dimensions. Food is not solely sustenance for the body; it's a vessel of prana, the life force that animates us. The quality of this life force is influenced by the choices we make. Opting for fresh, seasonal, and locally sourced foods infuses our meals with a higher pranic value. This elevates the nourishment we receive, touching not only the physical body but also the subtle energies that shape our existence.

By acknowledging food as prana, Ayurveda encourages a conscious approach to eating one that transcends the act of consumption and becomes a sacred ritual. Being conscious lets us link with the natural energy in our food, enabling us to use its strength for our overall health.

Moreover, Ayurveda illuminates the profound interplay between our mental, physical, and spiritual realms. Through meditation and mindful eating, we promote a peaceful mind and acknowledge the energy in food. This begins a transformative path of nourishing not just our bodies, but also our minds and spirits.

Ayurvedic Nutrition: Beyond the Plate

Daily Routines and Ritucharya: Ayurveda, a tapestry woven with holistic wisdom, extends its embrace beyond the mere act of eating. It gently whispers that life's symphony is composed not solely of the foods we choose, but also the rhythms we dance to. Within this philosophy lies the art of crafting daily routines that harmonize with our doshas and the ebb and flow of the seasons. These routines become a symphony of balance, nurturing our well-being.

Ritucharya, the dance of seasonal routines, embodies Ayurveda's profound connection with nature. As the seasons shift, so do our bodies needs. These ancient rhythms guide us to adjust our lifestyle, diet, and practices in alignment with the world around us. Just as leaves fall and blossom anew, our habits transform to synchronize with nature's symphony.

Mindful Eating Practices: At the heart of Ayurvedic nutrition, lies the quiet practice of mindful eating. It's a voyage beyond just eating, urging us to relish each bite with appreciation. Ayurveda guides us to eat in a calm, focused setting, without disruptions, enabling us to truly be present with our nourishment. This conscious involvement leads to a stronger link with the sustenance that supports us.

In the realm of Ayurveda, mindful eating is not a mere technique but a transformative experience. It nurtures our bodies and nurtures the relationship we share with food. By savoring each bite, we acknowledge the miracle that unfolds with every meal the fusion of nature's bounty with our being. This practice heightens our awareness, cultivates gratitude, and elevates our connection with both the plate and the world around us.

Ayurveda for Spiritual Well-being

Ayurveda is the traditional healing system from India that is literally translated as 'the science of life.' Through healthy daily practices and aligning with natural rhythms, one can prevent disease and create health on a daily basis. And although the outcome of Ayurvedic lifestyle and medical treatment is a healthy body and mind, the true aim of Ayurveda is to connect us to a deeper experience of who we are.

Ayurveda is true body-mind-spirit medicine that allows us to understand, appreciate, and integrate all aspects of who we are.

Ayurveda is a consciousness-based healing system. This means that the foundational principle in Ayurveda is that our true nature is one of infinite potential because consciousness is the ground state of who we are.

As humans, we have a physical experience that we call the body as well as a mental experience that we call the mind. Both experiences are constantly changing, in every moment, therefore by their very nature, are impermanent.

The constant and unchanging self that is aware of the physical and mental experience is described in Ayurveda as pure consciousness, also known as spirit. It is that within which all experience is occurring. The beauty of this description is that we start to understand that each and every choice we make influences the changing system that we call body and mind.

And when we understand our true nature as consciousness, or spirit, we have a greater appreciation for the importance of spiritual well-being, which is a connection to that true Self.

What is Spiritual Well-Being

Spiritual well-being is a multidimensional concept. It does not necessarily refer to any specific religious or spiritual practice but instead includes several characteristics such as a sense of meaning in life, purpose, a connection to something greater than our individual selves, and transcendence. Connection can include connection to oneself, others, nature, or a higher power. Transcendence includes the experience of existence that is beyond the physical body and/or beyond space and time. As opposed to a social construct, spirituality is a naturally occurring and personal phenomenon.

As a physician, having this complete understanding of well-being is invaluable in helping guide patients on a journey of physical, mental, emotional, and spiritual health. And the importance of spiritual well-being is being increasingly appreciated and validated through science. Through validated questionnaires that measure our spiritual well-being, it has been shown that a higher level of spiritual well-being is associated with better overall health and well-being.

Multiple studies have shown that increased spiritual health can result in improved psychological well-being and physical health as well as improved coping skills. In addition, in certain populations, spiritual health can be more important for quality of life than physical health. Higher spiritual well-being can also reduce anxiety and depression in patients with cancer and lead to improved quality of life. Therefore, addressing one's spiritual well-being needs to be recognized as part of a complete medical system as it is in Ayurveda.

The Brain and Spiritual Experience

Although the field is relatively new, there are many interesting studies looking at the brain and spiritual experiences. There are specific areas of the brain that seem to be associated with a felt-sense of connection outside of oneself, a core component of spirituality. This experience involves areas of the brain such as the parietal cortex. The parietal cortex is involved in the experience of a 'sense of self,' meaning an individual self, therefore during meditation or other spiritual experiences, there is a decrease in activity of the parietal cortex, thus contributing to a sense of being something greater than an individual identity.

Another area of the parietal cortex, the posterior parietal cortex, is involved in spatiotemporal processes (the experience of the human body in time and space) and one study reports a blunting of activity in this area when subjects recounted a personal spiritual experience. In addition, there was a decrease in areas of the brain associated with the stress response, which supports the subjective data showing a decrease in anxiety and depression with spiritual experience. The researchers concluded that there are neural mechanisms associated with spiritual experiences and that future studies that increase our understanding of these brain changes could help facilitate the integration of spirituality into treatment and prevention in areas of mental health conditions in particular.

How to Cultivate Improved Spiritual Well-being

Spirituality does not necessarily imply any particular practice or belief therefore each individual can choose which practices work for them. Some of the practices that contribute to an increase in spiritual well-being include meditation, prayer, mindfulness, contemplation, connecting with nature, to name a few. For others these experiences can occur while listening to music, volunteering, or while engaging in focused and meaningful work. Just as we need healthy habits for physical and mental well-being, it is equally important to have regular practices to cultivate spiritual well-being.

Research has proven how important this is. In a 2017 study, it was shown that within 5 days of an immersion into an Ayurvedic lifestyle program, people can experience a sense of non-dual awareness, which is a sense of transcendence--oneness with everything, or identifying with the entire universe. This Ayurvedic immersion program involved several daily Ayurvedic lifestyle practices, an Ayurvedic diet, aligning with biological rhythms, Ayurvedic massages, as well as daily meditation and yoga. Some of the outcomes included a sustained sense of gratitude, self-compassion, and spirituality after returning home.

Ultimately, when we engage in Ayurvedic lifestyle practices, we calm the body and mind so that we can experience our true nature. A well-known verse from an ancient Ayurvedic text states "Ayurveda Amritanam," which is translated as "Ayurveda is for immortality." This refers to the true result of Ayurveda which is to help us connect to our Universal and ever-present self and experience more peace, harmony, and connectedness, which results in better personal and collective well-being.

Yoga and Its Relation to Positive Psychology

In particular, the practice of yoga is crucial to this study. The foundation of yoga is in line with the recent shift of focus to positive psychology, since the development of awareness and stillness is a key point in yoga. Whereas a purely medical perspective (which was the main focus before positive psychology arose) focused on merely reducing negative symptoms, positive psychology and yoga seek to accept the current situations and stimuli as they come and not to evaluate. Yoga fits with this approach, because it is a way of practicing these traits. Yoga for example focuses on the contemplative practice of focused attention and controlled breathing. Also, reducing external stimuli and viewing emotions as being temporary.

The conceptual background of yoga has its origins in the philosophy of ancient India. There are multiple schools of yoga, all of which have their unique way of practice (i.e., Iyengar, Viniyoga, Sivananda). The schools differ in elements of yoga, such as physical postures (asanas), breathing techniques (pranayama), relaxation and meditation which ultimately cultivates 'higher states of consciousness'.

It is often important to see the meditation and yoga practices outside the context of the eastern philosophy. Practically seen, the physical exercises (asanas) is associated with patient's physical flexibility, coordination and strength, whereas the breathing practices and meditation calm and focus the mind to develop greater awareness and diminish anxiety. Other reported beneficial effects are reduction of distress, improvements in resilience, mood and metabolic regulation.

The aforementioned dynamics of yoga consists of three key components that have known general effects on mental health, which are intention, attention and attitude. Exerting these three factors in yoga practice, it can increase muscular strength, range of motion, flexibility and sleep quality. Furthermore, it has been found that yoga can relieve stress and conditions of anxiety that impact physical and mental health conditions, primarily depression. Especially for physical conditions, the effects of increasing muscular strength, flexibility and range of motion could be important since they impact the physical part of an individual.

More and more it is stated that negative mental symptoms are overlooked in the treatment of physical diseases. Because of the physical nature of the disease, the physical cause and symptoms draw most of the attention. Because of this reason, interventions with the aim of improving mental health have been overlooked as well. Though there is often relatively too little attention for mental health in physical conditions, there are clues that improving mental health in physical condition is rather important. The aforementioned studies in this chapter have put forth some thoughts that the experience of the physical condition could be less painful and troublesome.

Mental Health

To be able to clarify what the effects of yoga are on mental health in physical, chronic conditions, one must first determine what 'mental health' actually is. The most common definition of 'mental health' is given by the World Health Organisation. They postulate it as the following: "mental health is a state of well-being in which the individual realizes his or her own abilities, can cope with the normal stresses of life, can work productively and fruitfully and is able to make a contribution to his or her community". As can be seen, in this definition multiple factors come forward, which are well-being, effective functioning and being able to contribute to the near outside world.

In line with the medical perspective on mental health, mental health was purely seen as the absence of mental illness. Positive psychology postulates that this view does not do justice to the whole meaning of 'mental health'. Although negative symptoms such those of anxiety and or depression have a crucial impact on the individual, mental illness represents only part of a person's functioning and mental health. Keyes (2005) states that the main focus of the medical perspective is aimed at negative symptoms and to reduce these in order to bring forth the positive mental health of the individual. Seligman et al. (2000) join this statement by concluding that this medical perspective isn't capable of fully preventing mental disorders. Thus, it can be stated that, for an individual to be happy, not only should there be an absence of negative symptoms, but the presence of positive experiences as well.

Furthermore, it is important to define these 'positive experiences'. The hedonic approach consists of emotional well-being, which is defined as the amount of positive feelings that are present, the amount in which negative are absent and the amount in which people are satisfied with their lives. Whereas the hedonic approach concerns optimal experiences and emotional components of mental health, the eudaimonic approach focuses on optimal functioning and meaning in both the individual life (psychological well-being) as well as the social life (social well-being). The eudaimonic approach states that well-being is self-realization through the fulfilment of one's own personal potential. Westerhof and Bohlmeijer (2010) state that six criteria are important in this self-realization, which are purpose in life, personal growth, autonomy, environment control, self-acceptation and positive relations. In sum, mental health according to positive psychology isn't just the mere absence of negative experiences, but the presence of positive ones as well. The positive ones can be divided into emotional, psychological and social well-being. Concluding, this view on mental health will be employed: 'improvement of positive experiences based on the hedonic and eudaimonic approaches, and a decrease in negative symptoms such as negative mood states (e.g. anxiety or depression) and illness'.

Yoga And Cardiopulmonary Conditions

Blood Pressure and Hypertension

Innes et al. reported on 37 studies investigating the effects of yoga on blood pressure and hypertension, among them 12 RCTs, 12 non-randomized clinical trials, 11 uncontrolled studies, 1 cross-sectional study, and 1 single yoga session examination. Most reported a reduction of systolic and/or diastolic pressure. However, there were several noted potential biases in the studies reviewed (i.e., confounding by lifestyle or other factors) and limitations in several of the studies which makes it "difficult to detect an effect specific to yoga".

Ospina et al.'s AHRQ cites two studies which found small, insignificant improvements of systolic (weighted mean difference = -8.10; 95 per cent CI, -16.94 to 0.74) and diastolic blood pressure (weighted mean difference = -6.09; 95 per cent CI, -16.83 to 4.64) in favour of yoga when compared to no treatment. When compared to health education, yoga interventions resulted only in small and insignificant improvements of systolic blood pressure (weighted mean difference = -15.32; 95 per cent CI, -38.77 to 8.14) and diastolic blood pressure (weighted mean difference = -11.35; 95 per cent CI, -30.17 to 7.47).

Pulmonary Function: Raub also examined studies evaluating yoga's effects on lung function in healthy volunteers and patients with chronic bronchitis and asthma. In healthy volunteers practicing yoga, there are reported improvements of various parameters of lung function with breathing control techniques, specific postures, and/or relaxation techniques.

However, these improvements were "not consistent and depended upon the length of yoga training, the type of yoga practice used (e.g., breathing exercises and yoga postures), and the type of subject". Raub also cited some studies on patients with asthma describing improvements in peak expiratory flow rate, medication use and asthma attack frequency. In a double-blinded RCT with placebo-control, there were only a few small and insignificant improvements in lung function variables. Thus, more rigorous trials are needed to clarify the value of yoga breathing practices for patients with asthma.

Yoga and Metabolic/Endocrine Conditions

Glucose Regulation: The effects of yoga on risk indices associated with insulin resistance syndrome, risk profiles in adults with type 2 diabetes mellitus, and the management of type 2 diabetes mellitus. Innes et al. identified several studies on the effects of yoga on insulin resistance syndrome-associated variables, that is, 2 RCTs, 2 non-RCTs, and 8 uncontrolled clinical trials. These studies reported postintervention improvement in various indices in adults. However, the results varied by population (healthy adults, adults at cardiovascular disease risk, adults with type 2 diabetes, etc.) and study design.

The management of type 2 diabetes mellitus and concluded that the reviewed trials "suggest favourable effects of yoga on short-term parameters related to diabetes but not necessarily for the long-term outcomes." However, the duration of treatment in the reviewed studies was variable.

The AHRQ cites two studies comparing yoga versus medication which reported a large and significant reduction of fasting glucose in individuals with type 2 diabetes in one study, and a smaller but still significant improvement in the other study. The authors discussed differences in the study populations, and interventions as possible explanation for the observed heterogeneity of results.

Menopausal Symptoms: The menopausal symptoms and analyzed 3 RCT, 1 N-RCT, and 3 uncontrolled clinical trials. Although some studies reported beneficial effects, "the evidence was insufficient to suggest that yoga is an effective intervention for menopause". RCTs, which addressed effects of yoga on menopausal symptoms, particularly psychological symptoms, somatic symptoms, vasomotor symptoms, and/or urogenital symptoms. However, yoga was associated with small effects on psychological symptoms, but no effects on "total menopausal symptoms, somatic symptoms, vasomotor symptoms, or urogenital symptoms".

Yoga and Musculoskeletal Conditions

Musculoskeletal Functioning and Pain

There were 3 systematic reviews and 2 other reviews on the effects of yoga on musculoskeletal function, chronic pain conditions, and pain-associated disability. Two reviews specifically addressed low back pain or arthritis, while the other reviews summarized studies on various chronic pain conditions, most with a focus on musculoskeletal conditions and associated disability.

Posadzki et al. included 11 RCTs with variable methodological quality and found that 10 of 11 studies reported significantly greater effects in favour of yoga when compared to "standard care, self care, therapeutic exercises, relaxing yoga, touch and manipulation, or no intervention." A recent meta-analysis on pain intensity/frequency, and pain-related disability included 5 RCTs with single blinding, 7 RCTs without blinding, and 4 non-RCTs. Yoga for the treatment of back pain (6 studies), rheumatoid arthritis (2 studies), headache/ migraine (2 studies), and other indications (i.e., hemodialysis, irritable bowel syndrome, labour pain, etc.).

All of these studies reported positive effects in favour of the yoga interventions. There were moderate treatment effects with respect to 5 pain, and pain-related disability. Despite some study limitations, there was evidence that yoga may be useful for several pain-associated disorders. Thus, well-designed larger scale studies with adequate controls for confounding factors and more thorough statistical analyses are needed to verify these promising findings.

With respect to chronic back pain, the studies indicate that yoga was more effective than the control interventions (including usual care or conventional therapeutic exercises), albeit some studies showed no between group difference. Two recent and properly powered trials of yoga for back pain were published and reported clinically meaningful benefits for yoga over usual medical care from 6- to 12-months postrandomization, but not over an intensive stretching intervention.

Known Effects of Yoga on Mental Health in Chronic Diseases

The studies for this meta-analysis include osteoarthritis, fibromyalgia, rheumatoid arthritis, chronic lower back pain, multiple scleroses and breast cancer. All these conditions are viewed as chronic conditions which share a physical nature. Disorders/diseases are thought of as chronic (1) when they impact an individual's life tremendously in several aspects and (2) exist longer than 3 months. To this day, several effects of yoga on mental health have already been found. Several systematic positive effects of yoga on depression for example. Yoga has also been found to positively affect anxiety and fear conditions. For the condition multiple sclerosis, it has been found that patients scored significantly higher after a 6 month course on the SF-36 (Short Form health-related quality of life) for the scales of emotional well-being, overall quality of life and the mental health composite. Furthermore, breast cancer patients reported an overall significant higher quality of life, an improvement in emotional functioning and less disturbed mood states.

Present Study: To this day, there is still relatively little known about the effects of yoga and meditation on mental health in different physical conditions or diseases. There are multiple reasons why there should be more attention for yoga and its effects. Several articles and meta-analyses recommend a meta-analysis for an overall effect of yoga on physical conditions. Therefore, in form of a master thesis, a meta-analysis will be conducted concerning the effects of yoga on mental health in chronic, physical conditions. This study distinguishes itself in that it uses a broader definition of mental health, which includes both the medical and positive psychology perspective. Furthermore, this study focuses not on diseases in general, but specifically on physical, chronic conditions. Concluding, it can be said further research is needed in the field of yoga effects on mental health in physical, chronic diseases. In this study, this will be done using several articles from a systematic search focusing on yoga impacting psychological outcomes and specified to chronic physical conditions.The primary question is: "What effects can be found of yoga on mental health in physical, chronic conditions?".

This will be attempted to answer with the following foci: (1) What is the overall effect of yoga on mental health in all conditions? (2) Some moderators could play a role, and the following will be checked: 1. the type of condition, 2. the type of control group and 3. the type of outcome (being able to make a distinction between types of outcomes is important because of the definition of mental health, which incorporates both the medical and positive psychology perspective). Furthermore, two mediators will be taken into consideration, namely 4. the total amount of yoga practice (because there might be a learning effect) and 5. the quality assessment score (there might be an effect that generally the lower the quality of the chapter, the higher the reported effect size and vice versa). And lastly, there might be publication bias. This will be checked in the analyses.

Selection of Studies: This research is conducted as a meta-analysis. Firstly, several articles concerning effects of yoga have been selected out of a systematic search, which was formed in earlier research. Ten Damme (2013) and Kruese (2013) systematically searched on Cochrane library using 'yoga' in the record title. Cochrane searches for effect studies and randomized controlled trials.

Quality Assessment: For the quality assessment, eleven studies were used and independently checked by another reviewer. The methodological quality of the studies was assessed using a short scale of seven criteria tailored to yoga studies and criteria established by the Cochrane collaboration. The quality checklist consisted of the follow questions: (1) Adequate subject randomization: randomly done by computer or an independent, blinded source, (2) Baseline comparability: were study groups comparable at the beginning of the study and was this explicitly assessed or were baseline imbalances appropriately corrected, (3) Power analysis: is there an adequate power analysis and/or are there at least 50 participants in the analysis, (4) Completeness of attrition follow up data: an explicit attrition analysis or the loss of follow up <50 per cent, (5) Handling of missing data: the use of intention-to-treat analysis (as opposed to an analysis based on mere completers), (6) Study integrity: is the study design followed and exerted as planned and (7) Quality of yoga: does the yoga trainer have an official yoga certification and the required experience to give lessons (which is at least a thousand hours). When the study meets a criterion, the study was rated as a 1 and was rated 0 when the criterion wasn't met. Furthermore, the studies were assessed as having a high, medium, low or poor quality. High was assessed when the study met six or seven criteria, medium when four or five were met, low when two or three were met and lastly poor when one or none were met. The quality assessment of the studies can be found. Disagreements were resolved by consensus. This was the case with two of the 77 ratings. Interraterrreliability was 0.93.

Meta-analysis: In a meta-analysis, the effects found in the selected studies are converted into a standardized effect size. These effect sizes can be compared with measures from other measurement scales. The Hedges g was chosen to be the effect size for the relevant constructs of the studies, which were calculated using the tool 'Comprehensive Meta Analyses'. A Hedges g is calculated by subtracting the mean score of the experimental group from the mean score of the control group, and dividing this outcome by the pooled standard deviations from both groups. According to Hedges and Olkin (1985), the magnitude of the Hedges g effect size can be interpreted using the conventions of the Cohen's d effect size. An effect size of around 0.2 is small, around 0.5 is medium and around 0.8 can be interpreted as a large effect size. These conventions are used for this meta-analysis as well.

Heterogeneity: As one tries to use the meta-analysis to estimate a combined effect from a group of studies which are similar in one or more ways, there needs to be a check that the effects found in the individual studies are similar enough, so that one can be confident that a combined estimate will be a proper reflection of the set of studies. Although, the individual estimates will vary by chance, some variation is to be expected.

To check whether there is more variation than would be expected based on chance alone (which is called statistical heterogeneity), this must be checked. Heterogeneity was tested in this meta-analysis using the following two indicators. The Q-statistic, which rejects the null-hypothesis of homogeneity when Q is significant, indicates that true effect sizes probably vary from study to study. The second indicator is the I^2-statistic.

The percentage of this statistic shows the study-to-study dispersion because of true difference, above and over random sampling error. When the value is a percentage of zero, there is no indication of dispersion. 25 per cent will be considered as low, 50 per cent as moderate and 75 per cent as high. When heterogeneity is significant, a random effect model will be chosen in the analysis. In this random model, effect sizes may differ, giving right to true variation in effect sizes between studies. This way, the likelihood of type-II errors is reduced.

Outliers which are outside the confidence interval of the pooled effect size are advised to be removed when a common effect size is assumed. All studies were taken into account and outliers were considered and not automatically removed from this study, though the removal of Hedges $g > 2.5$ was planned.

Yoga Philosophy and Ayurveda as base for Yoga therapy

To deal with menopause symptoms with Yoga Therapy tools we need to understand the Yoga and Ayrveda view of human structure. Nathamuni's "Yoga Rahasya" describes stages of human life.

Yoga practice is different for people in different age.

1. Srsti Krama - Period Of Active Learning And Growing. Girls Were Prepared For The Future Life. Asana Part Is The Most Important Here (4:2:1)
2. Sthiti Krama - Period Of Stability - Yoga Is For Good Health And Also For Therapy If Needed. Asana Part Is Less And The Main Tool Is Pranayama (2:4:1). Prana Stores Our Energy. In This Period Women Have A Lot Of Responsibility, A Lot Of Things To Do And Not So Much Time For Themselves. It Is Period Of Fertility And Also Menopause Starts. Practice Must Give More Energy And To Maintain Good Health. Pranayama As A Main Tool Helps To Calm Down Very Quickly Giving Stability Instead Of Agitation.
3. Laya Krama / Adhyatmika Krama - Last Stage Of Life, Free Of Responsibilities, Time For Yourself, To Observe What Is Inside Of Your Heart, Also Preparation For Leaving From This Life. Yoga Pracctice is more meditative. Asana and pranayama must be done in smaller parts (1:2:4)

Focus is different for every stage, but every stage prepares the next one. During the period of menopause most women still lead active lives, Stithi krama, with many responsibilities at work and many still have youngsters living at home. Teenage life and menopause in the same family may be a challenging situation. There could be possibility that there are small children in a family because nowadays women getting birth in middle age. They need to take care of their physical and psychological health.

Health, Disease and Three Doshas

Ayrveda's seers isolated three forces which are particularly important, because they permit us to understand associations that exist between seemingly unconnected casual pathways and manifested symptoms within an organism. These forces are called the three doshas.

The word dosha means "fault," "mistake," "imperfection," although the doshas are paradoxically forces that both preserve an organism`s balance and rhythm when they are themselves balanced, yet will disturb its harmony when they are disturbed. Like prana, these three doshas are invisible forces which can't be directly perceived. Only their actions can be demonstrated, through the bodily substances, which are their vehicles.

These include (but are not limited to) nervous impulses for vata, bile for pitta, and mucus for kapha. These three doshas are condensations of the five mahabhutas - the five "great elements"

- o Vata, the body's principle of kinetic energy, is in change of all motion in the body and mind.
- o Kapha, the principle of potential energy, is the stabilizing influence in the living being; it also lubricates and maintains.
- o Pitta, which is in charge of all transformation in the organism, controls the balance of its kinetic and potential energies. The three doshas pervade the body, working in every cell at every instant, but they concentrate themselves in those tissues in which they are particularly required:
- o Vata is particularly active in the brain, nervous system, the heart, colon, bones, bone marrow, lungs, bladder.
- o Pitta concentrates in the brain, liver, spleen, small intestine, endocrine glands, skin, eyes, blood.
- o Kapha is most prevalent in the brain, joints, mouth, head and neck, stomach, lymph, pleural cavity, pericardial cavity and fat. Each of the doshas has five varieties, or subdoshas. Although these subdoshas tend to act as if they were distinct entities, they are merely specializations of the three doshas, created by Nature to perform specific tasks.
- o The five kaphas are manifest in body lubricants, including stomach mucus, pleural and pericardial fluid, saliva, synovial fluid, and cerebrospinal fluid.
- o The five pitas appear in transformative substances, including the digestive juices, haemoglobin, melanin, rhodopsin, and various neurotransmitters.
- o The five vatas divide the body into spheres of influence according to the direction of their motion: forward and back in the chest, upward in the head, circular in the digestive tract, outward and inward in the periphery, and downward in pelvis.

Even though they are imperceptible to our senses, the three doshas are still forms of matter.

They are more conscious matter than is the matter that makes up the body, which allows them to influence the body efficiently, and they are less conscious than prana, the thinking mind, and the emotions.

These higher structures can therefore efficiently control the doshas - but only in those people who have carefully aligned their prana, thinking mind, and emotions with the higher consciousness of the soul and the spirit. Others tend to align their awareness's with what is going on their bodies - which allows them to fall prey to imbalance of the dosha forces.

Vata, pitta, and kapha are "waste products" created during the subtle metabolism of the higher forces that are prana and its associates, tejas (the universal fire that discriminates and digests, also called agni) and ojas (the subtle glue that integrates body, mind, and spirit together into a functioning individual).

Proper elimination of these physical wastes helps to maintain healthy levels of the doshas within the body: urine is vehicle for removing the kapha force, sweat carries away excess pitta force, and defecation expels excess vata force.

When an organism is healthy, little waste is produced; when it is poor health, waste will accumulate. This is one of the main reasons why those who possess good health tend to amass more of it, and those who are sick will usually get sicker until they change their ways. Like all other substances, the three doshas also possess qualities, and their increase or decrease in your system depends upon the similar or antagonistic qualities of everything you ingest - physically, energetically, mentally, emotionally, and spiritually.

All substances and all activities increase and decrease the three doshas according to their qualities. In particular, it is almost always the case that anything dry increases vata, anything hot increases pita, and anything heavy increases kapha, for vata is the only dry dosha, pitta the only hot dosha, and kapha the only heavy dosha.

If we wished to express this reality in awareness terms, we might say that vata communicates dryness to the organism, that pitta's message to a person is heat, and finally, that kapha proclaims heaviness throughout the being.

Ayurveda, Spirituality and Meditation

Ayurveda, the traditional healing system of India, is often looked at as a way of optimizing the functioning of the body. Ayurveda is capable of assisting in the healing of many conditions as well as extending life itself. The knowledge of Ayurveda has its roots in the Vedas, the sacred texts of India from which many spiritual philosophies and religions have sprung. These include Hinduism, Buddhism, Jainism, Yoga and others. It is a science not only of the physical body, but it goes beyond into the understanding of consciousness itself.

Ayurveda's sister, Yoga, is quite well known for its physical stretching exercises. Yoga is actually much more than this-it is a complete science and philosophy leading to enlightenment. Likewise, Ayurveda is much more than a science of understanding what foods are right for you. It is a science of using health as the basis of one's journey toward enlightenment. In fact, Ayurveda and Yoga are two sides of one coin. Ayurveda keeps the physical body healthy so that one can pursue spiritual goals, while yoga is the path of spirituality. Ayurveda is not a religion any more than yoga is a religion. They are spiritual sciences applicable to one's journey regardless of religious faith. Both sciences support a person on their journey toward self-realization or the direct knowing of their nature as spirit or soul. Scriptural study, whether it comes from the East or West, illuminates this journey.

Ayurvedic psycho-spirituality is based on the idea that we are all souls growing and evolving toward enlightenment or reunification with God. This can easily be viewed as entering the gates of heaven-for what is more heavenly then becoming one with God? Along this journey of our evolution there are naturally challenges which inspire us to grow and evolve. Some come to us in the form of health challenges; others are challenges in relationships or finances. They are, in a sense, gifts-for without them, there would be no motivating force behind our growth as spirits.

The three gunas are the grounds from which we come to understand ourselves emotionally and spiritually. Gunas are defined as the qualities of nature.

Sattva is the quality of clarity and purity. When our minds are sattvic, or pure, there is a natural innate connection between ourselves and God. With this awareness, our highest most virtuous qualities manifest. Our minds are much like a still lake and the light that reflects through it is the light of God.

Rajas is a state of activity and distraction where we forget our true nature as spirit and get wrapped up in the dramas of our lives. As a result we get caught in the experience of emotion and the challenging feelings of fear, worry, anxiety, anger, resentment, and attachment. If you imagine the clear lake of sattva, rajas is that lake after a rock has been thrown in and now it is disturbed. Each wave is a challenging emotion. Tamas is a state of darkness and inertia. In this state of being, not only are we unaware of our connection with God or spirit, but we spiral down into our own darkness and become harmful to ourselves or others. With our darker nature being dominant, we take actions such as violence or vindictive behaviours, or possibly addiction and suicide. Any harmful act reflects our own tamasic nature. If you recall the clear lake of sattva which had become rajasic when the rock was thrown in, now it has been stirred up and is muddy. The darkness is tamas.

It is our spiritual journey to move from dark to light, from ignorance to awareness, or from tamas to sattva. It is said in Ayurveda that Rajas and Tamas are the causes of disease. The actions taken and the emotions felt by the rajasic and tamasic mind upset the balance of the three Doshas, leading to physical disease. Sattva is the sole cause of health. Disease cannot affect the sattvic person-the one who has awakened into the light, therefore we could say that disease is the end result of forgetting our true nature as spirit. Once we forget, we act out of harmony with nature. These actions bring about disease. Healing involves the cultivation of harmony or sattva.

Ayurveda sees disharmony as the sole cause of disease. Healing takes place through a harmonious relationship with our environment. Ayurveda prescribes many regimens to bring about harmony or sattva in our lives. These regimens are numerous and to the beginner can quickly seem overwhelming to perform. Recommended actions include eating slowly in a peaceful environment, using proper aroma and colour therapy, going to bed early, awakening with the sun or earlier, applying oil to the body, meditating, doing yoga, and many more.

Students often ask why it is so difficult to adopt a harmonious lifestyle. The answer is simple. It is because we are not yet fully awakened to our spiritual nature. How can we live in harmony if we are not connected to our higher purpose in life? Without knowledge of higher awareness, it is our human nature to act as though we are only our senses and our mind. Our senses fear what is uncomfortable and desire only what gives us pleasure or great highs. The creation of harmony in our lives brings with it a rejection of that which brings us our highs, for each high is just a fleeting moment destined to pass and leave us desiring more.

Ayurvedic and yogic practices bring us peace, not highs. They sustain us; they do not burn us out. Yet to get to this place, one must go through the fire of awakening our self awareness. This process is honest and not always pleasurable. With honesty about ourselves at first there is discomfort and pain, so we move away from it. We drop those practices which, though difficult, lead to harmony and light because the light hurts our eyes. So how do we go about creating harmony? How do we become successful travelers on our journey?

There are many roads of empowerment but none is greater than our own direct self experience of God. This is achieved primarily through meditation and prayer. In the quietude of consciousness lies the light of God, the infinite. This light can fill us and sustain us, it can empower us to create change. The more that we come to know our nature as God or spirit, the more we are empowered to act harmoniously. The process begins for many with formal meditation. It ends when we meditate every action in our lives. When our lives become a meditation, ego slips away, exposing our true nature. Now we are ready to join pure consciousness, pure awareness. We become one with God.

Ayurveda and Yoga: Synergies for Complete Wellness and Self-Realization

Ayurveda and yoga are two ancient sister sciences that have been used together for centuries to promote complete wellness and self-realization. Ayurveda is a holistic system of medicine that focuses on restoring balance to the mind, body, and spirit. Yoga is a mind-body practice that uses physical postures, breathing exercises, and meditation to promote physical, mental, and spiritual well-being.

Ayurveda and yoga have a number of synergies that make them particularly complementary when practiced together:

Diet and lifestyle:

Ayurveda recommends following a diet and lifestyle that is tailored to your individual dosha type. Yoga can help you to develop a more mindful approach to your diet and lifestyle choices.

- Dosha balance: Ayurveda teaches that good health is dependent on keeping the three doshas in balance. Yoga can help you balance your doshas by practicing postures, breathing exercises, and meditation that are appropriate for your dosha type.
- Physical health: Ayurveda recommends herbal remedies, massage therapy, and other treatments to promote physical well-being. Yoga offers a variety of breathing exercises and

asanas that can strengthen and tone the body, improve flexibility, and reduce stress.

- Mental health: Ayurveda recommends treatments and herbal medications to promote mental well-being. Yoga offers a variety of meditation and relaxation practices that can help to calm the mind and reduce stress.
- Spiritual well-being: Both Ayurveda and yoga recognize the interconnectedness of the mind, body, and spirit. Ayurveda teaches us to build a lifestyle in accord with spiritual well-being as it is essential for overall health and well-being. Yoga offers a variety of practices, such as meditation and chanting, that promote spiritual growth and development.

Overall, Ayurveda and yoga are two powerful tools that can be used together to promote complete wellness and self-realization. By following an Ayurvedic diet and lifestyle, practicing yoga postures and breathing exercises, and meditation, you can achieve a state of physical, mental, and spiritual well-being.

Yoga and Ayurveda

Yoga is one of the most extraordinary spiritual sciences that mankind has ever discovered. It is like a gem of great proportions, containing many facets whose light can illumine the whole of our lives with great meaning. Going back over five thousand years, it is one of the few spiritual traditions that has maintained an unbroken development throughout history. Comprehending all aspects of the human being and the world of nature, it can unfold all the higher powers that are accessible to us both internally and externally.

Yogic methods cover the entire field of our existence - from the physical, sensory, emotional, mental, and spiritual to the highest Self-realization. It includes all methods of higher evolution in humanity - physical postures, ethical disciplines, breath control, sensory methods, affirmations and visualizations, prayer and mantra, and complex meditative disciplines. Yoga understands the nature and interrelationship of the physical, subtle and formless universes into the boundless infinite beyond time and space, and shows us how these also exist within each human individual.

Yoga is the fruit of the teachings of the Himalayan sages, going back to what yogis regard as the beginning of this particular world age or cycle of civilization some ten thousand years ago. It is said to carry on the traditions of earlier, spiritually advanced teachings which present civilizations have forgotten. Yoga is a distillation of wisdom from the myriad of sages throughout the ages, the ongoing legacy of the spiritual urge of humanity, as adapted to the particular requirements of each age and each person. It is like a wide and luxurious banyan tree spreading out our higher potentials and giving them strength and nourishment.

Like yoga, with which it has grown, Ayurveda possesses a long history with many layers, much diversity and a continuous development that makes it relevant for all people and all times. Ayurveda is one of the most remarkable holistic medical systems in the world. It covers all aspects of health and well-being - physical, emotional, mental and spiritual.

It includes all methods of healing from diet, herbs, exercise and lifestyle regimens to yogic practices and meditation. With its unique understanding of individual constitution, Ayurveda provides the insight for each person and each culture to create a way of life in harmony both with the world of nature and our higher Self. It offers optimal health and development for all creatures by its profound understanding of natural law.

Following in the footsteps of yoga, which already has a worldwide presence, Ayurveda is emerging as one of the most important global systems of mind-body medicine. It shows us how to understand the language of nature, the language of life, so that we can live in harmony with the greater universe, not evolving only for ourselves but bringing benefit to all creatures. Ayurveda contains the secrets not only for healing the individual but also for uplifting society, all creatures and the planet itself.

Yoga and Ayurveda are sister sciences that developed together and repeatedly influenced each other throughout history. They are integral parts of the great system of Vedic knowledge which states that all the universe is One Self and that the key to cosmic knowledge lies within our own minds and hearts. As Vedic disciplines, yoga and Ayurveda work together to enhance their great benefits on all levels. They can be integrated with related Vedic or yogic sciences of astrology, architecture, music and language for an even broader approach.

Yoga is first and foremost a science of Self-realization. Its concern is spiritual practice, mainly through meditation, to take us beyond the sorrow and ignorance of the world. It teaches us how to move from our outer bodily and ego-bound identity to our immortal Self that dwells within the heart. Yoga provides the key to all spiritual development, which in the Vedic sense is gaining knowledge of our true nature beyond time, space, death and suffering

Ayurveda is primarily a science of Self-healing aimed at relieving the diseases of body and mind. This does not mean that Ayurveda is merely a method of personal healing which doesn't require help from therapists or doctors. In fact, Ayurveda says that medical practitioners are indispensable in dealing with the complexities of disease and the variabilities of health requirements. Ayurveda as Self-healing means that it is concerned with restoring wholeness, with our inner Self as its ultimate goal, which is spiritual healing.

Ayurveda's concern is alleviating both bodily and mental diseases and promoting both physical and psychological well-being. Yet the ultimate goal of classical Ayurveda, like classical yoga, is Self-realization - the highest form of Self-healing. Ayurveda shows us how to attain optimal health not for outer enjoyment but to provide a wholesome foundation and sufficient energy to pursue the yogic quest.

The link between yoga and Ayurveda is prana, or the life-force. Yoga is the intelligence of prana seeking greater evolutionary transformations, while Ayurveda is its healing power, seeking to consolidate the life-systems it has already developed. Together, Ayurveda and yoga afford a complete discipline, one which can transform our existence from the physical to the deepest spiritual levels of our being with extraordinary vitality and creativity on all levels.

Yoga and Ayurveda in the West

Yoga is a common term in the Western world today, where yoga classes can be found in every city or neighborhood. Most people identify yoga with the physical postures or asanas that are the most evident side of the system. While yoga asanas can afford a good doorway into the vast temple of yoga, they are hardly the entire structure or its central deity. Eventually, most who look into yoga will come into contact with its broader and more spiritual practices, such as mantra and meditation.

Ayurveda is similarly becoming known in the West today as a special system of natural medicine. There are ayurvedic centers in most cities in the country. Ayurvedic herbs can be found at most health food stores. The idea of ayurvedic constitutional types has been presented in a number of popular books and magazines. However, the physical side of ayurvedic healing through diet and herbs is only part of the system. Its inner aspect, healing the subtle body and the mind (which includes yogic practices and meditation), is the other and perhaps more important half.

A number yoga centers offer ayurvedic therapies and the two sciences are generally studied together. However, many people who have been introduced to yoga from a physical model may not be fully aware of the importance of its ayurvedic connection. This may include various yoga teachers and yoga therapists, who may themselves have no ayurvedic training.

Traditionally, in India, yoga dealt with the spiritual side of life, what we have introduced as the path of Self-realization. Ayurveda, on the other hand, dealt with both physical and mental disease as well as with the prescription of lifestyle regimens. Yoga as therapy or exercise was traditionally prescribed in an ayurvedic context. Classical yoga therapy was ayurvedic both in theory and in application. This fact should be borne in mind by those using yoga today for healing purposes. They should not ignore the potential benefits of adding ayurvedic insights to yoga therapy. They should learn to understand the ayurvedic effects of yogic practices and not merely try to define yogic healing in terms of modern medicine or modern psychology alone.

The combined study of yoga and Ayurveda is of great importance for each discipline and for helping us understand the whole of life that both sciences address in such a profound manner. Restoring wholeness in body, mind and spirit is what we are all seeking, both individually and collectively.

Chapter 5

Ayurveda and Medicine

Introduction

Ayurveda, an ancient Indian system of medicine, emphasizes holistic health by balancing mind, body, and spirit. It utilizes natural remedies, dietary adjustments, herbal treatments, and lifestyle modifications to prevent and treat illnesses. Ayurvedic principles focus on individualized care, considering each person's unique constitution and environmental factors.

While rooted in traditional wisdom, Ayurveda is increasingly integrated into modern healthcare, offering complementary approaches to conventional medicine. Its emphasis on preventive care, wellness promotion, and personalized treatment makes Ayurveda a valuable addition to the medical landscape, contributing to a more comprehensive and patient-centered approach to health and healing. The central concept of Ayurvedic medicine is the theory that health exists when there is a balance between three fundamental bodily humours or doshas called Vata, Pitta and Kapha.

- Vata is the air principle necessary to mobilize the function of the nervous system
- Pitta is the fire principle which uses bile to direct digestion and hence metabolism into the venous system.
- Kapha is the water principle which relates to mucous, lubrication and the carrier of nutrients into the arterial system.

All Ayurvedic physicians believe that these ancient ideas, based in the spiritual knowledge discovered by the Rishis and Munis, exist in harmony with physical reality. These Ayurvedic concepts allow physicians to examine the homeostasis of the whole system. People may be of a predominant dosha or constitution, but all doshas have the basic elements within them.

Ayurveda holds that the tastes of foods or herbs have specific physiological effects. Those tastes that transform after digestion (Vipaka) are more powerful.

Sweet - Madhura

Sweet foods nourish, cool, moisten, oil, and increase weight

Sour - Amla

Sour foods warm, oil, and increase weight

Salty - Lavan

Salty foods warm, dissolve, stimulate, soften, oil, and increase weight

Bitter - Katu

Bitter foods cool, dry, purify and decrease weight

Pungent - Tikta

Pungent foods warm, dry, stimulate, and decrease weight

Astringent - Kasaya

Astringent foods cool, dry, reduce stickiness.

Ayurveda - Basic Concepts

Ayurveda is an ancient medicine system of the Indian subcontinent. It is said to have originated in India about 5000 years back. The word Ayurveda is a conjugation of two Sanskrit words 'ayus', meaning 'life' and 'veda', meaning 'science', thus ayurveda literally means the 'science of life'. Unlike other medicinal systems, Ayurveda focuses more on healthy living than treatment of diseases. The main concept of Ayurveda is that it personalizes the healing process.

According to Ayurveda, the human body is composed of four basics-the dosha, dhatu, mala and agni. There is immense significance of all these basics of the body in Ayurveda. These are also called the 'Mool Siddhant' or the 'basic fundamentals of Ayurvedic treatment'.

Dosha

The three vital principles of doshas are vata, pitta and kapha, which together regulate and control the catabolic and anabolic metabolism. The main function of the three doshas is to carry the byproduct of digested foods throughout the body, which helps in building up the body tissues. Any malfunction in these doshas causes disease.

Dhatu

Dhatu can be defined as one, which supports the body. There are seven tissue systems in the body. They are as Rasa, Rakta, Mamsa, Meda, Asthi, Mjja and Shukra which represent the plasma, blood, muscle, fat tissue, bone, bone marrow and semen respectively. Dhatus only provide the basic nutrition to the body and it helps in the growth and structure of mind.

Mala: Mala means waste products or dirty. It is third in the trinity of the body i.e. doshas and dhatu. There are three main types of malas, e.g. stool, urine and sweat. Malas are mainly the waste products of the body so their proper excretion from the body is essential to maintain the proper health of the individual. There are mainly two aspects of mala i.e. mala and kitta: Mala is about waste products of the body whereas kitta is all about the waste products of dhatus.

Agni: All kinds of metabolic and digestive activity of the body takes place with the help of the biological fire of the body called Agni. Agni can be termed as the various enzymes present in the elementary canal, liver and the tissue cells.

The Body Matrix

Life in Ayurveda is conceived as the union of body, senses, mind and soul. The living man is a conglomeration of three humours (Vata, Pitta & Kapha), seven basic tissues (Rasa, Rakta, Mansa, Meda, Asthi, Majja & Shukra) and the waste products of the body such as faeces, urine and sweat. Thus the total body matrix comprises of the humours, the tissues and the waste products of the body. The growth and decay of this body matrix and its constituents revolve around food which gets processed into humours, tissues and wastes. Ingestion, digestion, absorption, assimilation and metabolism of food have an interplay in health and disease which are significantly affected by psychological mechanisms as well as by bio-fire (Agni).

Panchamahabhutas: According to Ayurveda all objects in the universe including human body are composed of five basic elements (Panchamahabhutas) namely, earth, water, fire, air and vacuum (ether). There is a balanced condensation of these elements in different proportions to suit the needs and requirements of different structures and functions of the body matrix and its parts.

The growth and development of the body matrix depends on its nutrition, i.e. on food. The food, in turn, is composed of the above five elements, which replenish or nourish the like elements of the body after the action of bio-fire (Agni). The tissues of the body are the structural whereas humours are physiological entities, derived from different combinations and permutations of Panchamahabhutas.

Health and Sickness

Health or sickness depends on the presence or absence of a balanced state of the total body matrix including the balance between its different constituents. Both the intrinsic and extrinsic factors can cause disturbance in the natural equilibrium giving rise to disease.

This loss of equilibrium can happen by dietary indiscrimination, undesirable habits and non-observance of rules of healthy living. Seasonal abnormalities, improper exercise or erratic application of sense organs and incompatible actions of the body and mind can also result in creating disturbance of the existing normal balance.

The treatment consists of restoring the balance of disturbed body-mind matrix through regulating diet, correcting life-routine and behaviour, administration of drugs and resorting to preventive Panchkarma and Rasayana therapy.

Diagnosis

In Ayuveda diagnosis is always done of the patient as a whole. The physician takes a careful note of the patients internal physiological characteristics and mental disposition. S/He also studies such other factors as the affected bodily tissues, humours, the site at which the disease is located, patients resistance and vitality, his/her daily routine, dietary habits, the gravity of clinical conditions, condition of digestion and details of personal, social, economic and environmental situation of the patient.

The diagnosis also involves the following examinations:

1. General physical examination
2. Pulse examination
3. Urine examination
4. Examination of the faeces
5. Examination of tongue and eyes
6. Examination of skin and ear including tactile and auditory functions.

Treatment

The principal objectives of Ayurveda include maintenance and promotion of health, prevention of disease and cure of sickness.

Treatment of the disease consists in avoiding causative factors responsible for disequilibrium of the body matrix or of any of its constituent parts through the use of Panchkarma procedures, medicines, suitable diet, activity and regimen for restoring the balance and strengthening the body mechanisms to prevent or minimize future occurrence of the disease.

Normally treatment measures involve use of medicines, specific diet and prescribed activity routine. Use of these three measures is done in two ways. In one approach of treatment the three measures antagonize the disease by counteracting the etiological factors and various manifestations of the disease. In the second approach the same three measures of medicine, diet and activity are targeted to exert effects similar to the etiological factors and manifestations of the disease process. These two types of therapeutic approaches are respectively known as Vipreeta and Vipreetarthkari treatments.

For successful administration of a treatment four things are essential. These are:

1. The physician
2. The medicaments
3. The nursing personnel
4. The patient

The physician comes first in order of importance. S/He must possess technical skill, scientific knowledge, purity and human understanding. The physician should use his/her knowledge with humility, wisdom and in the service of humanity. Next in importance comes food and drugs. These are supposed to be of high quality, wide application, grown and prepared following approved procedures and should be available adequately.

The third component of every successful treatment is the role of nursing personnel who should have good knowledge of nursing, must know the skills of their art and be affectionate, sympathetic, intelligent, neat & clean and resourceful. The fourth component is the patient himself who should be cooperative and obedient to follow instructions of the physician, able to describe ailments and ready to provide all that may be needed for treatment.

Ayurveda has developed a very vivid analytical description of the stages and events that take place since the causative factors commence to operate till the final manifestation of disease. This gives this system an additional advantage of knowing that possible onset of disease much before the latent symptoms become apparent. This very much enhances the preventive role of this system of medicine by making it possible to take proper and effective steps in advance, to arrest further progress in pathogenesis or to take suitable therapeutic measures to curb the disease in its earliest stage of onset.

Types of Treatment

The treatment of disease can broadly be classified as Shodhana therapy (Purification Treatment): Shodhana treatment aims at removal of the causative factors of somatic and psychosomatic diseases. The process involves internal and external purification. The usual practices involved are Panchkarma (medically induced Emesis, Purgation, Oil Enema, Decoction enema and Nasal administration of medicines), Pre-panchkarma procedures (external and internal oleation and induced sweating). Panchkarma treatment focuses on metabolic management. It provides needed purificatory effect, besides conferring therapeutic benefits. This treatment is especially helpful in neurological disorders, musculo-skeletal disease conditions, certain vascular or neuro-vascular states, respiratory diseases, metabolic and degenerative disorders.

Shamana therapy (Palliative Treatment): Shamana therapy involves suppression of vitiated humours (doshas). The process by which disturbed humour subsides or returns to normal without creating imbalance of other humours is known as shamana. This treatment is achieved by use of appetisers, digestives, exercise and exposure to sun, fresh air etc. In this form of treatment, palliatives and sedatives are used.

Pathya Vyavastha (Prescription of diet and activity): Pathya Vyavastha comprises indications and contraindications in respect of diet, activity, habits and emotional status. This is done with a view to enhance the effects of therapeutic measures and to impede the pathogenetic processes. Emphasis on actions such as dos and donts of diet is laid with the aim to stimulate Agni and optimize digestion and assimilation of food in order to ensure strength of tissues.

Nidan Parivarjan (Avoidance of disease causing and aggravating factors): Nidan Parivarjan is to avoid the known disease causing factors in diet and lifestyle of the patient. It also encompasses the idea to refrain from precipitating or aggravating factors of the disease.

Satvavajaya (Psychotherapy): Satvavajaya concerns mainly with the area of mental disturbances. This includes restraining the mind from desires for unwholesome objects and cultivation of courage, memory and concentration. The study of psychology and psychiatry have been developed extensively in Ayurveda and have wide range of approaches in the treatment of mental disorders.

Rasayana therapy (use of immunomodulators and rejuvenation medicines): Rasayana therapy deals with promotion of strength and vitality. The integrity of body matrix, promotion of memory, intelligence, immunity against the disease, the preservation of youth, lustre and complexion and maintenance of optimum strength of the body and senses are some of the positive benefits credited to this treatment. Prevention of premature bear and tear of body tissues and promotion of total health content of an individual are the roles that Rasayana therapy plays.

Diet and Ayurvedic Treatment

In Ayurveda, regulation of diet as therapy has great importance. This is because it considers human body as the product of food. An individuals mental and spiritual development as well as his temperament is influenced by the quality of food consumed by him / her.

Food in human body is transformed first into chyle or Rasa and then successive processes involve its conversion into blood, muscle, fat, bone, bone-marrow, reproductive elements and ojas. Thus, food is basic to all the metabolic transformations and life activities. Lack of nutrients in food or improper transformation of food lead to a variety of disease conditions.

Basic elements of Ayurvedic Medicine

Ayurvedic medicine with its roots in India, originated during the Vedic period. As a medicinal theory that complements the concept of allopathic medicine; Ayurvedic medicine is geared to the principle of five elements. According to its basic premise not only the universe but the human body which is a part of the universe is constituted by five essential elements of earth, air, water, fire and ether. The medicinal theory of Ayurveda, which has human body in its prime focus, enshrines the composing units of human body in the following manner.

According to it human body is constituted by:

- o Tasa dhatu or plasma
- o Takta dhatu or blood
- o Mamal dhatu or flesh
- o Medha dhatu or fat
- o Majja dhatu or marrow and
- o Sukra dhatu which include semen and female reproductive organs.

Similar to the Elizabethan concept of 'humors' as necessary tools of balance in the human body, Ayurvedic medicine dwells on the proper balance of wind, bile and phlegm. According to the century's ancient Orientalmedical practice, imbalance in the mentioned elements of wind, bile and phlegm; gave rise to defects or 'dosas' in human body and that a healthy metabolic system rests on a rightful balance of these elements which existed in equal measures in the human body.

In keeping with the concept that there are twenty essential qualities or 'guna' typical of each and every substance of the universe, Ayurvedic medicine upholds the application of the remedial measures when any of the fundamental qualities are disturbed on account of the imbalance in the 'vatas' of wind or air; bile or pitta and 'khapa' or phlegm. Its therapeutic regimen rests on the devices of exercise, meditation and massage.

It dwells on the belief that by way of the mentioned regimens of exercise, meditation and massage imbalance in the physiological system can be rectified. Besides that, a healthy system striking the right balance between its composing humors; thrives on healthy digestion and required excretion of toxic elements.

Ever since the later Vedic age; the medicinal system of Ayurveda was classified into eight separate disciplines. Involving different regimens of treatments seeking to cater to different organic system of human physiology, there are areas catering to internal medication, pediatric, psychiatry, surgery, toxicology, child bearing capacities, revitalisation of the immunity, and that serving to rectify the disorders in eye, ear, nose and throat. As a medicinal concept holistic in purpose; it not only upholds the maintenance of proper balance; but also emphasizes a moderate expression of instinctive urges and desire with sleep, food consumption, sexual and other activities being carried out in proportional measures. 'Charaka Samhita' throws significant light on the diagnostic procedures of Ayurvedic medicine. The tenfold method of disease diagnoses involves the examination of patient's build up or constitution with accurate measurement of his height, weight and structure, assessing the nature and essence of his abnormality; recognition of factors which may lead to stability. It also involves an assessment of his diet peculiarities and necessary correction to be made therein. The vital factors of his age, stamina, digestive and psychiatric capabilities are also kept in mind while deducing the cause, origin and the nature of disease.

Similar to the allopathic mode of treatment, another of the fundamental tenets of Ayurvedic medicine involves the study and analysis of symptoms and pathogenic development of a disease. The therapeutic measure also bears in mind the factors of effects and side effects; whether it has been able to get rid of the original factor and the symptomatic factors exhibited by the disease it seeks to rectify.

The medicines used as part of Ayurvedic therapy are made of herbs and various aspects of the natural flora. For the remedial procedure of certain diseases animal and alcoholic elements are also made use of. Extracts of plants and animals are used in forms of tar, oil and paste meant for topical application. Emphasizing basically on external application and massage, there are those meant for oral consumption as well. Modern time has witnessed a steady revival in the popularity of Ayurvedic medicine as holistic and alternative mode of treatment.

Dinacharya

In order to keep the tridoshas in a state of healthy equlibrium and digestion & metabolism (agni) in proper order, Ayurveda prescribes for each individual a specific daily routine (dina - day & acharya - behaviour). The various stages to this daily routine, influenced by the specifics of your prakriti, that will enable you to make the most out of your life, are:

Arising

Since our biological clocks are attuned to the rising and setting of the sun, it is obviously better to awake at sunrise in perfect synchronisation to the natural clock. An ideal time to let the body cells soak in the strength of a tempered sun to be charged for the day. Drinking a glass of luke-warm water helps flush out all toxins accumulated overnight in the body.

Natural Urges: The last portion of the night being ruled by vata - involved in the process of elimination - dawn is the best time to eliminate the body's physical waste. Proper elimination also helping remove the kapha that naturally accumulates overnight. Defecation once or twice daily is the best.

Preferably not immediately after a meal. But urination then is wise. Examine your eliminations each morning and if you notice any disturbance indicating poor digestion, go on a fast. It will allow the body rest to correct the system before disease sets in. Never suppress the natural physical urges as elimination, hunger, thirst, sleep, sneezing, yawning, vomiting, flatus and ejaculation, for it will lead to discomfort and even disease.

Cleanliness: Thorough washing of the limbs, face, mouth, eyes & nose purifies the bodies sense organs. Best done with a bath in clean water, it should accompany brushing of the teeth (should be repeated after every meal), scraping off a toxicated coating of ama from the tongue, occasional gargling of salt water with a pinch of turmeric to keep gums, mouth & throat healthy, proper cleaning of the nose and the ears and washing the eyes with warm water held in mouth for moments (saliva being very good for the eyes). Keep your hair trimmed, nails filed and wear clean clothes. Feel free to use perfumes in moderation and feel good.

Exercise: Either passive like massage or active like aerobics or both as in yoga postures, regular exercise increases the body's stamina and resistance to disease by facilitating the immune system, clearing all channels, promoting circulation & waste disposal, and destroying fat. Done regularly, it can reduce anxiety but become addictive. Depending on age & body type, kaphas can go for heavy exercises, pittas should do it in moderation and vatas should perform yoga and not aerobics. Never exert more than half your capacity, during illness, just after a meal and without rhythmic breathing. Swimming, walking and even laughing are excellent options.

Massage: Necessary for every person, a regular self-massage with herbal oils is usually adequate but needs to be supplemented with professional attention occasionally. It makes the skin supple, controls vata by reducing its cold, dry, light, rough & erratic qualities, enhances blood circulation, encourages quicker removal of metabolic wastes and relaxes the body. Follow the normal direction of hair growth, use a little extra oil over the body's vital parts, massage the scalp and head at least weekly and just the soles of your feet if short of time.

Meditation: Ideal for disciplining the mind and removing stress & strain, it is best done after a quick bath to cleanse yourself. Critical in satisfying the mind's hunger, when done well it is so nourishing that even the body can survive on less.

Control of desire, or mental hunger, is the key to longevity and immortality. Anything can be meditation so long it is sincere and heartfelt. The simplest and healthiest involves the sun and its golden colour is deemed the most nourishing and productive. While this routine acts as a critical shield of defence against the destabilising influences of an external environment, by using selective choice in some of the other factors mentioned below you can easily improve upon the condition of your total health.

Dinacharya Towards Ayurveda

The reason for this is that most healthy and happy state is most natural state, and vice versa. Intrinsic to this natural state is the basic intelligence of everything from how a baby should take its first step to how the sperm should enter the egg to conceive the baby in the first place, to how a cell should remember when to live and when to die. Dinacharya is one of the best things that can do to stay in balance, prevent disease and treat almost any disease.

Today's society is so alienated from Nature. Who knows what day of the cycle the moon is in To really heal must return to balance and know place in the Universe. One way to describe the daily cycle is in terms of the doshas, Vata, the air element; Pitta, the fire element; and Kapha, the water element. Vata is dominant from 2 to 6 in the morning and afternoon. Kapha is dominant from 6 to 10 in the morning and evening, and Pitta is dominant during mid day and midnight. Keep in touch with these energies during the day and move with them, not against them.

Waking: From 2 until 6, or until dawn, the Vata element is dominant. Sometime during this period before dawn should wake up. In Ayurveda the night is divided into 16 periods from sunset to sunrise.

The ideal time to arise is during the 14th period which is about 2 hours before dawn, around 4:30 to 5. This is the time when there is the most sattva in the air. It is the most fresh and pure time of the day. Some exceptions to this rule of rising are the very young, the old, parents with small children, and people with fevers or diarrhea.

Breathe

Elimination: As soon as possible empty colon and bladder. If wait until later in the morning or during the day are slowly poisoning and creating an opportunity for chronic conditions to arise.

Clean The Senses: View of the world and will change if purify senses everyday. Wash the eyes with rose water and Triphala to purify the sight. Wash ears and apply a tiny amount of sesame or almond oil in them to purify hearing. Brush teeth and scrape tongue with a tongue cleaner to purify mouth and sense of taste.

Monitor the condition of body by observing the coating on tongue every morning. Gargle with warm water or herbal tea or a quarter cup of sesame oil to purify voice and strengthen teeth. Finally do Jal neti and put a little oil in nose to purify the sinuses and sense of smell. The traditional Dinacharya also recommends that inhale the smoke of medicinal herbs every morning to purify the mind, head, face, neck and lungs.

Oil Massage: Abhyanga is the name for oil massage. The morning abhyanga is typically a self massage. It is one of the main ways that Ayurveda keeps us strong and prevents us from aging. A major part of aging is the drying out of tissue that results in slower transport of nutrients into the cell and body and toxic wastes out of the body. Oil massage removes this dryness, removes stagnated flows and organs, and nurtures mind and body. It also makes skin look great if use the right oil.

Exercise: Vyayama is the name for physical exercise. This is usually yoga but it can be anything including a walk, tai chi, a swim or whatever. This early morning exercise removes stagnation in the body mind, strengthens the digestive fire, reduces fat and gives an overall feeling of lightness and Joy as it fills body with good Prana.

It is not to be strenuous, no quarter mile sprints or racquetball, but more meditative and easy. In fact, exercising at one fourth to one half of capacity is recommended. want long deep breaths to absorb the Prana, not short quick shallow breaths. Too much exercise will aggravate Vata and the blood and imbalances will follow. The exercise will also help the oil that just put on soak deep into body and nourish all tissues.

Bathing: After exercise bath to remove any excess oil and dirt. Both showers and bathtubs are recommended in the classics. Usually warm water baths are suggested, but care should be taken not to put very warm water on the neck and head, as this will throw off balance. Bathing increases the digestive fire, especially if the water is a little cold. Put on clean clothing after the bath and apply essential oils as wish. I always put a tilak on forehead with sandalwood oil and use lavender instead of deodorant.

This is also the time to put on gems if want. Gems and good clothes can increase intelligence and longevity, destroy inauspiciousness and attract good vibes. The point is that finish the bath feeling and looking so great that are ready to face even God. And indeed that is next.

Meditation: For a few minutes to an hour sit down and see who really are, focus on focus, put attention on Awareness. See and Be only Consciousness. This is the most important aspect of Dinacharya. The whole day, indeed the whole world, revolves around THIS. Simply be quiet. Sit in Peace as Peace for just a little while.

Breakfast: Take a light breakfast. like to drink a thick fruit-spirulina-herb-bee pollen-etc drink for breakfast. Western science has studied the aging process for some time and has come up with only one practice that is definitely anti-aging. This is to minimize calories while maximizing nutrients.

Think of this when are deciding what to eat and fill mind with gratitude and Love for food as eat. Also, may think that nobody does fire ceremonies anymore, but according to Ayurveda every time eat are offering food to the fire of digestion so that this fire can carry the offering to the gods, and that

Lunch: Got up six or seven hours ago, ate only a light breakfast. Now are really hungry. This is great. If want to really digest food well it is best to put it on a hot fire and hunger indicates that have one ready to go.

Eating food before the previous meal is digested is considered one of the main causes of disease. It is also one of the hardest habits to get out of in our society where there is so much food everywhere. This is the main meal of the day so eat a healthy nutritious meal that has moderate calories. After the meal it is good to take a little walk, a couple hundred steps only, to help the food digest.

Sundown: Sundown is a special time of balance between day and night. In this balance it is easier for mind to stop long enough. This is the time for evening prayers and meditations in many cultures around the world.

Dinner: Eat around 6 to 7. This meal should be lighter than lunch. In fact, people doing spiritual practices often skip it entirely so that their early morning practices are crystal clear instead of having their awareness dulled and loaded down because dinner is still being processed. After dinner take a Peaceful walk with family and friends.

Ease: From dinner to bedtime just take it easy. Spend time with family, read, and relax.

Bedtime: Around 10 go to sleep so that can get 6 to 7 hours of sleep before 4:30 am. A good practice is to massage the soles of feet with a calming oil before going to bed. This will calm system and promote well being. And remember to take Triphala before sleep. It is also a good time to take calming calcium citrate for strong bones and nerves. In the evening is the time to make Love with Beloved, in a beautiful nurturing uplifting merging. Men should try not to ejaculate, as this loss of sperm means a loss of vital energy in the form of Ojas.

Pharmacology of Ayurveda

The materia medica of the Ayurveda, composed of the five basic elements, has been categorized according to the derivatives of these elements. They include: taste (rasa), potency (virya), taste of the digestion product (vipaka), properties (guna), specific properties (prabhava) and action (karman). Taste (rasa) is six fold: sweet (madhura), sour (amla), salty (lavana), sharp (tikta), bitter (katu) and astringent (kasaya). Each taste is composed of two of the five elements. The condition of the food substances after digestion is also expressed in terms of taste (vipaka), however it can only be sweet, sour or sharp.

The properties (guna), are grouped in 10 pairs, each one complementary to the other: heavy and light, cold and hot, fat and dry, slow and sharp, stable and labile, soft and hard, clear and slimy, smooth and raw, fine and massive and viscous and liquid. The potency (virya) of a drug is defined as its capability to express its property. Sometimes, potency is grouped in the same way as the property, but for practical reasons, it is usually expressed in terms of hot (ushna) and cold (shita).

The specific property (prabhava) distinguishes two drugs that have the same taste, taste after digestion and potency. This might be due to the composition of the drug or the location in the body where the drug acts. Finally the action (karman) of a drug on the body is expressed in terms of the three doshas. A drug can increase or decrease the vata dosha, the pitta dosha and the kapha dosha. The drugs used in Ayurveda are made by several processes from vegetable and mineral raw materials.

Mostly plant alkaloids are the active ingredients. Obviously barring some chemical changes it is mostly natural deviates.

Concept of 'AMA' in Ayurveda

Ama is a peculiar concept in Ayurveda (for which modern chemistry has no correlate). It is an important factor in a cause of disease and in modification of disease process.

Role of Ama: Ama originates from improperly digested toxic particles that clog the channels in body. Some of these channels are physical and include the intestines, lymphatic system, arteries and veins, capillaries, and genitourinary tract. Others are nonphysical channels called nadis through which energy flows. Ama toxicity accumulates wherever there is a weakness in the body, and this will result in disease

Causes of 'Ama' production: Agnimandya: Low digestive fire. Normal activity of digestive fire is essential for the complete and proper digestion of food. But due to low digestive fire the food is not properly digested, and toxic product is formed.

Therefore its absorption becomes sluggish and it gets retained in the intestine for a longer time. Due to this retention it becomes fermented or even putrefied. This toxic product remains unabsorbed in the intestine because of its incomplete digestion and it is the root cause of all diseases.

Dhatu-Agnimandya: Low Tissue Fire: Tissue fire plays an important role in the process of formation of tissues from the nutrient substances (of the particular dhatu). Hence when the power of the tissue fire of a particular tissue is diminished, either in the liver or in a particular channel, the formation or utilization of that tissue becomes incomplete and ama is produced. Such tissues containing ama are called Sama tissues-tissues with ama.

This type of pathology is seen in various diseases. In diabetes, fat and muscle tissues are formed as "Sama tissues" because of the low tissue fire of the fat and muscle tissues. Hence the normal functional activities of these tissues are hampered. In obesity a similar type of fat tissue is produced due to low tissue fire of fat tissue.

A peculiar thing observed in these two conditions is that, though there is low tissue fire, there is no associated low digestive fire; on the contrary digestive fire becomes sharper. In all other types of low tissue fire there is an associated low digestive fire.

Mala Sanchaya: Accumulation of Waste Products

Agni is the energy responsible for transformation of food substances into body tissues. In the first stage it produces nutritious substance, which is converted to tissues in the second phase of digestion, which is called secondary or tissue digestion.

Here the action of tissue fire takes place on nutrient food substances, and different tissues are produced. This is the anabolic activity of tissue fire. (M.N.)

The tissues produced by this process are utilized for the liberation of energy required for each and every activity of the body. During this process the tissue substances are again digested, disintegrated, and utilized for the liberation of heat and energy by the tissue fire.

This is the catabolic process. During this activity of disintegration of tissues certain minute waste products are formed.

They are called subtle waste products or kleda. Up to a certain limit the existence of these is essential for the body, and the excess is excreted from the body. When this excretion becomes inadequate due to excessive production or its defective excretion, it gets accumulated in the body-which results in the formation of toxic substance- Ama.

Dosha Sammurcchana-Interaction or Amalgamation Between Vitiated Doshas

Every dosha has certain qualities, which are antagonistic to the qualities of other doshas-e.g. the dry and light qualities of Vata are antagonistic to the oily and heavy qualities of Kapha.

Similarly the hot quality of Pitta is antagonistic to the cold quality of Kapha and Vata. Therefore when two or three doshas become severely vitiated and combined, they produce interaction between them. In such conditions opposite qualities, instead of nullifying each other interact and produce a toxic substance.

Krimi Visha -Bacterial Toxins When an infection is caused by the pathogenic organisms, they liberate a toxic substance.

Properties of ama: It is always in the form of incompletely digested substance. Hence it is non-homogenous, has a very bad or foul odor which can be experienced only when it is combined with excretory products such as sweat, urine, and feces, or when products such as sputum, vomit, etc., are expelled from the body. It is very sticky. It produces lethargy in the body.

Symptoms of Ama: Srotorodha: Obstruction- This can occur in any large, small, or minute channel, when it is indicated by stagnation and disturbance in transport, and metabolism can occur even at the cellular level.

The commonly observed obstructions are in the liver (affecting the passage of bile), the urinary tract, the fallopian tubes, the blood vessels, the respiratory tract, etc.

Weakness or reduced working power in any part or organ is due to the difficulty produced by ama in the contraction and relaxation of the musculature of the part, even when the organic structure of the muscle is normal.

Obstruction of the movement of Vata- Ama on one side causes disturbance in the action of the musculature of the part or organ, and on the other side it causes disturbances in the conduction of nerve impulses, and ultimately the activity of the concerned part becomes reduced or stopped. lack mental clarity and energy and feel weary and unenthusiastic

Heaviness and Lethargy: Tongue is coated especially upon awaking in the morning. Metabolic disturbance. Due to various diseases such as obesity, diabetes, etc., metabolic disturbance is produced. (Ash. Su. 13 /23)

Signs of Ama: Feeling heavy, muzzy headed, unclear thinking, aches and pains, bloating, gas, skin blemishes, fever, lack of energy, stickiness, foul smells (breath, sweat, urine, stools, phlegm), sinking stool, mucous in stool, turbid urine, lack of appetite or taste, indigestion, sticky/sweet taste in the mouth, copious phlegm. Pulse; deep, dull, slippery Tongue; thick, greasy coating.

Modern signs of ama: High triglycerides, atherosclerosis, late-onset diabetes, high blood sugar levels, some forms of depression, rheumatoid factor, the presence of H. pylori bacteria, leukocytosis or leukocytopenia (deficient and excess white blood cells), excess antibodies, Candida albicans in the gut and uterus, blood urea, gout, excess platelet count, High IgE levels from allergic reactions, excess red blood cells, gall stones as a sign of excess bile, kidney stones as a sign of un-metabolised calcium and oxalates, high liver enzymes (ALT, AST), intra-occular pressure (glaucoma), bacterial infection, high temperature, tumours.

Effects of ama: When such toxins come in contact with dosha, tissues, or waste product, it produces sama dosha, sama tissues and sama mala. In Ayurvedic texts symptoms of the sama and nirama stage of the doshas, tissues, and waste products are described for all the diseases. Ayurveda attributes cause of any disease to an imbalance in one or all of the doshas and for successful treatment of a particular disease physician has to determine, weather the imbalanced dosha is 'Sam' or 'Niram'

Treatment of Ama

Herbs

Anti-vata: Fresh Ginger, Linseed, Nutmeg, Garlic, Asafoetida, Cumin, Black Pepper, Fennel, Castor oil. Also try Asafoetida Formula, which is very useful for clearing wind, bloating and spasms from the intestines.

Anti-pitta: Kalmegh, Aloe Vera, Fennel, Coriander, Guduchi, Neem. Also try Amalaki formula that contains cooling herbs to clear heat toxins from the system.

Anti-kapha: Ginger, Cumin, Black pepper, Pushkaramoola, Punarnava, Tulsi, Vacha, Guggul. Also try the famous Ayurvedic formula called Trikatu, renowned for its heating properties that can literally digest toxins.

Specific Therapies: Sweating, fasting, hot water, wind and sun therapy, vigourous exercise, Panchakarma.

Anti-ama Diet: Emphasise pungent, bitter, astringent flavours

Fruit: No sweet fruit, only sour - cranberry, lemon, lime, grapefruit

Vegtables: Steamed sprouts, steamed vegetables - some raw is good for pitta. Lots of greens; microalgae - especially chlorella. No root/ sweet vegetables or mushrooms

Grains: No bread/ pastries. Less wheat and oats. Kicharee; barley, quinoa, millet, rye, rice

Beans: Mung

Nuts: None, some pumpkin seeds

Dairy: None. Goats' milk is slightly astringent and is less Kapha forming

Meat: No shellfish, fish, fats, red meat, pork, eggs

Oils: None. Ghee okay in small quantities as are mustard or linseed oils, which are drying

Sweetners: None. Sugar is ama forming. Honey is okay (2 tsp/ day).

Drinks: Ginger, cinnamon, cardamom, fennel, dandelion root coffee.

Immunity (Vyadhikshamatva) in Ayurveda

When etiological factors come into contact with the body they try to produce disease. At the same time the body tries to resist the disease. This power of the body, which prevents the development of diseases or resists a developed disease, is called vyadhikshmatava. It is commonly observed that certain persons do not develop a disease even after coming into contact with the relevant etiological factors, while others become victims of the disease.

The reason is that when the resistive power of the body is sufficiently strong it destroys the causes. A beautiful simile is used in Manusmriti to illustrate this fact: when a seed is sown in non-fertile soil it is destroyed.

Immunity depends upon the maintenance of the equilibrium of doshas and the healthiness of tissues and channels. Similarly the strength of the body is related to immunity and it also depends upon the healthiness of tissues. The factors, which are related to the healthiness of tissues, are:

- o Birth in a country where people are naturally strong
- o Birth at a time when people naturally gain strength
- o Favourable disposition of time (pleasant and moderate climate)
- o Excellence of the qualities of the sperm and the ovum
- o Excellence of the ingested food
- o Excellence of the physique
- o Excellence of mind
- o Favourable disposition of the race and species.

Exercise

Cheerful Disposition during Sexual Indulgence: This strength is attainable from three sources-constitutional, temporal, and acquired. Constitutional strength is that gained from the time of the formation of the fetus onwards. Hence it is dependent on the healthiness of sperm and ovum and also on the excellence of time and place. The temporal strength is the one, which is gained from the favourable condition of time, such as youth, and favourable season.The acquired strength is one, which is achieved by the proper combination of diet, exercise, and other regimens.

Avyadhisaha Sharirani: Individuals incapable of resisting diseases. Obese individuals, Emaciated persons, Those who have improper physiology of the musculature, Those with defective blood, Those who have defective bone tissues, Emaciated and weak persons, Those nourished with unwholesome food, Those who have feeble minds

We know that excessively obese or excessively emaciated persons are very weak. Similarly, the strength of the body depends largely upon the healthiness of tissues, especially healthiness of the muscle, blood, and bony tissues. Hence persons in whom these three tissues have improper physiological functions are naturally very weak.

Persons who consume unwholesome food are also very weak, as their tissues are not properly nourished. And lastly, strength of the body also depends upon the mental health. Hence persons having feeble minds are also weak. Therefore it may be inferred that the common factor of all these eight types of individuals who cannot resist diseases is their weak constitution.

Vyadhikshama Sharirani: Individuals having good resistance against diseases. On the other hand, individuals whose physical constitutions are of a type opposite to the eight types mentioned above are capable of resisting diseases. If a person's physical and mental strength is of a high degree then naturally his immunity is also good and such persons can resist diseases very well. Individuals whose bodies are neither too corpulent nor too emaciated, who possess healthy and good musculature, blood, and bone tissues, who are well nourished with wholesome and sufficient food and who have strong minds are capable of resisting diseases.

Persons having proportionate bodies and musculature, compactness of the body, and healthy sense organs are not overcome by the onslaught of diseases. They can withstand hunger, thirst, and the heat of the sun, cold weather, and physical exertion. They can also digest and assimilate food properly.

Amongst the factors responsible for immunity, the greatest importance has been assigned to the healthy condition of the three tissues-blood, muscle, and bone. In our opinion the reasons for this are:

Here is a typical relation of between these three tissues and tridosha-i.e. between blood and Pitta, muscle and Kapha, bone and Vata. The healthy condition of these three tissues will naturally maintain equilibrium of the three doshas, which is also required for resisting disease.

The white cells of the blood are the force, which fights against any infection and prevents any foreign substance from entering the body. The plasma of the blood contains gamma globulins, which are antibodies. Muscular tissue also produces these gamma globulins.

Red bone marrow in the bones is the organ of the reticulo-endothelial system responsible for the manufacture of the red and white cells of the blood.

Ashtau Nindita [Eight undesirables]. There are eight types of undesirable constitutions: too tall, too short, too hairy, hairless, too white, too black, too corpulent and too emaciated.

These constitutions are considered undesirable because they do not possess sufficient resistive power against diseases. The qualitative and quantitative proportions of the tissues are not proper in them. The measurement by finger (anguli parimana) of the body and the compactness of the tissues is also abnormal.

In our opinion these eight types of undesirable constitutions are mainly related to some sort of hormonal dysfunction of the body. The dysfunction of thyroid, gonads, adrenal cortex, and pituitary is related to obesity. Hyperactivity of the thyroid causes wasting of muscles and develops wasting.

The excessively tall constitution is associated with disturbances in the anterior pituitary, which produces gigantism. In this condition a person becomes abnormally healthy. He also becomes impotent and cannot resist diseases. Dwarf constitution is also associated with disturbances in the pituitary.

In conditions such as Frolich's syndrome and Cushing's syndrome such dwarf constitutions are produced. Excessively hairy and hairless are associated with dysfunction of the pituitary, adrenal cortex, and gonads. The advanced modern medicines are also unable to cure these eight conditions even today.

Skin Care in Ayurveda

Skin is the seat of a sense organ. The senses of touch, pain, temperature, pressure are felt by it. It is a Matruj Avyava i.e. derived from mother or having maternal origin.It gives external covering to the whole body. The seven layers of skin get their nutrition from Mansa Dhatu {muscle tissue}. It is known as an UpDhatu (secondary tissue product) of the Raktadhatu (blood) because it only mimics the Dhatu's in beholding the body. It does not do Poshan Karma i.e. do not give nutrition to the other Dhatus.

As skin is an Upadhatu of the Raktadhatu, it is a mirror that reflects the qualities of the Raktadhatu (blood) and the Rasadhatu (body's plasma tissue).Hence it is a common saying that 'glowing skin is the result of good quality Rasa and Rakta'.

No amount of bleaching and facial massage or application of make-up through dexterity of a skilled beautician can hide the shallow look if the skin is unhealthy.

Conversely, a healthy skin will always look attractive even when devoid of make-up.

Characteristics of a person with ideal skin(Twak Sar/Ras Sar)

People with ideal skin have soft, oily, thin, smooth and lustrous skin.

They have soft, thin, scanty, oily, black and deep-rooted hair.

Eye-brows and eyelashes are black and smooth.

They have good eye - sight.

In their eyes, pupils, cornea and sclera are very well differentiated.

Mouth, Lips, Palate and Tongue are unctuous and oily.

These persons do not suffer from skin diseases and their wounds heal quickly.

They are intelligent and learned and have the necessary means and wealth to beget worldly pleasures.

They like music.

They love their family, nation, estate, and property.

They enjoy a long, healthy and happy life.

Ayurvedic Skin: The first step in the holistic Ayurvedic approach to skin care is finding out ayurvedic skin type.

Vata skin is in generaly dry, thin,delicate and cool to the touch, easily gets dehydrated, and is very vulnerable to the influence of dry windy weather. Vata skin may age faster, and tends to be dry, rough and flaky when out of balance.

Pitta skin type tends to be fair, sensitive, soft, warm, and of medium thickness. less tolerance to hot food, less tolerance to fieriness in temperament. Pitta skin types tend to be more prone to freckles and moles than the other skin types. When out of balance, Pitta skin can flare up in rashes, rosacea, acne, or sunspots.

Kapha skin tends to have all the qualities of water and earth - it can be oily, thick, pale, soft, cool and more tolerant of the sun. Kapha skin tends to age slower and form less wrinkles than the other two types. Kapha skin types may struggle with dull complexion, enlarged pores, excessive oil, blackheads, pimples, moist types of eczema and water retention.

"Combination" skin can be Vata-Pitta, skin that is both dry and sensitive, Kapha-Pitta-skin is oily and sensitive, and Vata-Kapha-skin that is generally dry with some oily zones.

The ayurvedic approach to caring for combination skin takes into account environmental and seasonal factors. a person with Vata-Pitta skin would follow the recommendations for Pitta skin in summer and Vata skin in winter. The Kapha-Pitta type would follow Pitta recommendations in summer and Kapha recommendations in winter. The Vata-Kapha type would be best served by generally following Vata guidelines, with extra cleansing of the oily zones.

Vata Skin Care: For Vata skin to stay youthful, skin care products used should be very nurturing. They must include some essential oils or herbs in combination, which can nourish the skin and rehydrate it, otherwise it may be susceptible to wrinkles and premature aging.

Going to bed on time, eating regular meals, and following a regular daily routine are essential components of a holistic approach to Vata skin care, as are eating foods that help balance Vata and nourish the Vata skin. Suggestions for caring for Vata skin: Vata skin types, for instance, will want to eat more warm, unctuous foods and favour the sweet, sour and salty tastes to balance the dry, rough, moving Vata dosha.

Provide added nourishment to skin by including organic milk, whole grains and green leafy vegetables in diet. Drink lots of lukewarm water everyday for internal hydration. Eat plenty of sweet juicy fruits, they help cleanse the body from within and provide hydration as well.

Include a little healthy fat such as Ghee (clarified butter) or olive oil in diet for added lubrication.

A warm oil self-massage is excellent for keeping skin lubricated. Use a gentle, all-natural moisturizer to keep facial skin hydrated. Provide added deep lipid support with facial oil. Get plenty of rest so mind as well as body have the opportunity to recharge. Use a gentle, moisture-balancing cleanser and splash face with water several times when cleanse.

Pitta Skin Care: The Pitta skin type needs both cooling and nurturing. Use skin care products that help enhance resistance to the sun. Avoid tanning treatments and therapies that expose delicate, sensitive skin to steam for extended periods of time. The ayurvedic herb Flame of Forest can help protect Pitta skin from photosensitivity. But like other ayurvedic herbs, it needs to be used in combination with other herbs for a balanced effect on the skin.

Suggestions for caring for Pitta skin: Pitta skin type thrive on sweet, bitter and astringent tastes, as found in sweet, juicy fruits, rose petal preserve, and cooked greens. Avoid hot, spicy foods. Stay away from harsh, synthetic cosmetics; they can damage sensitive skin and cause breakouts.

Avoid hot spicy foods and an excess of deep-fried foods, they add heat to an already fiery constitution. Eat lots of sweet juicy fruits and have some rose petal jam in cool milk every day. The rose is considered cooling for mind, body and emotions. Use cooling oil, such as coconut oil, for the daily massage. Cook with cooling spices such as fennel and licorice. Take extra care to protect skin when go out in the sun. Use gentle, natural skin care products for cleansing and moisturizing. Provide added lipid support, such as facial skin oil, every other day.

Kapha Skin Care: "Kapha skin, because of its thickness and oiliness, is more prone to accumulate ama - toxins under the skin.

People with Kapha skin need to do detoxification on a regular basis, both internal detoxification and external detoxification to flush toxins from the skin," says Mishra.

Scrubbing the skin with a gentle exfoliating clay can help external cleansing. Kapha skin types may also need to take herbal formulations to cleanse the skin from within.

Suggestions for caring for Kapha skin: The oiliness of Kapha type skin calls for a diet that is warmer, lighter, less oily, and free of heavy, hard to digest foods. Eating more bitter, astringent and pungent tastes help stimulate digestion and balance Kapha skin.Avoid too many sweet foods or deep-fried foods, they add to the oiliness in the skin. Exercise everyday to improve circulation.

A daily warm oil massage can also help circulation. Eat plenty of organic vegetables and fruits to help cleanse the body from within. Cleanse skin twice everyday; exfoliate with a mud-mask at least once a week. Cook with warming spices such as ginger and black pepper to stoke the digestive fire and inhibit the accumulation of ama inside the body.

Nourishment for skin: Besides following the diet for skin type, following foods are terrific skin-enhancers: leafy green vegetables; easily digested proteins such as paneer, milk, tofu, sunflower seeds; foods high in zinc such as quinoa; and beta-carotene-rich foods such as carrots and sweet cherries. Almonds and walnuts support the skin with their protein and lubricating fat content.

Some skin-friendly spices include turmeric to nourish the first four layers of the skin; cumin to rid the body of ama; black pepper to cleanse the channels, and fennel to balance the transformational ability of the skin.

All antioxidant-rich fruits and vegetables, such as pomegranate, apple, pear, and bitter, green leafy vegetables are also excellent for the skin. Eat only fresh, whole and organic foods. Stay away from packaged, canned, frozen, processed, and packaged foods.

Effect of stress on skin: There are three types of stress, and all three impact the skin in different ways.

Mental stress starts a chain reaction that ends in a drying out the moisture in the skin. Thinning, dryness and the shrinking of the 'shrotasa' (microchannels) that carry nutritive fluid to the skin result in wrinkles and stress lines. Emotional stress also affects the skin-just notice how anger or embarrassment can turn face red. This shows the connection between emotions and the skin. If emotional stress becomes chronic, the result is acne, sun sensitivity, and other Pitta-based problems.

Physical stress: Exercising too much, working too much, or straining the body over a period of time causes physical stress. This causes the drying out of skin moisture and rough, aged skin.

To counteract mental stress, maintain a Vata-pacifying diet and daily routine. To bring emotional stress into balance, follow a Pitta-pacifying diet and routine. For physical stress, try to limit exercise or work to fifty percent of physical stamina.

Treatment for skin disease: Ayurveda has stated that skin diseases occur primarily due to sluggish liver function, which leads Pitta and Kapha Dosha dysfunction when toxins build up and the liver is overwhelmed, then the impurities show up in break-outs and other skin problems.

Another vital factor that contributes to healthy appearance is the clean bowel: hence the need for regular and complete bowel evacuation. In order to achieve this, a mild laxative like Trifala and a light diet are advisable if one suffers from constipation. Also, be sure to drink lots of water throughout the day to help flush out the impurities. In spring sip hot water to help melt the ama (digestive impurities) that have accumulated. Scientifically treatments have been classified as shodhana & shamana.

Sodhan Chikitsa: When doshas are vitated in large guantity & disease is chronic then shodhan chikitsa should apply first. Acharyas have classified shodhana as Basti, Vaman, Virechana, Raktamokshana (Blood letting) & nasya.

Shaman Chikitsa: When doshas are minimally imbalanced & the body is weak. Shaman Treatment is more important. Shaman treatment can be classified as external & internal. Administration of proper food, medicines by mouth is internal treatment & the application of medicated oil, lepo (ointment), etc is external treatment.

Ayurveda has said that for all skin diseases 'Khadira' is best as oral medicine and 'Aragwad' is best for local application. Shirish, Lamajjak, Nagkesara and Lodhra are used for Hyperhydrosis and as an anti sweating agent. Tejpatra, Ambu, Lodhra, Abhay {Khas} and Chandan are used as Daurghandya- har {to prevent body odour} Charaka has mentioned a group of 10 drugs, which are promoters of complexion.

They are known as the 'Varnya Dravya': Chandan (Sandalwood), Lal Nagkesar (Fragrant Poon), Padmaka (Himalayan Cherry),Ushir (Cuscus Grass), Madhuka (Liquorice), Manjishtha (Madder), Payasa (White Yam), Shita (White Scutch Grass), Lata (Black Scutch Grass).

Shata Dhout Ghruta (100 times washed ghruta): Traditional Ayurvedic Skin Cream - It's completely natural and chemical free.

Very useful for achiving radient and glowing skin. Shatadhout Ghruta is preapred from organic ghee (made from cow milk) by washing it repeatedly 100 times using specific method prescribed in Ayurveda. This process transforms the ghee into a soft,cooling, nourishing, silky cream.

Recommended use: It is an excellent Astringent, Moisturiser, Anti-wrinkle & Cleansing cream. Can be used as a daily moisturizer on the face (or whole body) or for facial massage. Also, has calming effect on reddish or burned skin, and on eczema and rosacea.

Ayurveda and Modern Medicine

Modern medicine is recognizing that we must consider the nature of the individual in health and disease. It is not enough to give the same treatment to everyone suffering from the same disease. Their individual makeup should be considered because it causes the symptoms and development of the disease to vary considerably.

Ayurveda contains perhaps the world's best system of constitutional types that helps us treat each individual appropriately. It classifies people according to the three doshas or biological humours of Vata, Pitta and Kapha, (which correspond roughly to the air, fire and water elements energized by the life-force).

From these three main types derive many subtypes and conditions, resulting in a unique analysis of each individual's specific health condition.

This typology is not the product of any single factor like the current popular blood types in naturopathic medicine, but reflects the whole range of biological manifestations including body frame and weight, facial features, digestive tendencies, disease tendencies and psychological indications of emotional temperament and mental acuity. Ayurvedic books contain such typology tests and Ayurvedic doctors spend much time determining the individual nature and needs of each patient based upon these considerations.

Ayurveda treats the individual more so than the disease, which it sees as a by product of imbalances within the person.

It makes the individual important and strengthening his or her vitality the goal, regarding the disease manifestation as secondary and derivative.

It says that the same individual will be prone to various diseases that reflect their individual make-up and energies. Therefore, Ayurveda can provide treatment that covers not only a specific illness but all the potential diseases that the individual is likely to fall prey to over time.

Modern medicine is realizing the importance of disease prevention. It is not enough to treat diseases after they arise. This is like trying to put out a fire after it has already started and done some damage. Real treatment consists of preventing the disease from arising in the first place. And many diseases that are difficult to treat once they are fully developed can be prevented, if caught early enough.

Ayurveda is based upon a firm foundation of disease prevention, which is not simply a matter of regular medical check-ups but requires a healthy lifestyle in harmony with one's own individual constitution and unique life-circumstances. Disease arises mainly from a breakdown of the balance of internal energies in a person, not merely from external pathogens, however powerful these may be. Ayurveda's main method of long term treatment is to strengthen our internal energy (ojas).

This is similar to modern medicine's effort to strengthen the immune system, which is the energy of our body to defend itself from outside attacks.

But Ayurveda has a better understanding of this internal energy and its connections with mind and consciousness. It views our vital energy not merely as a biochemical phenomenon but as a product of the mind and prana and includes how we think, breathe and use our senses in its methods of healing.

Ayurveda and Consciousness

In the modern world we are gradually discovering the importance of the mind and emotions in the disease process. Ayurveda is inherently a mind-body medicine. Its doshas or biological humours are not simply physical pathogens, elemental imbalances or dietary indiscretions but include the effects of impressions, emotions and thoughts. The doshas reflect the consequences of emotional toxins like anxiety, anger and attachment on our physiology.

What junk food does to the body, junk impressions, such as our mental diet of violent movies, does to the mind, rendering it dull and heavy.

Negative emotions impact our health by adversely disturbing our internal organs, weakening the liver and heart which carry emotions. Disturbed thoughts impact our health through unbalancing the flow of energy through the nervous system. Disease always has a psychological component, and psychological disorders impact our vitality in a negative way.

Ayurveda emphasizes the role of consciousness in health and disease. It understands the workings of the mind on an organic and energetic basis just as it does the workings of the body, so that we can provide proper nutrition and exercise for the mind as well. It teaches us to be conscious how we live, what we eat, how we move and how we think so that we can bring the healing power and insight of consciousness into our existence.

Whatever we give consciousness to, we help improve, just as exposure to sunlight helps plants grow. This spiritual side of Ayurveda is not a matter of religious dogma, occult hocus pocus or New Age fantasy but part of the sophisticated spiritual sciences of Yoga and Vedanta, with which Ayurveda is intimately connected.

Yoga and Ayurveda

The role of the mind in immunity has been stressed in both Yoga and Ayurveda. In rejuvenation treatment for increasing immunity this has been made very clear by many Ayurvedic texts. Similarly, Yoga texts have given methods to increase the strength of mind for this purpose.

One should adopt all the procedures for increasing the Sattvic quality of mind-sattvic diet and sattvic behaviour. Ayurveda has explained the ethical regimen for the same purpose. Increased sattva is related to good pain tolerance, a health-conscious attitude, and increased immunity.

Ayurveda is based on a medically relevant philosophy with a distinctive perspective towards human life. It views man as a microcosm of the universe. Ancient Indian physicians asserted that both nature and man are made up of the same matter, the five gross elements: earth, fire, air, water and space;additionally, man has consciousness. Man is a combination of body, mind and self; physical and psychological processes are inseparable and interact, both expressions of the life force.

The treatment is given to the psychophysical organism (Bhutatma) and not to one or the other part of the body.

Ayurveda views the human being as a whole constituted of body, mind, intellect and self. The body is said to be of two types: the gross body, Sarira, which is observable and perishable, and the subtle body, Sukshma- deha, made up of elements like mahat, ahankara and sensory organs. The subtle body cannot be perceived.

Ayurveda views the human being as a whole person and not as a machine but how does it look upon male and female? The male is the giver of seed, nourished by the female, the field. The seed has potential for life; the field is inanimate. Both Caraka and Susruta use the word field for the womb.

The language of Beeja and Kshetra sees woman as an object and hence a lesser being. The four goals of life, the system of four stages of life which provide a context for moral life, are not for her.

Her duties are mainly two - giving birth and acting as a sexual partner. In her youth she is in the custody of her father or brother. Later on, the husband has a right over her and in old age she is under the control of her sons. She is always a dependent being. Medical treatment by Ayurveda has the effect of controlling a woman's life. Ayurveda does not permit the practice of abortion because it violates the principle of non- violence.

This forces a woman to reproduce against her will. Ayurveda sees women as having a certain social status. Women are seen as objects of enjoyment for men. Medical treatment for a woman is meant to keep her fit to perform these two functions.

The notions of physical and mental cleanliness, necessary parts of Ayurveda, are also intimately related to the ideas of purity and pollution, and used to deprive women of the right to participate in certain rituals, or during certain periods.

Because of its commitment to the western scientific perspective, biomedicine cannot and does not have a just approach to women's problems. Despite its holistic point of view, Ayurveda does not provide a nonexploitative alternative, because of its commitment to religious beliefs,.

The Need for a New Form

Medicinal systems are created by human beings, so they can be changed by them as well. This requires the evolution of a new perspective. The issue is not the hegemony of this or that system but how we use it for the health of all human beings. Both systems are influenced by socio- cultural practices that appropriate and use techniques to fulfill political purposes. At this level, one's understanding of ethics and commitment to values become important.

Biomedical ethics is limited to interpersonal relations such as those between doctor and patient or patient and health care institution. Questions such as a patient's right to health, to refuse treatment, a doctor's duty to save and not kill, his commitment to his profession, problems of maintaining severely brain- damaged human beings on life support systems, infanticide, abortion, mercy- killing, are 'paramedical' problems. There is no viable and consistent relationship between the theoretical basis of biomedical medicine and the value-framework in which it operates. Ethical issues either remain at the periphery or are redundant.

Ayurveda is based on a philosophy of life. Man as a miniature of the cosmos must represent the order and organisation of nature. A healthy life is based on order and discipline. It presupposes a harmonious relation to nature and society, while preserving the integrity of one's personal private world.

The world extends beyond the natural world to the social and private worlds. Man uses his imagination to create a culture, based on normative values, with goals of life which provide space for all stages, from birth to death. Thought and action are geared to move from self- centreed interest to the broadest possible social vision.

Activities such as art, science, philosophy, and medicine belong to this larger context. Every inquiry supplements and nourishes the others. Life becomes a whole; different ways of relating oneself to others and to nature exhibit different lifestyles.

Ayurveda therefore prescribes a medically relevant lifestyle which includes proper diet, proper exercise and proper mental attitude. This is reflected in day-to-day practice, dinacharya.

Thus ethics becomes an integral part of Ayurveda. In this ethics, obligation is the keyword. Human beings are part of a social world and they have an obligation to nature, society and to themselves. These obligations are determined according to varna and ashrama.

However, this system of specific values (visesa- dharmas) presupposes a hierarchical structure: all human beings are not equal; they do not have rights independent of caste, gender and social status. Women do not have any status in terms of varna; hence there is no question of their having basic rights like right to life, right to freedom of thought and action. (Men also do not have rights but have obligations.)

Today, we are committed neither to Ayurveda nor to bio- medicine but have a confused attitude to both systems. The same confusion exists at the level of evolving a new ethics. On the one hand, we are more inclined to use biomedicine and are receptive to the new ideas of basic human rights. On the other hand, our psyche is governed by traditional values.

Therefore, constructing a new ethics becomes an ambitious task. This task cannot be restricted to evolving a new methodology to interpret moral rights and obligations. It requires the creation of a new form of life based on general values equally applicable to all human beings.

Raso Vai Yoga

The word 'Yoga' comes from the Sanskrit root 'Yuj' which means union or 'to bind.' Yoga is the science of union with the divine, with truth. Ayurveda, Yoga and Tantra are ancient disciplines that have been practiced in India for centuries. They are mentioned in the scriptures of the Vedas and Upanishads. The purpose of each practice is to help the individual to achieve longevity, rejuvenation and self-realization.

Ayurveda and Yoga are sister sciences. Ayurveda is the science of the body and only when the body has become healthy, fit then is the individual considered ready to study the spiritual science of yoga. Yoga brings man to natural state of tranquility, which is equilibrium. Yogic practices help to bring natural order and balance to neuro-hormones and to the body's metabolism, improving endocrine metabolism.

These practices naturally treat stress and stress-related disorders. Yogic exercises have both a preventive and a curative value. The philosophy of Yoga was the systematized and co-coordinated by Patanjali in his 'Yoga Sutras.' Patanjali described the eight limbs of Yoga and Yogic practices for the quest of the soul.

These are the Yama (the natural regulation of the nervous system), Niyama (discipline), Asana (posture), Pranayama (rhythmic control of the breath), Prtyahara (contemplation), Dharna (concentration), Dhyana (meditation), Samadhi (the state of awakening, perfect equilibrium).

Asanas

The third limb of Yoga is Asana, or a series of physical postures. Mastering these postures brings steadiness, health, lightness of limbs, natural equilibrium and encourages fitness of mind. They create a fine physique, which is strong and elastic without being muscle-bound, and helps to keep the body free from disease. Ayurveda indicates which type of Yoga is suitable for each person, according to his constitution. In the commentaries from Charakacharya and Shushrutacharya

Raso Vai Yoga classes

The yogasan that we practice has the preciseness, sequencing, emphasis on alignment with staying in the pose for a certain duration and properness of the posture, derived from great Aiyangar traditon.. But at the same time it is flowing, have gentleness, with no goal to achieve but to relax in the pose, no pushing but agreeing with the body and at the same time being total and aware in each movement.

Yoga is there to not only to keep body mind in harmony and healthiness but also a way to seek the inner by fusing meditative ness into it. In the yoga classes techniques of meditation are practiced too, helping to bring one to the centreedness which in turn makes the practice of Yoga more multidimensional and fulfilling.

Our Yoga classes brings out a powerful cumulative effect and the methods of working results not only achieving a firm body, relieving stress, eliminating aches and pains, improving posture getting many ailments treated along the way but also brings a tranquility and meditative ness to the person.

The Potential of Ayurveda

It is well known that the oldest of all the sciences in the world is the science of life, Ayurveda.Traditionally it is believed that Maharishi Bharadwaja was the first human being to have been deputed to acquire the first knowledge of Science of Life Ayurveda from Indra, the king of gods.

Indra is supposed to have acquired this knowledge from Ashwins and they from Prajapati. Finally it is from Brahma that this supreme knowledge was acquired. Brahma is stated to have acquired this knowledge as Revealation through Yogic Samadhi.

Thus, even though, it was revealed knowledge, revealed in deep yogic state of Samadhi, this knowledge of Ayurveda or Science of Life was enriched later by the practical and experimental means, adhering to the 'Scientific Method' of the Modern Science, an essential requirement for the development of any Science.

The scientific method of Modern Science is founded on the principle of:

a. Observation
b. Hypothesis / anti-thesis
c. Experimentation and
d. Proof. Was the Scientific method of Modern science followed by Ayurveda? The answer is 'yes' - The notion of Hypothesis was known in Ayurvedic texts as Charaka Samhita as "Ooha" and the anti-thesis was called "Apoha".

Thus we find that both hypothesis and anti-thesis were used along with observations and experimentation. Therefore, we have to conclude that 'revealed knowledge' was continuously enriched by experimentation along with the appropriate hypothesis, which can be generalized into the laws of science when supported by 'proof'. What is the 'proof' in a medical science such as 'Ayurveda' The proof is its efficacy - the treatment - the cure or prevention of a disease or malady.

We all know that Ayurveda indeed works - the treatment has its beneficial results - even today. Ayurveda is the oldest medical system of the world, which works even today - The therapy and cure are universally known.Among all the tests (or proofs) the test of the time is the most challenging.

Survival of the fittest - Ayurveda has survived the test of the time - not for a few centuries (as in the case of other medical systems) but for thousands of years - for millennia altogether! Which medical system has survived the test of the time, more than Ayurveda.

Bibliography

Anesaki, Masaharu: *Nichiren, the Buddhist Prophet,* Cambridge, Harvard University Press, 1916.

Aronson, Harvey B.: *Love and Sympathy in Theravada Buddhism,* Delhi, Motilal Banarsidass, 1980.

Bechert, Heinz: *Buddhismus, Staat und Gesellschaft in den Landern des Theravada Buddhismus,*. Weisbaden, Otto Harrassowitz, 1966.

Beckwith, Christopher: *The Tibetan Empire in Central Asia,* Princeton, Princeton University Press, 1987.

Cleary, Thomas: *Entry into the Inconceivable: An Introduction to Hua Yen Buddhism,* Honolulu, University of Hawaii Press, 1983.

Dargyay, Eva M.: *The Rise of Esoteric Buddhism in Tibet,* Delhi, Motilal Banarsidass, 1977.

Dowman, Keith: *Masters of Mahamudra: Songs and Histories of the Eighty-Four Buddhist Siddhas,* Albany, SUNY Press, 1985.

Eppsteiner, Fred: *The Path of Compassion: Writings on Socially Engaged Buddhism,* Berkeley, Parallax Press, 1988.

Frauwallner, E.: *The Earliest Vinaya and the Beginnings of Buddhist Literature,* Rome, Istituto Italiano per il Medio ed Estremo Oriente, 1956.

Gethin, R. M. L.: *The Buddhist Path to Awakening: A Study of the Bodhi-Pakkhiya Dhamma,* Leiden, E. J. Brill, 1992.

Gombrich, Richard F.: *Buddhist Precept and Practice,* Delhi, Motilal Banarsidass, 1991.

Hakeda, Yoshito S.: *Kukai, Major Works,* New York, Columbia University Press, 1972.

Inada, Kenneth K.: *Nagarjuna. A Translation of His Mularmadhyamaka-karika with an Introductory Essay,* Tokyo, Hokuseido Press, 1970.

Jacobson, Nolan Pliny: *Buddhism, the Religion of Analysis,* London, Feffer & Simons, 1974.

Karetsky, Patricia Eichenbaum: *The Life of the Buddha: Ancient Scriptural and Pictorial Traditions,* Lanham, University Press of America, 1992.

Law, Bimala Churn: *A History of Pali Literature,* London, Kegan Paul, Trubner & Co., 1933.

Lerner, Eric: *Journey of Insight Meditation: A Personal Experience of the Buddha's Way,* New York, Schocken Books, 1977.

Mookerjee, Satkari: *Buddhist Philosophy of Universal Flux,* Delhi, Motilal Banarsidass, 1980.

Nagao, Gadjin: *Madhyamika and Yogacara: A Study of Mahayana Philosophies,* Albany, SUNY Press, 1991.

Nanananda, Bhikkhu: *Concept and Reality in Early Buddhist Thought,* Kandy, Buddhist Publication Society, 1976.

Nyanatiloka, *A.: Guide through the Abhidhamma Pitaka,* Kandy, Buddhist Publication Society, 1971.

Ortner, Sherry B.: *Sherpas through Their Rituals,* Cambridge, Cambridge University Press, 1978.

Pande, G. C.: *Studies in the Origins of Buddhism,* Allahabad, University of Allahabad, 1957.

Powers, John: *Wisdom of Buddha: The Samdhinirmocana Sutra,* Berkeley, Dharma Publishing, 1994.

Rogers, Minor and Ann: *Rennyo: the Second Founder of Shin Buddhism,* Berkeley, Asian Humanities Press, 1991.

Saso, Michael: *Tantric Art and Meditation: The Tendai Tradition,* Honolulu, University of Hawaii Press, 1991.

Sprung, Mervyn: *The Problem of Two Truths in Buddhism and Vedanta,* Boston, Reidel, 1973.

Swearer, Donald K: *Me and Mine: Selected Essays of Bhikkhu Buddhadasa,* Albany, SUNY Press, 1989.

Takakusu, Junjiro: *The Essentials of Buddhist Philosophy,* Honolulu, Office Appliance Co., 1956.

Thomas, E. J.: *The Life of the Buddha as Legend and History,* London, Routledge & Kegan Paul, 1927.

Tucci, Guiseppe: *The Theory and Practice of the Mandala,* New York, Samuel Weiser, 1973.

Watanabe, Fumimaro: *Philosophy and its Development in the Nikayas and Abhidhamma,* Delhi, Motilal Banarsidass, 1983.

Wells, Kenneth E.: *Thai Buddhism, Its Rites and Activities,* Bangkok, Christian Bookstore, 1960.

Williams, Paul: *The Reflexive Nature of Awareness,* London, Curzon, 1997.

Index

A

Ancient Conceptions; 18.
Ashtanga Sangraha; 8.
Ayurveda; 1, 2, 3, 4, 5, 6, 7, 9, 10, 25, 26, 27, 32, 33, 34, 35, 36, 37, 38, 39, 40, 41, 42, 43, 44, 45, 46, 47, 48, 50, 52, 54, 55, 56, 57, 62, 63, 64, 66, 67, 68, 69, 71, 72, 73, 74, 75, 76, 82, 86, 87, 88, 89, 90, 91, 92, 93, 94, 95, 110, 111, 112, 113, 114, 115, 116, 119, 120, 121, 122, 123, 124, 125, 126, 127, 128, 129, 130, 131, 132, 135, 136, 139, 140, 141, 142, 143, 144, 145, 146, 147, 148, 151, 152, 153, 154, 155, 156, 157, 158, 159, 167, 170, 171, 172, 173, 174, 175, 176, 177, 178, 179, 180, 182, 183, 184, 185, 186, 188, 189, 190, 191, 192, 195, 196, 199, 203, 204, 205, 206, 207, 208, 209, 210, 211, 212.
Ayurveda Based; 131.
Ayurvedic Elements; 72.

B

Balancing Pitta; 61, 68.
Basic Concepts; 179.
Big Picture; 111.
Blog Details; 81.
Blood Pressure; 162.
Body Elements; 70.

C

Chronic Diseases; 164.
Complete Wellness; 173.
Cultivating Mental Clarity; 91.

D

Developmental Theories; 97.
Dinacharya; 127, 128, 129, 131, 186, 188, 189, 190.

E

Eastern Embodiment; 103.
Ecological Approach; 23.
Endocrine Conditions; 163.
Enhancing Mental Health; 124, 125, 126.
Existential Phenomenology; 98.

G

Great Inner Adventure; 90.

H

Health; 2, 4, 5, 6, 13, 38, 53, 96, 97, 102, 128, 135, 136, 137, 141, 144, 147, 150, 153, 154, 158, 169, 170, 173, 177, 178, 190.
Holistic Approach; 140, 141, 154.

I

Identifying Pitta Dosha; 67.
Interactive Behaviourism; 22.
Internal Cleaning; 9.

K

Kapha Body Type; 64, 83, 84, 85.
Kapha Imbalance; 62, 63.

L

Lifestyle Modifications; 124, 141.

M

Mental Constitution; 116.
Mental Illness; 123, 136, 137, 139, 140.
Mental Peace; 146.
Mind Designers; 21.
Modern Medicine; 204.
Musculoskeletal Conditions; 164.

N

Natural Lifestyle; 39.

P

Pathya Ahara; 136.
Pharmacology; 191.
Physical Activity; 149.
Pitta Body Type; 65, 82, 84, 85.

R

Raso Vai Yoga; 209, 210.
Rigid Notion; 108.

S

Simple Definition; 35.
Skin Care; 199, 200, 201.
Soul Connection; 1.
Spiritual Experience; 158.
Spiritual Lens; 93.
Spiritual Significance; 153.
Stress Management; 6, 146, 147.
Stress Reduction; 144, 145.
Sushruta Samhita; 1, 7, 8, 50, 53.

T

Treatment; 5, 17, 70, 122, 139, 141, 182, 183, 184, 195, 203.

U

Understanding Ayurveda; 3.
Understanding Doshas; 86, 87.

V

Vata Body Type; 65, 66, 82, 83, 84, 85.
Vata Imbalance; 58.

W

Waste Products; 193.

Y

Yoga; 5, 39, 52, 85, 87, 90, 93, 95, 96, 112, 126, 127, 136, 138, 149, 159, 160, 162, 163, 164, 165, 167, 168, 171, 173, 174, 175, 176, 177, 206, 209, 210, 211.
Yogic Diet; 151, 152, 153.